What People Are Saying About
Chicken Soup for the Sports Fan's Soul . . .

"Sometimes when I'm happy, I cry. This book made me very happy."

Jack Buck
Baseball Hall of Fame sportscaster

"This book allows us to listen to a wonderful sound. It is the beat of the true heart of sport. You can hear it in the words of love and soul and respect that seldom find their ways to the sports pages."

Will McDonough
columnist, *Boston Globe*

"Here is a sumptuous buffet of stories, revealing some surprising aspects of the sporting scene and offering a better understanding of why players in all competitive activities must keep their cool. This reminds us as parents and fans to do the same, never allowing highly charged emotion to override good judgment. (There are better ways to get your name in the paper.) A most enjoyable reading experience."

Hank Ketcham
creator of *Dennis the Menace*

"Sports has a unique capacity to make us feel better about ourselves. This book tells us why!"

Barry Mano
president, National Association of Sports Officials

"This book touches the heart, soul and funny bone. It puts sports in the right perspective. Everyone should read it. Sports fans will love it."

Ron Barr
host, *Sports Byline USA*

"A great gift idea for all fun-loving, referee-ridiculing, umpire-baiting armchair experts!"

Gil Stratton
CBS Sports

"These stories show why sports in school is important. It gives a way to connect and help our family life. Academics, arts and athletics—all part of a three-legged stool. It's all about life. Terrific."

Gene Upshaw
executive director, NFL Players Association

"A great gift idea for all fun-loving armchair quarterbacks like me."

Dan Dierdorf
analyst, CBS Sports

"Wonderful stories about dedication and persistence. I was inspired to go to the next level."

Les Brown
motivational speaker

"After being a part of the professional sports community for over thirty years, it is exciting to read stories that inspire and motivate, as well as provide fun. These stories present a unique look at the games and the people of the sports world. WONDERFUL READING!!"

Ed T. Rush
director of officiating, National Basketball Association

"This book, *Chicken Soup for the Sports Fan's Soul,* takes you back to an earlier time, an honest time when sports were played by those with hearts for their game."

Gordon Forbes
pro football editor, *USA Today*

"Sometimes it's easy for fans to forget that those larger-than-life warriors, often just images on a television screen, are real people, full of conflicting emotions, passions and fears. These stories show the whole range of human experience, from thrilling victories to gut-wrenching sorrow, but best of all, hope and inspiration is a common thread in each fascinating story."

Joe Starkey
play-by-play broadcaster, San Francisco 49ers

"In my line of work I'm around world-class athletes all the time. *Chicken Soup for the Sports Fan's Soul* celebrates the athlete in all of us!"

Robin Roberts
ESPN/ABC sports anchor

CHICKEN SOUP FOR THE SPORTS FAN'S SOUL

101 Stories of Insight, Inspiration and Laughter from the World of Sports

Jack Canfield
Mark Victor Hansen
Mark & Chrissy Donnelly
Jim Tunney

Health Communications, Inc.
Deerfield Beach, Florida

www.hci-online.com
www.chickensoup.com

We would like to acknowledge the following publishers and individuals for permission to reprint the following material. (Note: The stories that were penned anonymously, that are public domain, or that were written by Jack Canfield, Mark Victor Hansen, Mark Donnelly, Chrissy Donnelly and Jim Tunney are not included in this listing.)

Roger Maris and Me. Reprinted by permission of Andy Strasberg. ©2000 Andy Strasberg.

Stadium Nights. Reprinted by permission of Bob Greene. ©1992 Bob Greene.

Thanks, Mom! Reprinted by permission of Steve Young. ©1999 Steve Young.

If It Makes Him Happy. From *Up Close and in Your Face with the Greats, Near-Greats and Ingrates of Sports.* ©1993 Roy Firestone, c/o Selnick & Associates, Inc., P.O. Box 56927, Sherman Oaks, CA 91413.

A True Champion. Reprinted by permission of Carole Yamaguchi and Anita Gogno. ©2000 Carole Yamaguchi and Anita Gogno.

(Continued on page 358)

Library of Congress Cataloging-in-Publication Data

Chicken soup for the sports fan's soul : 101 stories of insight, inspiration, and laughter from the world of sports / Jack Canfield . . . [et al.].

    p.   cm.

    ISBN 1-55874-876-8 (hardcover : alk. paper) — ISBN 1-55874-875-X (trade paper : alk. paper)

    1. Sportsmanship.   2. Athletes—Conduct of life.   3. Sports—Anecdotes.

I. Canfield, Jack, date.

GV706.3 .C45 2000

796—dc21

                              00-059660

Publisher: Health Communications, Inc.
            3201 S.W. 15th Street
            Deerfield Beach, FL 33442-8190

Cover design by Lisa Camp
Cover photos by ALLSPORT Photography, Stephen Dunn (Mark McGwire);
Al Bello (Monica Seles); Jonathan Daniel (Michael Jordan); Otto Greule Jr. (Joe Montana);
David Cannon (Lee Trevino); Mike Powell (Kerri Strug and Kristi Yamaguchi)
Typesetting by Lawna Patterson Oldfield

With gratitude, we dedicate
Chicken Soup for the Sports Fan's Soul
to Jim Murray (1919–1998)
who understood that sports were played—
and prayed about and reveled over and swallowed up—by
regular folks like you and me and Murray himself.

"I've never been unhappy in a ballpark,"
he said, and his writing reflected that joy and appreciation.
But he wrote about all sports, and from all viewpoints
—the press box, locker room, parking lot, sideline, mound,
goalpost, ring or rink. He won the Pulitzer Prize in 1990 for
commentary (there isn't a category for sportswriting) and was
named National Sportswriter of the Year fourteen times by
the National Association of Sportswriters and Sportscasters,
twelve of them consecutively. These recognitions, and an
ardent following of sports fans worldwide, came to him
because Murray recognized that a person's dreams, whether
ending in victory or loss, arise from the soul, and that's
what he wrote about—the souls of the players and coaches
and owners and fans that make sports meaningful.
We miss you, Jim, and know that you are writing
compelling glimpses of the angels right now.

Contents

3. HIGHLIGHTS AT ELEVEN

4. ON TEAMS AND SPORTSMANSHIP

5. INSIDE THE GAME

6. OVERCOMING OBSTACLES

7. FAMILY DAY

8. WISDOM OF THE GAME

9. ROAR OF THE CROWD

Acknowledgments

Chicken Soup for the Sports Fan's Soul has taken over three years to write, compile and edit. At times it's been a marathon and at times it's been a sprint, but at all times it's been an incredible journey. As with all projects of this magnitude, we received important help from many caring people. We would like to thank the following people:

Our families, who make up our collective home team. Thank you for giving us love and support.

Patty Aubery, thanks for your enthusiasm and guidance, and for always being there for us.

Patty Hansen, you are a guiding light of friendship, love and encouragement. Thanks for being such a great *Chicken Soup* role model. Thanks to Elisabeth and Melanie for your friendship and hospitality.

Inga Mahoney, thanks for your warm hospitality and support.

Christopher Canfield, thanks for inspiring us with your free-spirited and carefree approach to life.

Linda Tunney, thanks for your warm heart and deep understanding of the importance of this book to sports fans everywhere.

Hilda Markstaller, at ninety-three years young, you are the original sports fan. Thank you for being such a font of wisdom and for passing on your love of sports.

Kelly Garman, thanks for everything. Your participation has made this a much better book! Debbie Merkle and Paul Van Dyke, thanks for your help and encouragement along the way.

Heather McNamara and D'ette Corona, thanks for your expert editing and guidance. Your input has been invaluable.

Nancy Autio, thanks for all of your help in the permission process, as well as your friendship.

Leslie Riskin, Veronica Romero, Teresa Esparza, Robin Yerian, Joy Pieterse, Kristi Knoppe, Dee Dee Romanello, Shanna Vieyra, Dave Coleman, Tanya Jones and Cindy Holland, thanks for providing the daily support that makes it possible to focus on a project like this.

Deborah Hatchell, thanks for being there at all of the key points along the way.

Lisa Williams and Michelle Adams, thanks for taking good care of Mark and his grueling schedule, which allows him to travel the world to spread the word of *Chicken Soup for the Soul*.

Laurie Hartman, Maria Nickless and Tracy Smith, thanks for also helping to expand the reach of the *Chicken Soup* message.

Peter Vegso, we've said it before, and it's still true: We thank and honor you for your heartfelt desire to make a positive difference in the world.

Terry Burke, your team's contributions, your personal excitement for sports and your friendship make this an especially fun project. We also thank the entire sales and marketing team for their enthusiasm.

Christine Belleris, Lisa Drucker, Allison Janse and Susan Tobias, it's always a pleasure working with you.

Kim Weiss, thanks for helping us get the word out and inspiring sports fans everywhere.

The entire Health Communications team, your

professionalism, dedication and teamwork are an inspiration.

A very special thank you goes out to the many people who took hours reading and grading our top stories. Your guidance and feedback were invaluable: Fred Angelis, Jeff Aubery, Patty Aubery, Nancy Autio, Frank Bennett, Ken Blanchard, Ty Boyd, Leonard Broughton, Timi Brown, Jim Cathcart, Mike Chamberlin, Dan Clark, D'ette Corona, Charlotte Daniels, Clancy Dixon, Ken Flowers, Mike Frank, Bud Gardner, Chris Garman, Kelly Garman, Dennis Garrison, Jay Gentry, Marilyn Gustafson, Shari Hastey, Jim Heffernan, Robert Hentry, Darrell Imhoff, Karen Johnson, Mike Johnson, Nell Jones, Tom Krause, Stanley Kwan, Elaine Langlois, Barbara LoMonaco, Jack Lowe, Tor Matheson, Margaret McCall, Roger McGarrigle, Art McNally, Heather McNamara, Vera Merkle, Linda Mitchell, Shiela Murray-Bethal, Bob Neale, Jeanne Neale, Byron and Gloria Nelso, Jack Niro, John Oldach, Ducky O'Toole, Janet Tunney Peck, Carolyn Phillips, Vickie Rayson, Cynthia Renfro, Mark Sanborn, Ed Scannell, Shelly Scott, Tom Seamon, Gordon Paul Smith, Tery Stratton, Herb True, Marilyn Van Dyke, Al Walker, Warren Welse and Brent Wilder.

We also thank everyone who submitted the thousands of stories, letters, poems and quotes that we reviewed for possible inclusion in the book. While we weren't able to use them all, we were touched by each one. Your stories provided us with constant encouragement and reinforcement that we were on the right track. Thank you all!

Introduction

When it comes to bringing out the best in the human spirit, there is nothing quite like sports. There is an intensity and a richness inherent in every sporting experience that amplifies our emotions and our connection with the moment and, indeed, with ourselves. We somehow feel more *there*, as if we are momentarily transported to a universe where the colors are more brilliant, the sounds more vibrant and pure, the emotions at once more powerful and poignant. On a very basic level that we seldom consider, it is how we wish we could feel all of the time. It is this transcendent quality of sports that inspired us to collaborate on *Chicken Soup for the Sports Fan's Soul*.

We compiled this book hoping to celebrate all that is good in the world of sports. From major leaguers to little leaguers, from hockey stars to figure skaters and from horse racing to the Iditarod, the stories in this book highlight the positive and transformative nature of sports. These stories will inspire you, provide you with insights into the game of life and leave you with a newfound appreciation for sports in general. This book is for anyone who has ever enjoyed watching or participating in any sport, from a professional athlete to a weekend warrior, from a soccer mom to the diehard sports fan who reads the sports section before the rest of the paper.

Written by people who were transformed through their experience in sports, these stories celebrate sports as a metaphor for life in a unique and insightful kaleidoscope of experiences. Like how a champion thoroughbred winning the Triple Crown can teach us more about coming from the heart than a roomful of coaches; or how "The Greatest" showing humility at the right time and in the right dosage can profoundly make an old man's day; or how a cancer-ridden figure skater demonstrates the power of passion and determination in overcoming the most extreme of obstacles; or how one of the winningest coaches of all time reminds us that it is perspective and attention to the little things that makes a true champion; or how the simple constancy of season tickets shared over the years between a grandfather, a son and a grandson creates a family bond that lasts a lifetime.

Winding through these and other stories in the book is the common thread of sports as one of our most important and powerful teachers. When we open ourselves to it, sports teaches us to focus and stay the course, or to develop a new strategy and rededicate ourselves to a goal. It teaches us the importance of teamwork and reminds us that we must strive to give our individual all. It teaches us to be humble in victory and gracious in defeat. At its best, sports will build us up and it will wear us down; it will build character and teaches us to overcome adversity.

Most importantly, sports will be there for us like an old friend when we need to visit that other universe where the colors are brighter, the sounds are more vibrant and every moment is lived to the fullest.

Share with Us

We would love to hear your reactions to the stories in this book. Please let us know what your favorite stories were and how they affected you.

We also invite you to send us stories you would like to see published in future editions of *Chicken Soup for the Sports Fan's Soul*. Please send submissions to:

Chicken Soup for the Sports Fan's Soul
P.O. Box 30880-SF
Santa Barbara, CA 93130
Fax: 805-563-2945

You can also visit or access e-mail at the *Chicken Soup for the Soul* site on America Online at keyword: chickensoup or at *www.chickensoup.com*.

We hope you enjoy reading this book as much as we enjoyed compiling, editing and writing it.

1

LOVE OF
THE GAME

Sports is life with the volume turned up.

Barry Mano

Roger Maris and Me

I grew up in the shadow of Yankee Stadium, and just fell in love with baseball.

When Roger Maris came to the New York Yankees from the Kansas City Athletics in 1960, I was eleven. I had been burned in a fire in August, so I was laid up for a while and followed baseball even more closely. I remember a headline that said Roger Maris "rejuvenates" the Yankees. I had never heard the word before, but it made me think this Roger Maris was someone special.

For me, there was something about the way he swung the bat, the way he played right field and the way he looked. I had an idol. In 1961 the entire country was wrapped up in the home-run race between Maris and Mickey Mantle and Babe Ruth's ghost. I cut out every single article on Roger and told myself that when I got older and could afford it, I would have my scrapbooks professionally bound. (Eight years ago I had all of them bound into eleven volumes.)

I usually sat in section 31, row 162-A, seat 1 in Yankee Stadium. Right field. I would buy a general admission ticket, but I knew the policeman, so I would switch over to the reserved seats, and that one was frequently empty.

I'd get to the stadium about two hours before it opened. I would see Roger park his car, and I would say hello and tell him what a big fan I was. After a while, he started to notice me. One day he threw me a baseball during batting practice, and I was so stunned I couldn't lift my arms. Somebody else got the ball. So Roger spoke to Phil Linz, a utility infielder, and Linz came over, took a ball out of his pocket and said, "Put out your hand. This is from Roger Maris."

After that, my friends kept pushing me: "Why don't you ask him for one of his home-run bats?" Finally, when Roger was standing by the fence, I made the request. He said, "Sure. Next time I break one."

This was in 1965. The Yankees had a West Coast trip, and I was listening to their game against the Los Angeles Angels on the radio late one night, in bed, with the lights out. And Roger cracked a bat. Next morning my high school friend called me. "Did you hear Roger cracked his bat? That's your bat."

I said, "We'll see."

When the club came back to town, my friend and I went to the stadium and, during batting practice, Rog walked straight over to me and said, "I've got that bat for you."

I said, "Oh, my God, I can't thank you enough."

Before the game, I went to the dugout. I stepped up to the great big policeman stationed there and poured my heart out.

"You have to understand, please understand, Roger Maris told me to come here, I was supposed to pick up a bat, it's the most important thing, I wouldn't fool you, I'm not trying to pull the wool over your eyes, you gotta let me. . . ."

"No problem. Stand over here." He knew I was telling the truth.

I waited in the box-seat area to the left of the dugout, pacing and fidgeting. Then, just before game time, I couldn't stand it anymore. I hung over the rail and looked down the dimly lit ramp to the locker room, waiting for Rog to appear. When I saw him walking up the runway with a bat in his hand, I was so excited I almost fell. I don't know what he thought, seeing a kid hanging upside down, but when he handed me the bat, it was one of the most incredible moments in my young life.

I brought the bat home, and my friends said, "Now why don't you ask him for one of his home-run baseballs?"

So I asked Roger, and he said, "You're gonna have to catch one, 'cause I don't have any."

Maris was traded to the St. Louis Cardinals on December 8, 1966—a dark day for me. That year, I went off to college at the University of Akron, in Ohio. My room-mate had a picture of Raquel Welch on his wall, and I had a picture of Roger Maris.

Everyone knew I was a big Maris fan. My friends said, "You say you know Roger Maris. Let's just go see." So six of us drove two and a half hours to Pittsburgh, Pennsylvania, to see the Cardinals play the Pirates. It was May 9, 1967. We got to Forbes Field two hours before the game, and there was No. 9. It was the first time I had ever seen Roger Maris outside of Yankee Stadium, and I figured he wouldn't know me in this setting. I was very nervous. Extremely nervous, because I had five guys with me. I went down to the fence, and my voice quavered: "Ah, Rog . . . Roger. . . ."

He turned and said, "Andy Strasberg, what the hell are you doing in Pittsburgh?"

That was the first time I knew he knew my name. "Well, Rog, these guys from my college wanted to meet you, and I just wanted to say hello." The five of them paraded by and shook hands, and they couldn't believe it. I wished Rog good luck and he said, "Wait a minute. I want to give

you an autograph on a National League ball." And he
went into the dugout and got a ball and signed it. I put it
in my pocket and felt like a million dollars.

In 1968, I flew to St. Louis, Missouri, to see Roger's last
regular-season game. I got very emotional watching the
proceedings at the end of the game. I was sitting behind
the dugout, and Rog must have seen me because he later
popped his head out and winked. It touched my heart. I
was interviewed by the *Sporting News,* who found out I had
made that trip from New York City expressly to see Roger
retire. The reporter later asked Maris about me, and Roger
said, "Andy Strasberg was probably my most faithful fan."

We started exchanging Christmas cards, and the relationship grew. I graduated from college and traveled the
country looking for a job in baseball. When the San
Diego Padres hired me, Roger wrote me a nice note of
congratulations.

I got married in 1976, at home plate at Jack Murphy
Stadium in San Diego, California. Rog and his wife, Pat,
sent us a wedding gift, and we talked on the phone once
or twice a year. In 1980, Roger and Pat were in Los
Angeles for the All-Star Game, and that night we went out
for dinner—my wife Patti and I, my dad, Roger and Pat.

When Roger died of lymphatic cancer in December
1985, I attended the funeral in Fargo, North Dakota. After
the ceremony, I went to Pat and told her how sorry I felt.
She hugged me, and then turned to her six children. "I
want to introduce someone really special. Kids, this is
Andy Strasberg." And Roger Maris Jr. said, "You're Dad's
number-one fan."

There is a special relationship between fans—especially
kids—and their heroes that can be almost mystical. Like
that time my five college buddies and I traveled to
Pittsburgh to see Roger. It's so real to me even today, yet
back then it seemed like a dream.

I'm superstitious when it comes to baseball. That day I sat in row 9, seat 9, out in right field. In the sixth inning Roger came up to the plate and, moments later, connected solidly. We all—my friends and I—reacted instantly to the crack of the bat. You could tell it was a homer from the solid, clean sound, and we saw the ball flying in a rising arc like a shot fired from a cannon. Suddenly everyone realized it was heading in our direction. We all leaped to our feet, screaming and jostling for position. But I saw everything as if in slow motion; the ball came towards me like a bird about to light on a branch. I reached for it and it landed right in my hands.

It's the most amazing thing that will ever happen in my life. This was Roger's first National League home run, and I caught the ball. Tears rolled down my face. Roger came running out at the end of the inning and said, "I can't believe it."

I said, "You can't? I can't!"

The chances of No. 9 hitting a home-run ball to row 9, seat 9 in right field on May 9, the only day I ever visited the ballpark, are almost infinitely remote. I can only explain it by saying it's magic—something that happens every so often between a fan and his hero. Something wonderful.

Andy Strasberg

Postscript: On August 3, 1990, I received a phone call from Roger's son Randy and his wife, Fran. They were calling from a hospital in Gainesville, Florida. Fran had just given birth to their first son. Fran and Randy wanted me to know that they named their son Andrew and asked if I would be his godfather. To this day I still can't believe that the grandson of my childhood hero, Roger Maris, is my namesake and also my godson.

Stadium Nights

To get the best out of a man, go to what is best in him.

Daniel Considine

In my time as a reporter, I have witnessed some impressive, moving and emotional things. But I had never seen anything like what I experienced during time spent with Michael Jordan in 1990 and 1991. Though his purely athletic feats were well-documented, I often saw things that made all the athletic heroics fade away.

One night after a game, Jordan approached his car, which the security guards had readied. There were so many people and so much noise, and about twenty feet away was a little boy in a wheelchair. Jordan was clearly in a hurry; he had his own son with him. So he opened his car door, and somehow saw the boy. He walked over, got down on the ground beside him and spoke. Jordan comforted the child, talking slowly. This was not something that had been set up by the team; the boy's father had just brought him there to get a close glimpse of Jordan. Though it was freezing, Jordan remained crouched down by the boy until his father could take a picture. Only then did he return to his car. You can't set out to learn how to do this. No one can tell you how or advise you on it; it comes from something deep inside. If nothing else good ever happens for that little boy, he will always know that, on that night, Michael Jordan included him in his world.

At another game, I met Carmen Villafane. Her disabilities were so severe, her physical limitations so pronounced, that strangers tended to avert their eyes. I wondered how she was able to have her wheelchair positioned on the floor behind the Bulls bench at every game. *She must come from a family with a lot of pull,* I thought.

Well, not exactly, I learned.

In talking to her, I discovered that about a year earlier she had made a valentine for Jordan. She had managed to get tickets to a game and give it to him. He opened it right there in front of her, read it and thanked her.

Months later, she saw him at an auto show, and he asked her why she hadn't been at any more games. When Jordan learned Carmen had only had that single ticket, he instructed her to call his office. Without much hope, she did, and the office staff knew all about her. They mailed tickets for the remainder of the season. The following season Jordan sent her more tickets and a handwritten note. The letter said: "I hope you enjoy the season ahead. I'm looking forward to seeing you at every game—Michael."

Carmen was not the only one touched by Jordan. One time I got to the stadium early and found him on the playing surface of the stadium with hours to go before game time. He grabbed a basketball and motioned to two of the teenage ball boys to guard him. They glanced at each other; this was new. They were accustomed to shagging balls for him, but tonight he was inviting them to play. I watched as the two ball boys dribbled and passed. Jordan chased them into a corner of the court, laughing with them, reaching for the ball, slapping it out of their hands. The unspoken, priceless message he was sending them was that they were good enough for this—they were good enough to play around with him.

Another time, I had written a column about a random act of kindness I had seen Jordan do for a child outside the arena. It was when all this was new to me, before I knew that he did this kind of thing all the time.

A reader called in response and told me he and his wife had been to a Bulls game and their car had broken down. "We were four blocks from the stadium, in a bad area, and at the corner under a streetlight was Jordan's car," he said. "He was standing outside the car, talking with some neighborhood boys. It was late at night and they were just talking."

Later I asked Jordan about these boys. He said the year before, he'd seen them waiting outside the stadium in terrible weather, wanting a glimpse of the Bulls. He brought them in with him to the game. "Now they wait for me on that corner every night. . . . They're just kids who seem like they really need someone to talk to," he told me. Jordan's wife later told me he asks the boys to show him their grades to make sure they are keeping up with their schoolwork.

Jordan remembers that once he was a kid learning how to lift a basketball into the air. He was once a boy who was told that he wasn't good enough. He remembers every detail of being cut from the basketball team when he was a high school sophomore. Jordan told me: "We stood there and looked for our names. Mine wasn't on the list. I looked and looked. It was almost as if I didn't stop looking, it would be there."

When reality set in that morning he was cut, Jordan went through the rest of the day numb. "Then I hurried into my house and I closed the door of my room and I cried so hard. It was all I wanted, to play on that team."

At the end of that high school season, Jordan worked up the nerve to ask the coach if he could ride along on the bus with the team to a district tournament. "The coach told me no. But I asked again, and he said I could come. When we got there, he told me the only way I could go in was to carry the players' uniforms. So that's what I did."

He told me he was glad the episode happened because it taught him what disappointment felt like, and he never wanted to feel that way again.

In those years that I spent with Jordan, the world I wrote about had become no less grim, no less dismaying than it had been the first time I'd walked into the stadium. Nothing was going to change that; if anything, this world of ours keeps spinning itself into crueler and more sorrowful shape.

But there is more than one way to look upon that world. Of all the things I'd taken away from all those stadium nights, maybe that was the most important: the knowledge that, if you look closely enough, amid the merciless and the bitter, there is always the chance that you may find comfort and the promise of something good.

Bob Greene

Thanks, Mom!

I have often been told that I am a quarterback with the mindset of a running back. People have always commented on my ability to scramble, yet that wasn't always my style. All professional athletes retain vivid memories of events that helped mold them into the players they are today. The following story marks the beginning of my scrambling techniques.

I was nine years old and playing in a competitive game of Pop Warner football. I played running back for the North Mianus Indians. We were playing against the Belle Haven Buzzards and our quarterback had tossed me the ball. I took a few tentative steps and while I was trying to figure out where I should run, I was tackled. It was an illegal neck-tackle that threw me on my back and knocked the wind out of me.

As I tried to catch my breath, I saw my parents run onto the field towards me. I thought, *Oh, gosh, please Mom, go back to the sideline.* You see, it was okay to have my dad run out on the field. His nickname is "Grit" and he was a running back himself while at Brigham Young University. But, it was certainly not cool to have my mother, Sherry, come charging over with him. They finally reached me and, much to my surprise, as my father bent down to see how I was doing, my mother leapt over me, ran several more yards and grabbed the kid who had tackled me. As she picked him off the ground by his jersey, she shook him and shouted, "Don't neck-tackle!"

Needless to say, I was fine, but I'm not sure my opponent ever recovered from the shock. From that moment forth, I learned how to scramble, and quickly. I lived in fear of being tackled and had visions of my mother storming on the field to reprimand the tackler. We were teased about that incident for years. Even through high school, if someone tackled me too roughly, friends would yell, "Go get 'em, Sherry!" So, through a little unintentional motivation from Mom, I learned there are tremendous advantages to scrambling and avoiding tacklers.

Steve Young

"I know it's what your mother taught you, but you don't have to thank him every time he hikes you the ball."

If It Makes Him Happy

Without humility there can be no humanity.

Don Buchan

Tom Hauser, who worked with Muhammad Ali on his biography, appeared on my show, *Up Close,* a few years ago as a stand-in for Ali. Ali had agreed to appear after many entreaties, and I was thrilled. Now suffering from Parkinson's disease, his speech is slow and difficult to understand. I knew the viewers wouldn't mind, that they would appreciate a chance to see that Ali, while down, isn't out, that his indefatigable spirit is still there. He had a last-minute change of heart, though, feeling that he wouldn't be able to be himself and Hauser came in his stead.

On that show Hauser told me a story that encapsulates the gentle love that Ali inspires wherever he goes.

On hearing that a Jewish old-folks home in New York would be torn down, leaving the old people homeless, Ali quietly bankrolled a new home. When it was finished he went to visit.

In one corner of the room was a very old man, by himself. Ali approached the man and did a mock fight with his fists. The man's face brightened. Bundini Brown, Ali's trainer, said to the old man, "Do you know who this is?"

The old man said, "Yeah, it's the champ!"

"That's right," Brown said.

The old man said, "I know him, he's the greatest, he's Joe Louis!"

Everyone chuckled, and Brown started to correct the old man, to tell him who this really was.

Ali stopped Brown and whispered to him, "If it makes him happy to meet Joe Louis, if that's who his hero is, let's not confuse him."

Ali earned people's respect, but from those around him, more than anything, he earned their affection. Their love.

Roy Firestone

A True Champion

When our second child was born, Jim and I thought she was perfect, but the doctor pointed out that her feet were turned inward. "Left uncorrected, it would be a problem," he told us.

We vowed to do anything we could to help our baby. When only two weeks old, I brought her back to the doctor, just as he had directed, and the doctor put her tiny feet into casts, her precious baby toes just barely visible. Because she was growing, I had to take her back to the doctor every two weeks to have each foot recast.

Eventually the casting was finished and it was time for corrective shoes and bars. Jim and I watched with hope and concern as she struggled to walk. Those first, awkward steps made us so proud. By the time she entered preschool, her steps appeared quite normal. Encouraged by her progress, we looked for something else to help strengthen her lower body.

As it turned out, she loved the ice!

When she turned six, we enrolled her in skating lessons and soon she was gliding like a swan. We watched in wonderment as she skimmed the ice. She wasn't the fastest nor the most coordinated skater. She had to work hard at every new movement, but she loved the ice and her dedication paid off. At fifteen, she competed in both pairs-skating and the ladies' singles at the 1988 World Junior Championships in Australia, winning both events! At the senior World Championships in 1991, she won the ladies' singles. Then we found ourselves filled with love and admiration in France, at the 1992 Winter Olympics, as our daughter, Kristi Yamaguchi, won the gold medal.

I thought back to the early years of challenge for Kristi—the years of fear for us as her parents, and the same years of frustration for her as a child who simply wanted to walk; the endless doctor visits; the arduous first baby steps with bars and corrective shoes. During those years, we didn't expect gold medals and a stunning professional career ahead of her. We stood in awe of Kristi herself, respecting her strength and dedication, and how far she had come on two tiny feet that had once been bound in heavy casts. In our eyes, Kristi had always walked with the grace of a true champion.

Carole Yamaguchi
As told to Anita Gogno

Mister D's Boys

A brief item in the local paper announced the death of James Dudley. He was seventy-six. It reminded me of the last time I had seen him alive. He was shuffling along the sidewalk near his home. His dog bounded ahead of him, head high, ears flopping, turning often to check on his master's painfully slow progress.

I had driven past Mr. Dudley many times over the last few years. But that day I decided to stop. The least I could do was say "thank you" for all those summers. Whether he remembered me or not, I thought he might appreciate it.

The obituary mentioned that James Dudley had been a high-school teacher. He had earned a master's degree from Boston University. He was "active" in tennis and squash. He played semi-professional baseball. These were things I hadn't known about him.

Towards the end of the obituary was a note that Mr. Dudley had been "supervisor of the summer program at the town playground for thirty years." This I did know.

Mr. Dudley's summer program was baseball. No arts and crafts, no kickball or dodgeball for him. Seven hours a day, five days a week, twelve weeks a summer, for thirty years, almost every boy in town played baseball with Mr. Dudley.

It wasn't Little League. We had no uniforms, no fixed teams, no age limits, no skill requirements, no assigned positions. We showed up whenever we could, parked our bikes behind the backstop and played ball. Mr. Dudley was always there. He was never sick, never late. For thousands of us, he was a fixture of our summers, one constant in the chaos of adolescence.

He called me "Cat." Perhaps that was the way his ears heard the other kids call me "Tap." I like to think it was because of my pantherlike quickness at scooping up grounders.

Mr. Dudley was a big, solid man with white hair and a sun-worn face. He could throw strikes all morning, grooving them for the little kids and spreading on what he called "a little mustard" for the older boys. Then, in the afternoons of the hottest, muggiest August days, he'd do it all over again.

But even though we played a lot of ball in those summers, and Mr. Dudley would offer mild suggestions now and then ("Gotta keep that tail down" or "You're stepping in the old bucket"), I never had the impression that he was particularly interested in making skilled ballplayers out of us. Democracy was his real game. Everybody had to play every position at one time or another, and anyone cussing out a kid who dropped a pop-up got a glare from Mr. Dudley that made him shut up quick.

A frequent visitor to Mr. Dudley's baseball diamond was a huge boy who frightened the rest of us. We all vaguely understood that Joey was "different." His vocabulary was limited to nonsense syllables, which he uttered with great ferocity whenever he was frustrated. Sometimes he grabbed one of us by the arm and shook us. Mr. Dudley would say softly, "Cut it out, Joey, and get up to bat. Let's see you hit one."

In spite of his size and strength, Joey was hopeless at

baseball. He didn't want to play in the field, but he liked to bat. So once a day the game stopped, and Joey stepped to the plate. Mr. Dudley underhanded the ball to him and Joey swung wildly. At some point the law of average dictated that he would connect. Then he would lumber around the bases while we kids in the field cheered and allowed the ball to dribble through our legs. Joey always got a "homer" out of it, and then he would retire for the day, calm and happy.

Occasionally a new kid might say, "Aw, does Joey have to play?" Then Mr. Dudley would answer quietly, "Everybody likes to play baseball."

I heard some older boys call Mr. Dudley "Jim," so at the advanced age of perhaps eleven, I tried it out on him. He didn't answer. The look he gave me contained no reproach, just disappointment. I finally settled on "Mister D," which satisfied both of us.

We were Mister D's boys, and we came and went. We grew up, went away to school and moved out of town. New boys came along to take our places. I'm not sure when Mr. Dudley retired from his playground job, but I imagine it coincided with the development of organized sports in the area. I guess the town fathers figured there was no need to replace Mr. Dudley. Or maybe there just wasn't anyone around who wanted to do what he did.

These were the things that went through my mind that day, shortly before Mr. Dudley died, when I decided to stop and say hello. I got out of my car and walked up beside him. "Mister D," I said.

He stopped and peered at me. He didn't seem to recognize me, which was all right. He hadn't seen me for close to thirty years.

"I used to play ball with you in the summer," I said. "You could pitch all day."

He nodded, but did not answer.

"So how's the old wing? Still got that rubber arm? Still spreading a little mustard on that hummer?"

He gave me a little smile. *A sad smile,* I thought. He whistled softly to his dog and began walking again. I moved along beside him.

"Anyway," I said lamely, "I wanted to thank you. You gave me a love for baseball. I played in college. I'm still playing softball. I've even coached, and I've tried to do it your way. Everybody plays all the positions. No favorites. Baseball has been very important to me. That was your influence."

He stopped again and put his hand on my arm.

"I know all that," he said softly. "I keep track of my boys. I know all that, Cat."

William G. Tapply

What Sports Is All About

My boy is only three years old, but I know the day will come when he asks me about the birds and the bees. That task, I will graciously leave to my wife, bless her. But in return, I will share with him a few of life's other important lessons.

The conversation might go something like this. . . .

"Dad?"

"Yes, son."

"Why do you like sports so much? I mean, what's it all about for you?"

"That's easy, son. It's about eye-black, stickum and pine tar. It's fourth and goal, first and long, and John 3:16. It's about tapping in a sixteen-foot putt for an eagle on the eighteenth after seventeen holes of triple bogeys. It's about divots, brush-burns, rally caps, the Miracle On Ice, and Lions, and Tigers and Bears (*Oh my!*).

"It's Goose Gossage, Bear Bryant and Catfish Hunter. Sweaty gym socks, the Boston Red Sox and the penalty box; ballpark franks, checkered flags and if you ain't rubbin', you ain't racin'. It's about sudden death, extra innings and being behind the eight ball; the Green

Monster, Wrigley ivy and Yankee pinstripes; goal-line stands, the terrible towel and the Dog Pound. RBIs, FGs, HRs, TDs, FTs and the 7–10 split.

"It's about tying flies, slimy worms, baiting the hook and having fun whether you catch a fish or not.

"It's about '. . . and down the stretch,' 'Let's get ready to *rrrumble*,' 'How ya hubba' and 'Holy cow.' Cans of corn, blue darters and playing pepper in the backyard until the sun goes down and you can't see the ball anymore.

"It's about the Music City Miracle (even though the Bills lost), the Immaculate Reception and the Drive. . . . The Thrilla in Manila, No Mas, and floating like a butterfly and stinging like a bee. It's about *Any Given Sunday, The Fish That Stole Pittsburgh,* and *Rocky* I through V (although V wasn't all that good) . . . mashed-potato mouthpieces, Little League baseball, Pop Warner football, face masks, shin guards, shin pads, the stand-up slide and natural grass . . . sunflower seeds, chewing gum and Gatorade.

"It's about driving the lane, finding your line and being in the zone; press boxes, dugouts, sidelines and that peanut guy who can hit you between the numbers from twelve rows down and hand you your change before you can open the bag.

"It's about still being in your seat long after the game is over because we were having too much fun to realize the game was over . . . grand slams, Hail Marys and the suicide squeeze . . . hearing *swoosh* before the buzzer, slap shots, wrist shots, sand traps, Ping-Pong, aces high and bull's-eyes.

"It's about tailgates, the tale of the tape and knocking a leaner off with a ringer; starting blocks, tackling dummies and spring training. The boys of summer, the rope-a-dope, who's on first, what's on second, and I don't know—third base.

"It's about Go Army, Beat Navy and how kids scream

'car' during street hockey games to let the goalies know they need to move their nets. It's about playing umpteen games of P-I-G and Around the World in the driveway until you finally beat your older brother.

"It's about cutmen who can make Frankenstein's monster look like Christie Brinkley, first basemen who can scoop up a dirt ball like it were rocky road and goalies who guard their nets like Fort Knox. It's about slumps, streaks and standing Os . . . the Ice Bowl, the Super Bowl, Lord Stanley's Cup, the Heisman and Touchdown Jesus.

"It's about the smell of your first baseball glove, the feel of your first lucky bat and the sound of your mother cheering at your first football game.

"In short, son, it's about the thrill of victory, the agony of defeat and everything in between.

"But most importantly, it's about passing all this on to your son one day as my dad did to me and I am to you."

William Wilczewski

You Were Great, Dad

There is always room for improvement, you know—it's the biggest room in the house.

Louise Heath Leber

It started out as an innocent game of basketball in my son's school. Ivan's gym teacher had come up with the nifty idea that maybe a few of the kids' fathers could get together one night to "work out."

The game became a regular Thursday gathering. Most times the kids would hang out and cheer us on. Actually, they'd cheer on their gym teachers.

"Sugg's the greatest," my boy gushed one night. Sugg, the teacher who had organized the game, had racked up twenty or thirty points over my outstretched palms. Listen, I know a boy has to have heroes other than his dad. I can handle that.

"Aw, he plays every day," I said. "Wait'll we get in shape."

"*Psych!*" my son said. I don't know exactly what this means, but I think it's some contemporary equivalent of "gotcha."

"He can't go to his right," I said.

"He doesn't have to," my nine-year-old laughed. He *laughed!*

"He's fat," I said.

"He's strong."

"He's *bald.*"

Ivan thought about this for a second. "Not bald," he said quietly. "A unique haircut."

This got me down. My wife said I was silly, that Ivan was just competing with me through Sugg. Well, if the kid wants to play basketball, let's play basketball. *Ivan* I can beat.

Eventually my game improved. This was partly because I began getting back into shape. Mostly, though, it was because I was working my tail off to win my son's approval.

"You outplayed your man," he said one night when I'd poured myself down onto the bench after a game.

"Really?" I was thrilled.

"Yeah, you had two steals, two rebounds, and you shot five for eight." I gave him a little hug and unlaced my sneakers with a mannered flourish. *This is ridiculous,* I was saying to myself. But I loved it.

Sugg announced that he had entered our Thursday-night group in a corporate basketball league. We would play a team sponsored by a large company.

I came home the next day with a green uniform. "Try it on! Try it on!" my daughter, Dani, screamed. I looked at my son. He sat on the couch, holding his hand over his mouth to hide a grin. I looked at my wife. "Try it on," she said.

I modeled for them.

"Why'd you pick number 12 instead of 33?" asked Ivan. The New York Knicks' current star center, Patrick Ewing, is number 33.

"I don't think they make Patrick Ewing jerseys in size thirty-eight portly-short," I said.

"Can we come to your first game?" Dani wheedled.

"No," I said. So they came.

The gym at the school was packed, and the corporate team was already on the floor. We came out in our shiny green outfits and formed a layup line.

"Don't anybody be tight," Sugg said. Ten tight faces smiled back.

"Go, Big Green!" my son shouted. The referee blew the whistle to start the game. On the bench, I cheered wildly at our first basket. I was determined to show my kids that being on the second team didn't diminish my enthusiasm. But I was flushed from the embarrassment.

We ran up a three-point lead by the fifth minute. Sugg signaled to me. "Twelve in for 35," I said to the scorer, and went in.

"Go, Dad!" Dani shouted.

The inbound pass came to me. I dribbled across midcourt. The corporate guys looked like trees. Green uniforms peeked out from behind them, waving their hands at me. I heard my daughter yell. I felt my son's eyes on the ball, on my hands, on my neck.

I passed to our best guy. He feinted right and drove left for a layup.

"Yeah, an assist!" my son yelled.

I remembered Little League, a count of no balls and two strikes, my father calling to me, "Okay, son, only takes one to hit it!"

This was Little League turned upside down. Now, with my own son cheering me, I felt the same way I'd felt before: furious that my supporter was being allowed to watch this very private battle I was having with my own inadequacies, yet elated to be playing in the full view of everyone I loved the most. *Heck, Ivan, if you want to call that an assist, then that's what it was.*

I dropped back for defense and accepted the cavalry

charge of the corporates. They passed to the guard I was defending. I bodied him. Whistles.

"Blocking! On 12 green!" the ref shouted.

I raised my hand and waved it a little, the way the pros do.

Corporates inbounded. I deflected the pass, and there was a scramble. Someone else's man shot and scored. Someone else's man. Thank goodness.

We ran back the other way. I was wide open, and the ball came to me at the foul line. I thought of ten thousand reasons not to take the shot, but none of them washed. So I put it up—and buried it.

"Yesssss!" shouted Ivan.

Sugg high-fived me when I came off. I sat down hard, breathing heavily, more from emotion than exertion. I looked over at Ivan and Dani and winked, the sweat running down my nose. You can have the agony of defeat.

We had the corporates by seven points at the half, but in the end we lost by four. My shot from fifteen feet out was my only score. My son read me the stats he'd been keeping in his head. "One for three, two assists, no turnovers. You were great, Dad."

"Daddy! Daddy!" my daughter chanted for a hug. I hugged her. "Ugh, sweaty," she said.

Later, over ice-cream sodas the kids chattered excitedly about Sugg and me and the game. "How do you feel?" my wife asked. She meant my knees and ankles, but I was only thinking of the agony and ecstasy. I felt good about not embarrassing myself. I felt great about my family. What had I learned?

That Dad doesn't have to be the high scorer to be the big hero. That your kids, when pressed, will probably do a better job of forgiving your inadequacies than you will of forgiving theirs. That I ought to shoot more when I'm open.

"You ought to shoot more when you're open, Dad," Ivan said.

"Right," I said. "When you're hot, you're hot."

Barney Cohen

IN THE BLEACHERS   By Steve Moore

IN THE BLEACHERS. © *Tribune Media Services, Inc. All rights reserved. Reprinted with permission.*

READER/CUSTOMER CARE SURVEY

We care about your opinions. Please take a moment to fill out this Reader Survey card and mail it back to us.
As a special "thank you" we'll send you exciting news about interesting books and a valuable **Gift Certificate**.

Please PRINT using ALL CAPITALS

First Name |_____| MI |__| Last Name |_____|

Address |_____|

City |_____| ST |__| Zip |_____|

Phone # (|__|__|) |__|__|__| - |__|__|__|__| Fax # (|__|__|) |__|__|__| - |__|__|__|__|

Email |_____|

(1) Gender:
○ Female
○ Male

(2) Age:
○ 12 or Under ○ 30-39
○ 13-15   ○ 40-49
○ 16-19   ○ 50-59
○ 20-29   ○ 60+

(3) Marital Status:
○ Married
○ Single
○ Divorced / Widowed

(4) Was this book:
○ Purchased For Yourself?
○ Received As a Gift?

(5) How many Chicken Soup books have you bought or read?
○ 1   ○ 3
○ 2   ○ 4+

(6) Did you enjoy the stories in this book?
○ Almost All
○ Some
○ No

(7) How did you find out about this book? *Please fill in ONE.*
○ Personal Recommendation
○ Store Display
○ TV/Radio Program
○ Bestseller List
○ Website
○ Advertisement/Article or Book
○ Catalog or Mailing
○ Other _____

(8) What FIVE subject areas do you enjoy reading about most? *Rank only FIVE. Choose 1 for your favorite, 2 for second favorite, etc.*

	1	2	3	4	5
Self-Help	○	○	○	○	○
Sports	○	○	○	○	○
Spirituality/Inspiration	○	○	○	○	○
Family and Relationships	○	○	○	○	○
Health and Nutrition	○	○	○	○	○
Business/Professional	○	○	○	○	○
Entertainment	○	○	○	○	○

3628027884

(13) Where do you purchase most of your books?
Please fill in your top TWO choices only.
- ○ Bookstore
- ○ Religious Bookstore
- ○ Warehouse / Price Club
- ○ Discount or Other Retail Store
- ○ Website
- ○ Book Club / Mail Order

(15) What type(s) of magazines do you SUBSCRIBE to?
Fill in up to FIVE categories.
- ○ Sports
- ○ Health
- ○ Business / Professional
- ○ World News / Current Events
- ○ General Entertainment
- ○ Other (please specify) _____

Do you have your own Chicken Soup story that you would like to send us?
Please submit separately to: Chicken Soup for the Soul, P.O. Box 30880, Santa Barbara, CA 93130

A Twenty-Four-Karat Friendship

The greatest good you can do for another is not just to share your riches, but to reveal to him his own.

Benjamin Disraeli

Jesse Owens seemed sure to win the long jump at the 1936 games. The year before he had jumped 26 feet, $8\frac{1}{4}$ inches—a record that would stand for twenty-five years. As he walked to the long-jump pit, however, Owens saw a tall, pit-eyed, blond German taking practice jumps in the 26-foot range. Owens felt nervous. He was acutely aware of the Nazis' desire to prove "Aryan superiority," especially over blacks.

On his first jump Owens inadvertently leaped from several inches beyond the takeoff board. Rattled, he fouled on his second attempt, too. He was one foul away from being eliminated.

At this point, the tall German introduced himself as Luz Long. "You should be able to qualify with your eyes closed!" he said to Owens, referring to his two jumps.

For the next few moments the black son of a sharecropper

and the white model of Nazi manhood chatted. Then Long made a suggestion. Since the qualifying distance was only 23 feet, 5½ inches, why not make a mark several inches before the takeoff board and jump from there, just to play it safe?

Owens did and qualified easily. In the finals Owens set an Olympic record and earned the second of four golds. The first person to congratulate him was Luz Long—in full view of Adolf Hitler.

Owens never again saw Long, who was killed in World War II. "You could melt down all the medals and cups I have," Owens later wrote, "and they wouldn't be a plating on the twenty-four-karat friendship I felt for Luz Long."

David Wallechinsky

Reach for the Stars

Let your soul stand cool and composed before a million universes.

Walt Whitman

When striving for the extraordinary, life often delivers gifts that transform us. One such immeasurable gift came to me at the end of the 1985 season.

It was a "Cinderella" season for the New England Patriots. We had started miserably, with four straight losses in which we managed to average less than one yard per rushing attempt. This pitiful showing earned us the unceremonious distinction of the worst rushing offense in the NFL.

We turned it around, though, thanks to spectacular plays by first one team member, then another, and the steady hands of quarterbacks Steve Grogan and Tony Eason. Thanks to teamwork, we pulled together a 10-4 record going into the next-to-last game of the season against Miami. Beat the Dolphins and we would lock a spot in the playoffs and make a try for the AFC championship for the first time in the twenty-five-year history of the Patriots. The sportswriters and broadcast analysts gave us no chance.

Since the game was scheduled for *Monday Night Football,* the pregame hype was as wild and ready as we were. On game day, the fans in the stands and on their couches at home were not disappointed. We gave 'em a dramatic, back-and-forth, feisty game punctuated with long bombs of desperate hope, and when it counted most, pinpoint accuracy from the Dolphins' Dan Marino. We proved the sportswriters right: we lost.

The season was down to one last chance. We had to pack our hopes and head home for a cold winter game against the Cincinnati Bengals. If we won that one, we could still make the playoffs in a wild-card spot.

That game was almost surreal. We felt like we could not be stopped. Most would have thought we were crazy, but we knew the offense, the defense and how the special teams were going to score. Even when we fumbled the ball, we had an intuitive sense that now our defense would get its chance to score. We were in the zone as a team, when everything seems effortless and time doesn't exist. The extraordinary seemed to unfold, always in our favor. Our home crowd was standing, cheering, *roaring* the entire game. You could literally feel the Bengals' will to win being drained out of them. We won that game 34–23 and claimed our team's greatest moment.

The atmosphere in the locker room afterward was giddy. Players, coaches, trainers, the media. Hugs, tears, laughter and flying champagne everywhere. A few players were so stunned they could only sit on benches and silently hug the moment. John Hannah sat with Pete Brock, Andre Tippet with Don Blackmon. Head coach Raymond Berry smiled, but I could tell he was already past this game, preparing his mind for the first round of the playoffs. We were contenders!

And then it happened. As I had done so many times after home games, I left the locker room, walked upstairs past the group of special guests and family members being held back by security. A woman reached through the ring of security and the clamor of celebration seemed to pause as I heard her ask, quietly but enthusiastically, for an autograph for her two boys. As I looked into her face I realized she was Christa McAuliffe, the woman who as America's Teacher-in-Space was about to head into space on the *Challenger*.

"Absolutely," I said. I was surprised to notice my hand trembling as I signed the paper she had presented. She smiled with a brightness and clarity I had noticed on television interviews. Without hesitation, I said, "And would you be so kind as to give me your autograph?"

She smiled even wider and her sons looked up at her in awe. "Mom," one of them whispered, "he wants your autograph!" I grabbed a piece of paper off a desk nearby and she signed it.

I knew what we had just done as a team was a triumphant life moment. We were making a run for the Super Bowl, the top prize for every professional football player. Yet, this accomplishment was eclipsed in my mind by a schoolteacher with a million-dollar smile and the courage, commitment and driving passion to inspire schoolchildren, teachers, national leaders, all of America and most of the world by living her dream.

I gave her a hug and said, "All the best for your flight. I admire you."

A few weeks later, I was in Hawaii for Pro Bowl Week. On Tuesday morning, January 28, 1986, I was in my hotel room watching the run-up to the *Challenger* liftoff, remembering Christa McAuliffe's easy friendliness and marveling at her grit, which was greater, surely, than any football player's, no matter how big, how willing to hit and be hit, how determined to do the best he can on the field. Off into space! This is in a whole different league. And then, my God, no! Plumes of white smoke. Just seventy-three seconds of excitement, and then tragedy.

I sat on the end of the bed, head in my hands, and cried. After a long time, I opened my briefcase, pulled out the piece of paper she had signed, taped it to the dresser mirror and left the room, closing the door quietly. I walked down the beach, thinking of her smile and her courage, trying to understand fate or at least accept it.

I walked for hours. When I stopped I didn't know where I was. I only knew where Christa was. I looked across the Pacific Ocean and repeated the words she had written to me:

"To Brian, Reach for the Stars. I'll be there."

Brian Holloway

2

DEFINING MOMENTS

There's no thrill in easy sailing
when the skies are clear and blue,
there's no joy in merely doing things
which anyone can do.

But there is some satisfaction
that is mighty sweet to take,
when you reach a destination that
you thought you'd never make.

Spirella

I Will Be There for You

*Other people may not have had high expecta-
tions for me . . . but, I had high expectations for
myself.*

Shannon Miller

In the gathering light of a cold November morning, I
walk onto the upper roadway of the Verrazano-Narrows
Bridge, which joins Staten Island to Brooklyn. It is closed
to traffic. I look across that enormous span and think, *Dear
Lord, have I bitten off more than I can chew?*

I am about to run my first New York City Marathon, the
annual 26.2-mile footrace through all five boroughs of the
city, ending on West Drive at 67th Street in Central Park.
I am with a small band of marathoners from Achilles, a
track club for disabled runners. We are starting early
because we will need extra time to finish the race. We are
an eclectic crew, on crutches or artificial limbs, in
wheelchairs.

I have multiple sclerosis, a degenerative neurological
disease. Medical science does not know what causes it or
how to cure it, and can't predict what symptoms will

come—or when. I could lose the ability to see, walk and speak.

For fifteen years I played by the rules and discarded the notion that I could still have an active physical life. The most exercise I got was whatever it took for me to get from my apartment to the subway and back again. Fortunately my symptoms did not worsen: I could walk, though I needed a cane to keep my balance.

But gradually I began to resent everything I had given up to MS, and I wanted those things back more than I've ever wanted anything in my life. I needed a dream, a goal—one that would ask for everything I had and still demand something more. I decided to run the New York City Marathon.

Early on in 1988, my friends kidded me about my new avocation. At work they started to call me Grete—after Grete Waitz, the Norwegian runner who had won eight New York City Marathons. The joke bloomed when my coworkers asked me how I would keep spectators from mistaking me for Grete during the race. "Easy," I told them. "I'll just carry a sign saying, 'I'm Not Grete.'"

That's what I'm wearing at the race now—a white shawl emblazoned with the legend "I'm Not Grete."

The starting horn is sounded. We're off, pushing, wheeling and skittering, each of us after our own fashion. A couple of miles and hours down the road, the crowds begin to assemble. At around the ninth mile the lead pack of male runners catches up to us. To avoid the risk of injury, we step up on the curb and watch the male leaders pass us by.

The pack disappears, and then the lead women arrive. Grete Waitz, all grace, power and beauty, is the front-runner. I stand aside and cheer her on. Finally, ten minutes after the first runners, there is an approaching thunder. The sidewalk shakes—and twenty thousand more people race by. I am unprepared for the intensity of feeling that this onrush of runners unleashes in me. All these dreams, all this energy. And I am part of it.

At 1:57 A.M. I finally get to the finish line. It's taken nineteen hours and fifty-seven minutes. I thrust my right arm into the air and let out a war whoop.

My first marathon is Grete Waitz's ninth and final victory, a record that will probably never be broken. I don't expect ever to see her again.

Then five years later Dick Traum, founder of the Achilles Track Club, honors Grete at his annual dinner. He seats me next to Grete. We're both shy, and we might have sat there in silence had Traum not introduced us. What absolutely floors me is that Grete knows who I am. She is astonished that anyone is willing to stay out on the course for twenty hours. She knows how exhausting two hours and twenty-five minutes can be.

We hit it off, and in no time we are chatting away. I even have my "I'm Not Grete" shawl with me, because I'm supposed to tell a story about it at the dinner. But I tell Grete another story.

The first year I ran the marathon, a New York paper took a picture of me at the finish line and ran it under the big picture of Grete. The next morning, on crutches and barely walking, I hailed a cab. As I got in, the driver looked at me. "Hey, I know who you are," he said in a thick Brooklyn accent. "You were in the paper today. You're that runner, the one that won the marathon, Grete What's-Her-Face."

At last I said the words I'd been waiting to say: "I'm not Grete." Then I told him, "I'm her older sister. People are always mistaking me for her."

"Yeah," he said. "I knew you looked just like her."

Grete thinks the story is hilarious. The dinner is just a few days before my sixth marathon, and she asks who will be there to record my finish. I tell her no one; I'll call in my time and get a finisher's medal later.

She says, "I really think someone should be there." Then Grete stuns me when she adds she "would be honored" if she could be that person. I protest that I have no idea when I'll finish. "It doesn't matter how long it takes," she says. "I will be there for you when you cross the finish line."

This year I do the race with a fibroid tumor pressing on my bladder and spine. It will take me twenty-eight hours to finish.

At 6 A.M. Grete arrives at the finish line, where a friend of mine tells her it will be at least another hour before I finish.

He also says there is no finisher's medal for me. Apparently someone stole a case of the medals.

"She has to have a medal," Grete says. She sprints out of the park, runs to her hotel room and wakes her husband, who had run the race the previous day. "I need your medal!" she says. "Someone needs it more than you do. If you have to have a medal, you can have one of mine." With that, she sprints back to the finish line.

I am still hours away, but Grete waits patiently for my arrival. At last I make the final turn into the park, salute the twenty-six-mile marker and begin the last 385 yards. The first thing I see is that two people are holding a tape across the finish line, the same tape the winners ran through almost a full day earlier. And then I see the person waiting behind the tape—Grete Waitz. She is determined that I experience the race no differently from the winner.

As I cross, Grete drapes the medal around my neck, and we collapse into each other's arms, sobbing with the emotion of the moment. She will be there for me every year after that.

Over the years we've gone together into New York schools to show kids both ends of the spectrum of winning. Here is a champion who talks about commitment and discipline, and shares her stories of triumph and defeat. And here is someone like me, who has the same satisfaction in achieving something of great personal significance.

For some of the kids, winning is a concept they never thought applicable to themselves. But Grete and I show them that, as the poster taped to my bedroom wall puts it, "The race belongs not only to the swift and strong—but to those who keep on running."

Zoe Koplowitz with Mike Celizic

[EDITORS' NOTE: *Grete Waitz was inducted into the National Distance Running Hall of Fame in 2000. Grete had never run a marathon before her New York City Marathon victory in 1978. When the Norwegian schoolteacher stopped running, she was the all-time leader in the New York City Marathon with nine victories (1978–1980, 1982–1986, 1988).*]

The Magic Bat

You may be disappointed if you fail, but you are doomed if you don't try.

Beverly Sills

Harry is every coach's dream kid: He shows up for every practice early, stays late and is enthusiastic. Harry is also every coach's nightmare: He has neither the instinct nor the physical talent for the game.

I stepped in as a stand-in coach for my son's Little League team when the regular coach got married. Somehow he thought a honeymoon took precedence over next Tuesday's game. How can you blame him? Our team hadn't won in more than two years.

As I accepted the fill-in spot, I promised myself that I would show no disappointment if we lost. That was the least I could do. The best I could do was give a good heart to the effort.

I met Harry at the first practice. A small, thin, awkward kid, his best throw was about five feet, which made the choice of fielding position difficult. And he was scared. Every time he came to bat, he would glance at the pitcher, lean the bat on his shoulder, close his eyes and wait until the misery of three pitches was over. Then he'd trudge back to the dugout. It was painful to watch.

I met Harry before Tuesday's game, took him aside and worked with him on keeping his eyes open. He tried, but it's tough to overcome the habit of fear. We were about to play a team that had beat us 22-1 the last time. It didn't seem a fortunate moment for a breakthrough. Then I thought, *Why not?*

I went to the dugout, got a different bat and returned to our practice area. "Harry," I said, "I want you to use this bat. It's the one for you. It's a magic bat. All you have to do is swing and it will hit the ball."

Harry seemed skeptical, but he said he would try. I hoped I wasn't complicating an already tough problem for Harry, but I wanted to try to help.

Our team was trailing from the first inning. No surprise in that, but we had some loyal parents in the stands to give constant encouragement to the kids.

On Harry's first at bat, I noticed he wasn't using his special bat, but I didn't step in. He struck out, as usual, and I decided to let it ride.

We were able to score from time to time. In the last inning, we were behind by only three runs. I was thinking about a "respectable outcome" speech to give the kids while packing up the gear. As the home team, we were last up. We alternated for five batters between singles with players safely on base and strikeouts. We had bases loaded and two outs. Only then did I notice that Harry was our last chance.

Surveying the field from my spot by first base, I saw the left fielder sprawl on the grass as Harry came from the dugout. He obviously expected no action. The right fielder was bothering some butterfly that was flitting about. The shortstop had moved well in, I suppose anticipating the possibility of a miraculous bunt. Clearly, the opposing players were already tasting the double-scoop ice cream cones they would go for after the victory.

Harry limped up to the batter's box. I noticed he had his usual bat. I called a time out, ran up to him and whispered, "Harry, this is the time for the magic bat. Give it a try. Just keep your eyes open and swing."

He looked at me in disbelief, but he said he'd try. He walked off for the special bat as I trotted back to first base.

First pitch, strike one. Harry didn't swing, but he kept his eyes open. I pumped my fist and gave it a little swing, encouraging him to swing. He smiled, got into his awkward stance and waited. He swung, eyes open, but missed. Strike two. That was the first real swing Harry had ever taken. Who cared if we won the game? I considered Harry a winner already.

The other coach yelled to his pitcher, "Fire one past him and end this thing!" I grimaced.

The pitcher threw a straight fastball and Harry swung. The magic bat did its trick. It found the ball, which flew over the shortstop's head.

Pandemonium erupted in the stands, in the dugouts, on the bases. I was cheering Harry to run to first as fast as he could. It seemed like an eternity. The left fielder called to the center fielder to get it. "You're closer!"

I kept cheering the runners. We had one in at home and three guys pouring it on from first to second, second to third, third to home. The second baseman yelled for the center fielder to get the ball to him. Excitedly, he obeyed, but the ball skipped across the grass and passed by the second baseman toward the right-field line. My job as coach was simple at this point. "Run, guys, run," I yelled.

Another guy scored. By this time, the entire team had joined the cheering, "Go, Harry, go Harry!" This was surely the longest distance Harry had ever run. He was panting as he headed for third and another guy crossed home.

The right fielder's throw was critical, and it was pretty good, but the third baseman muffed it. The ball scooted past him out of play. The rule: one base on an overthrow that goes out of play. Harry, exhausted, kept the push on as best he could.

About then, the first cry of "Grand Slam!" hit the air. Everyone joined in. When Harry reached home plate, about to collapse, his teammates lifted him as high as they could and chanted, "Harry, Harry, Harry!"

I ran over to the team to hug the proudest kid in America. Tears streaming, Harry looked up at me and said, "The bat, Coach, the bat."

I smiled and said, "No, Harry. It was you who hit the ball, not the bat."

David Meanor
Submitted by Don "Ollie" Olivett

"It doesn't work!"

Sofa Soccer

Perhaps you've been watching World Cup soccer on TV, and you're tempted to get up off the sofa and try the game yourself. Allow me, as a big believer in the benefits of exercise, to offer you these words of encouragement: Get back on the sofa.

I say this because recently I played in a soccer game (or "match") on a regulation soccer field or ("pitch"), and I wound up fearing for the safety of my most sensitive male anatomical parts (or "Roscoes").

I blame my wife. She's a sportswriter, and she covers South Florida's Major League Soccer team, which is called the "Miami Fusion." (This name represents the powerful bond that forms, in this multicultural melting-pot community, between your thighs and your car seat.)

I attend most of the Fusion games, because I like to sit in the press box and help the sportswriters by offering knowledgeable soccer observations such as, "I bet that hurts when they hit it with their heads!" and "There's the beer vendor!"

The reason I know so much about soccer is that I used to play it myself, as a college freshperson in 1965. The type of soccer I played was "intramurals," which comes from the Greek words "intra," meaning "guys," and "murals," meaning "who are not trying too hard." If the ball happened to come directly to us, we'd try to kick it, but we did not go looking to get involved.

So I remembered soccer as a casual, relaxing activity, which is why, when my wife and I were asked to play in a match between the media and the staff of the Miami Fusion, I said sure. I figured we'd jog around in the vicinity of the ball for a few friendly minutes, then go to a restaurant.

I was an idiot. I realized this the instant we arrived at the stadium. Most of the other people, on both teams, were serious, cleat-wearing soccer players. Some had played on professional teams, where they ate intramural players for their team snack. They were shouting Spanish soccer expressions that translate roughly to, "I shall kick the ball with great velocity, so stand clear, lest it pass through your torso and travel a great distance farther with your pancreas clinging to it!"

The other problem was the size of the playing field. It always appeared, from up in the press box, to be about the size of a football field, but when I actually stood on it, I realized that it was much closer, in terms of square footage, to Kansas. I became exhausted before the game even started merely from jogging to the middle of the field, where I had the following conversation with one of my teammates, a foreign journalist who spoke very limited English:

ME: What am I supposed to do?
HIM: Okay!
ME: No, really, I have no idea what to do.
HIM: Yes!

When the game started, I ran around in a sort of ampersand pattern. Every now and then, the ball would shoot past me, followed by people yelling in Spanish. One time the ball came directly toward me, and I was about to kick it when I heard cleated footsteps approaching from behind at an estimated 140 miles per hour. Because I am a free-thinking '90s guy, I'm not ashamed to say that it was a woman player who knocked me sideways like an inflatable Bozo doll and took the ball away. I AM ashamed to say that I was then replaced in the lineup by a man named Leo Muller who is—I swear I am not making this up—eighty-nine years old. Leo took up soccer in his late 60s, and he's in a league, and he played WAY better than I did, despite the fact that he has about the same foot speed as a geranium.

At halftime, my wife, who had also been running around out there somewhere, came to me on the sideline. I figured that, as a competitive person and sports journalist, she wanted to discuss tactics.

She said: "Do these shorts look too big?"

As a veteran male, I know it's a big mistake to answer that type of question, so I trotted onto the field for the second half. This was an even bigger mistake, because I wound up being part of a "wall." This happens when your team commits a foul, and the other team gets to kick the ball at your goal, so the players on your team line up in front of the kicker to try to block the shot. All the men put their hands over the part of their body they value the most, which needless to say is not their brains.

Fortunately, the ball was kicked in such a way that nobody in the wall will have to change choir sections, if you get my drift. Finally, after about a month, the game ended. I will frankly admit that the Fusion staff team was a lot better than the media team. But since the media get to write the story, I'm stating here, for the official record, that we won 158 to 3, and I personally scored nine touch-downs. So all in all, it was a lot of fun, and I look forward to playing soccer again. When they pry my cold, dead butt off the sofa.

Dave Barry

Whatever Works

Throw your heart over the fence and the rest will follow.

Norman Vincent Peale

Five-foot, three-inch Chris Robinson was seeing limited action with the basketball team at Sheridan Junior High School in Arkansas. As any fourteen-year-old would, he wanted to get off the bench into the games. So each day after practice he worked by himself in the gym—shooting, dribbling, shooting some more.

One day, after a long solo shooting session, he heard that the local bank was offering a twenty-five-dollar savings bond to anyone who could sink a shot from half-court during the halftime program the bank sponsored at all Sheridan High School home games. Since he was alone, Chris decided to try the long shot.

He walked to the midcourt stripe and looked at the hoop. He set his feet, took a deep breath and let loose with his best one-handed set shot. It fell far short of the goal. Chris retrieved the ball and tried a two-hander. It was a bit closer but nowhere near close enough. He stepped back from the midcourt stripe, took two giant steps and shot again. No luck. Next, he tried a full run-and-shoot two-hander; after that, a hop-skip-and-launch shot; and finally an underhand scoop shot.

All failed to make the distance.

One more try. This time he came up with the shot that would make Chris Robinson famous. Sort of.

He turned his back to the goal, dipped the ball down between his knees and with all his strength heaved the ball back over his head . . . and *swish*.

Astonished, he tried his shot several more times. He missed more than he made, but he seemed to have a knack that allowed him to make more of these shots than anyone would expect.

At the next home game, he couldn't wait for the half-time program. While his older sister, Courtney, played on the girls' varsity team, Chris ran around scrounging all the ticket stubs he could. He waited anxiously for the drawing that would give a ticket holder a chance for the bank's twenty-five-dollar bond. None of the numbers on his stubs were called.

He continued to practice his special shot. He felt confident that he could hit one out of three attempts. He wanted at least to get a chance. So every game he was there, scrounging ticket stubs, ready for a chance.

On the last game of the season, Chris sat in the bleachers with his ticket stubs spread out before him. By now, he was bargaining for ticket stubs, promising a percentage of his twenty-five dollars. The opportunity to try his shot before most of the 3,300 population of Sheridan meant far more than a savings bond. He listened for the numbers. He thought he heard one of them called! He scanned his stubs frantically. He didn't see the number. He went through them again. Surely, he had it! But no.

His heart sank. Then, an older boy a few rows back said,

"Hey, Chris, I've got it. There's no way I'm going out there and try that shot. Do you want it?"

Chris scampered up the bleachers, grabbed the ticket and ran down to hand the ticket stub to the halftime announcer, who looked at the ticket stub, smiled and handed Chris the basketball. He took the ball and looked at the goal. He looked at the crowd and saw mostly familiar faces.

"Make it, Chris!" someone yelled from the section where all the junior high kids sat for home games.

Chris slowly turned the ball in his hand. He saw Courtney standing near the goal, watching him with her fingers crossed. Chris bounced the basketball and carefully placed both heels on the edge of the half-court stripe. The crowd assumed he was facing the wrong goal. A voice bellowed, "Hey, Chris! Turn around, you're shootin' at the wrong basket!"

When it became apparent that Chris knew precisely what he was doing, there were a few whoops and shouts of encouragement, then the gymnasium grew quiet.

Taking a deep breath, Chris twisted around for one last look at the basket. Then he turned and looked at the basket that faced him. He looked to both sides, measuring. He paused, and then, holding the ball in both hands, dipped it between his knees, almost to the floor.

Chris fired the ball back over his head and waited. He didn't turn around to look. He watched for the reaction of his buddies seated in the top row of the bleachers. It seemed like an eternity. The ball, rotating slowly, descended quietly. Then, to the absolute delight and shock of the entire crowd, it went ... *phhffiiittt!*

Nothing but net.

Chris Robinson was famous. He was the kid who had made "that shot" ... "the shot heard 'round town."

Grady Jim Robinson

The Winner

Failure is not failure to meet your goal. Real failure is failure to reach as high as you possibly can.

Dr. Robert Schuller

It was the first swim meet of the year for our newly formed middle-school aquatics team. The atmosphere on the three-hour bus ride was electric with anticipation as the band of forty-eight adolescents thought of nothing but victory. However, the electricity turned into shock as our minnows filed off the bus and stared in disbelief at their muscle-clad Greek-god-like opponents.

The coach checked the schedule. *Surely there's been a mistake,* he thought. But the schedule only confirmed that, yes, this was the right place and the right time.

The two teams formed a line on the side of the pool. Whistles blew, races were begun and races were lost. Halfway through the meet, Coach Huey realized that he had no participants for one of the events.

"Okay team, who wants to swim the five-hundred-yard freestyle?" the coach asked.

Several hands shot up, including Justin Rigsbee's. "I'll race, Coach!"

The coach looked down at the freckle-faced youth and said, "Justin, this race is twenty lengths of the pool. I've only seen you swim eight."

"Oh, I can do it, Coach. Let me try. What's twelve more laps?"

Coach Huey reluctantly conceded. *After all,* he thought, *it's not the winning but the trying that builds character.*

The whistle blew and the opponents torpedoed through the water and finished the race in a mere four minutes and fifty seconds. The winners gathered on the sidelines to socialize while our group struggled to finish. After four more long minutes, the last exhausted members of our team emerged from the water. The last except for Justin.

Justin was stealing breaths as his hands slapped against the water and pushed it aside to propel his thin body forward. It appeared that he would go under at any minute, yet something seemed to keep pushing him onward.

"Why doesn't the coach stop this child?" the parents whispered among themselves. "He looks like he's about to drown, and the race was won four minutes ago."

But what the parents did not realize was that the real race, the race of a boy becoming a man, was just beginning.

The coach walked over to the young swimmer, knelt down and quietly spoke.

Relieved parents thought, *Oh, he's finally going to pull that boy out before he kills himself.*

But to their surprise, the coach rose from the concrete, stepped back from the pool's edge, and the young man continued to swim.

One teammate, inspired by his brave friend, went to the side of the pool and walked the lane as Justin pressed on. "Come on, Justin, you can do it! You can do it! Keep going! Don't give up!"

He was joined by another, then another, until the entire team was walking the length of the pool rooting for and encouraging their fellow swimmer to finish the race set before him.

The opposing team saw what was happening and joined the chant. The students' contagious chorus sent a chill through the room, and soon the once-concerned parents were on their feet cheering, shouting and praying. The room was pulsating with energy and excitement as teammates and opponents alike pumped courage into one small swimmer.

Twelve long minutes after the starting whistle had blown, an exhausted but smiling Justin Rigsbee swam his final lap and pulled himself out of the pool. The crowd had applauded the first swimmer as he crossed the line in first place. But the standing ovation they gave Justin that day was proof that the greater victory was his, just for finishing the race.

Sharon Jaynes

"I think we better have a little talk with Wilson after the meet."

CLOSE TO HOME. ©*John McPherson. Reprinted with permission of Universal Press Syndicate. All rights reserved.*

The Great Potato Pickoff Play

It was late in the season, and the Williamsport, Pennsylvania, Bills were going nowhere. Twenty-eight games out of first place in the Class AA Eastern League, they were facing an embarrassment of near-epic size.

Ball games had become a grim duty for Orlando Gomez, who had been coaching in the minors for ten years. An emotional man, Gomez might react to a loss one day with a compassionate postgame lecture, complete with a tearful "I luff you guys," and the next day challenge team members to a fistfight.

One of Gomez's least-popular moves that summer had been to send Bills catcher Dave Bresnahan back down to Class A ball. In every tight group of young men, whether convicts, soldiers, schoolboys or ballplayers, there is a character like Bresnahan.

Sending Bresnahan down to Class A ball seemed logical to Gomez. The team needed a change, Bresnahan was hitting under .200 and there was a kid in Kingston whom the Cleveland Indians, the Bills' parent organization, considered a prospect. What the manager could not have known was how important Bresnahan was to the team, the countless daily ways he motivated them.

In late July the Bills' starting catcher got hurt, and Bresnahan was called back. But by then the season was already a write-off. It was about this time that Bresnahan started talking about the potato.

No one knows how greatness comes to a man. For some it is a gift at birth; for others it comes through struggle. For Dave Bresnahan, it had come in a moment of blinding inspiration in junior college. He'd thought, *Wouldn't it be funny to use a potato in a baseball game?* But ball games had always seemed too important.

Now, twenty-eight games out, at the end of the season, the time had come. "I've always wondered if it would work," he said one night to Mike Poehl, a Bills pitcher. The pickoff trick would make a runner on third base believe that the ball, really a potato, was thrown by the catcher into left field. Then the runner could be tagged out at home with the real ball.

"You would have to have a potato shaped just the right size," Bresnahan explained.

Poehl laughed, but not heartily. The Indians' number-one draft pick in 1985, Poehl wanted badly to move up to the bigs, and more than anything he worried about his won-lost record. The stunt would be real funny, he told Bresnahan, as long as it didn't happen in a game he was pitching.

But most of the Bills loved the idea. It was the one thing they could look forward to, and it was decided that Potato Day would be Monday, August 3. The Bills were scheduled for a doubleheader against the team from Reading. Bresnahan had only one reservation. "What if they let the run count?" he asked first baseman Bob Gergan. So Gergan phoned a friend who worked as a major league umpire and explained the scenario. No clear rule would apply, said his friend. The ump would most likely send the prankster to the showers and move the runner back to third—no harm done—and have a good laugh about the whole thing later.

On Monday morning before the game, Bresnahan bought four choice spuds from Weis's market in Williamsport. Back in his kitchen, he scraped them bare. Then he whacked off the ends and whittled away until they were round. Next he tried to draw on seams with a red ballpoint pen, but the shaved potato was moist, and the ink wouldn't take. He began to worry. "What if the guy on third can see right away that it's not a baseball?" he asked Rob Swain, Brez's roommate and the Bills' third baseman. They took one outside to play catch. To Bresnahan's delight, the potato in flight looked like a baseball.

Bresnahan went to the ballpark that afternoon with a knot in his stomach. He set the carved potatoes on the shelf over his locker. On the lineup card Gomez had penciled him in as catcher for the first game. Poehl was scheduled to pitch.

That was that. Half-depressed and half-relieved, Bresnahan began dressing for the game.

"It's Potato Day!" one of the Bills shouted when he saw the carved spuds on the shelf. "Are you really going through with it?"

Bresnahan leaned over to Poehl. "If I decide to throw the potato tonight, is it all right with you?"

"No way," said Poehl. "I don't want a run counting against me."

Bresnahan shrugged to his teammates, as if to say, What can I do? They started ragging the pitcher.

"Lighten up, Mike," said Swain.

"There's nothing in the rule books about it, Mike," Gergan added. "The run can't count."

Poehl felt himself outnumbered.

"Do whatever you want," he said reluctantly.

The Bills were down 1–0 at the top of the fifth when

Reading's catcher, Rick Lundblade, singled and the next hitter sacrificed him to second. One out, man on second. Behind the plate, Bresnahan had butterflies in his gut. The moment was near.

With a left-handed batter up next, Bresnahan signaled for a low breaking ball inside, a pitch calculated to produce a grounder to the right side of the infield that would move Lundblade to third. Poehl's pitch worked like a charm. The batter grounded out to second, Lundblade was on third and the scene was set.

It's now or never, Bresnahan thought. He stood up and waved his catcher's mitt at home-plate umpire Scott Potter. "The webbing's busted," Bresnahan said.

Potter called time, waving Bresnahan to the dugout to get another glove.

Meanwhile, at third, Swain put his head down and turned away to keep from laughing. Poehl gazed at Lundblade and shook his head.

In the dugout, Bresnahan dropped his mitt and reached for another. The players sitting on the bench watched with a mixture of disbelief and hilarity. Gomez was oblivious.

Bresnahan trotted back to home plate with the potato cradled in his new mitt. As he crouched behind the batter, Bresnahan gingerly removed the potato from the mitt, cupping it in his right hand, which he draped over his right knee.

Lundblade took a lead off third. Out on the mound, Poehl reared back and fired the pitch low and outside. As Umpire Potter shouted "Ball," Bresnahan speared the pitch, leaped to his feet and threw the potato hard toward left field. Swain lunged and deliberately missed it.

At home, Bresnahan threw his catcher's mask to the ground and swore theatrically.

Unsuspecting, Reading third-base coach Joe Lefebvre screamed, "Go! Go! Go!"

Lundblade started home. Bresnahan was kicking the dirt. But just as Lundblade was about to lumber across home plate, a grinning Bresnahan turned and tagged him with the ball.

"Hey, Rick, you're out," he said.

Then Bresnahan rolled the ball back out to the mound and trotted off the field.

The whole stadium was silent for a moment. Meanwhile, the third-base umpire retrieved the potato in left field and jogged toward home plate. "You can't bring another ball on the field," Potter stormed.

"It's not a ball, ump; it's a potato," said Bresnahan.

Potter was fuming. "This is professional baseball," he sputtered. "You guys can't be out here showing me up. That run counts."

"You can't do that, ump," argued Swain, who had run in from third. "It's only a joke. Just do it over."

"No, the run counts."

"Come on, ump."

"The run counts!"

Orlando Gomez took it personally. He saw the stunt as Bresnahan's way of thumbing his nose at the manager for having sent him down to Class A earlier. When the inning was over, he took Bresnahan out.

The episode fired up the Bills. They came back to score four runs and win the game. Mike Poehl ended up with a five-hitter.

After the game, Gomez fined Bresnahan fifty dollars. His teammates immediately took up a collection.

The next morning's newspaper failed to see any humor in Bresnahan's prank, calling his caper "a foolish stunt" and quoting Gomez as saying, "Bresnahan did an unthinkable thing for a professional."

That same day, Gomez summoned Bresnahan to his office and fired him.

Bresnahan had figured he'd get tossed out of the game and probably get fined. But Gomez's decision floored him. For about an hour he was depressed, but then he called his dad to break the news. His father laughed so hard that Brez ended up coughing and crying with laughter himself. Bresnahan went back to the ballpark Wednesday to clean out his locker. On his way he stopped at Weis's market and bought a large bag of potatoes. He placed one potato on each of his teammates' lockers. Then he dumped the last one on Gomez's desk and left this note: "Orlando: This spud's for you!—Brez"

Mark Bowden

IN THE BLEACHERS   By Steve Moore

IN THE BLEACHERS. © *Tribune Media Services, Inc. All rights reserved. Reprinted with permission.*

Fair Play

Live with men as if God saw you, and talk to God as if men were listening.

Athenodorus

One day while golfing with colleagues in the insurance industry, I discovered yet another example of honesty being the best policy. I knew two of the men in our foursome, and was just getting to know our fourth—I'll call him Ace. By the third hole, I had learned his story, an object lesson for all of us.

Ace and his business partner had owned a property-and-casualty insurance agency. They had put in the years and the sweat, and the agency grew into a respected mid-size firm. It attracted the attention of one of the big conglomerates. After some negotiations back and forth, Ace and his partner decided to sell to the "big guns," agreeing to stay on as consultants and continue to do some selling. The paperwork was completed in a flash and everyone seemed pleased.

After a couple years, Ace and his partner felt they weren't active enough and decided they wanted to go back to running a brisker business, like they had before. The "big guns" said they couldn't, claiming they had agreed to never again work in insurance outside the big firm. Ace said, "Show me where we agreed to any such thing." The "big guns" claimed it had been an oral agreement. Ace knew there had never been such a discussion, much less an agreement, so he said, in effect, "See ya in court."

In court, the judge agreed an oral contract is as good as a written one, *if* it could be established there was a contract. His issue was whom to believe. After two days of listening to both sides insist their memory was the truth of it, the judge said, in effect, "It's basically a question of who do I believe, and in the absence of any real evidence, I have to go with my gut. My gut tells me to trust experience. The experience that's relevant here is that a number of years ago Mr. Ace played in the golf state championship. On the eighteenth, he hooked a drive into the rough. He was up and out in one, made his putt and everyone thought he had won the tournament, *except* that Ace admitted he had grounded his club in the hazard and declared a two-shot penalty on himself. No one had seen him ground his club. He could have slinked through and taken the win, but he didn't. He told the truth when he didn't have to, and I believe he's telling the truth now." Case closed.

Fair play *is* the best policy, in sports, in business, in all relationships, for all the right reasons, *and* for ones you can't anticipate at the time you make your choices. I have seen this truth exposed time and time again, and never more tidily proving the old saw—*virtue is its own reward*—than here.

Ed Marion

The Price of a Dream

Never look where you're going. Always look where you want to go.

Bob Ernst

I grew up poor—living in the projects with six brothers, three sisters, a varying assortment of foster kids, my father, and a wonderful mother, Scarlette Hunley. We had little money and few worldly goods, but plenty of love and attention. I was happy and energetic. I understood that no matter how poor a person was, they could still afford a dream.

My dream was athletics. By the time I was sixteen, I could crush a baseball, throw a ninety-mile-per-hour fast-ball and hit anything that moved on the football field. I was also lucky: My high-school coach was Ollie Jarvis, who not only believed in me, but taught me how to believe in myself. He taught me the difference between having a dream and showing conviction. One particular incident with Coach Jarvis changed my life forever.

It was the summer between my junior and senior years, and a friend recommended me for a summer job. This meant a chance for money in my pocket—cash for dates with girls, certainly, money for a new bike and new clothes, and the start of savings for a house for my mother. The prospect of a summer job was enticing, and I wanted to jump at the opportunity.

Then I realized I would have to give up summer baseball to handle the work schedule, and that meant I would have to tell Coach Jarvis I wouldn't be playing. I was dreading this, spurring myself with the advice my mother preached to us: "If you make your bed, you have to lie in it."

When I told Coach Jarvis, he was as mad as I expected him to be. "You have your whole life to work," he said. "Your playing days are limited. You can't afford to waste them."

I stood before him with my head hanging, trying to think of the words that would explain to him why my dream of buying my mom a house and having money in my pocket was worth facing his disappointment in me.

"How much are you going to make at this job, son?" he demanded.

"Three twenty-five an hour," I replied.

"Well," he asked, "is $3.25 an hour the price of a dream?"

That question, the plainness of it, laid bare for me the difference between wanting something right now and having a goal. I dedicated myself to sports that summer, and within the year I was drafted by the Pittsburgh Pirates to play rookie-league ball, and offered a $20,000 contract. I already had a football scholarship to the University of Arizona, which led me to an education, two consensus selections as All-American linebacker and being chosen seventh overall in the first round of the NFL draft. I signed with the Denver Broncos in 1984 for $1.7 million, and bought my mother the house of my dreams.

Ricky C. Hunley

Living to Ride

You have to set new goals every day.

Julie Krone

Kentucky. Saturday. May. An iridescent sky. A stampede of horses. The chance of a lifetime in a lifetime of chance. Everyone in pastels and hats and flowers, 144,110 people gathered in glad circumstances. "Until you go to Kentucky and with your own eyes behold the Derby," Irvin Cobb wrote, "you ain't never been nowheres and you ain't never seen nothin'." A race. An emotion. A turbulence. John Steinbeck wrote those words and these, "beautiful and violent and satisfying," after which, we may guess, he took a nap to rest up from the experience.

Saturday. May 1995. Her race done, Julie Krone came back with mud on her black boots and mud on her face and mud in her ears. All that had been shiny was now made brown by a fine mud thrown onto her in two minutes and more of her hard and dangerous work. Even iridescent days leave some dreamers dirty with dust.

Julie Krone tugged her yellow silks out of her white satin riding pants and walked in the paddock shadows.

Then she ran toward trainer Nick Zito and began a rueful recounting of the race. "Oh, Nick, oh my," she said. "Oh, Nick, the trip was so sweet, just so sweet."

Julie Krone's hands flew in demonstration. She held phantom reins close. She moved them a click to the right. She pushed her hands ahead. "Right where we wanted to be," she said with a smile. On her teeth, mud.

Julie Krone rides Thoroughbreds as well as anyone. She is the only woman ever to win a Triple Crown race, the Belmont Stakes. She feels a race's pace in ways that can be neither taught nor explained. A broken back, a broken ankle, a broken arm, a dozen concussions and a horse stampeding across her chest have not persuaded her to seek safety. She rides the way Bill Shoemaker rode. Waiting, watching, waiting for the time to move. Racetrackers call it sitting chilly.

She is thirty-one years old. At fifteen she came to Louisville for the first time. She and her mother "saved our quarters and dimes" to buy gas for the camper they drove from the family's little farm in Michigan and parked across the street from Churchill Downs. You had to be sixteen to work on the racetrack—so the mother went to a grocery store for paper, scissors and glue to doctor her daughter's birth certificate. By such a needful fraud did Julie Krone get two dollars an hour for walking horses after workouts.

Kentucky. Saturday. May 1979. The hot-walker Julie Krone stood on a barn on the backside and watched the horses move toward her, the sound rising, and then saw the stampede flash by, a blur of colors, a painting done by an artist trying to explain power and speed, a moment that all these years later is part of Julie Krone: "I imagined galloping down the stretch. I could hear the thundering hooves and the roaring crowd. I imagined them laying the roses across my lap. It was a great feeling of romance."

Julie Krone is a pixie. She is 4 feet 10½ inches tall, one hundred pounds. She has outsize blue eyes, pixie-cut blonde hair and a voice so tiny it might be a canary's. This pixie full of romance works in a game that can break your heart and your body. Her smiling explanation of how she has persevered: "Selective amnesia." As for injuries: "Mornings, some parts of me wake up slower than others." Why she does it: "If I'm not on a racetrack, I'm not alive."

When someone asked Nick Zito about using a woman rider, the trainer said, "I don't think of Julie as a girl. I think of her as a rider. A great rider. She has courage that cannot be measured."

So on a Saturday in May, looking to win his third Kentucky Derby in five years, Zito put Krone on Suave Prospect. Four women, including Krone three years before, had ridden in a Derby, but only Krone this time had a good horse. She said, "This is a horse sitting on a win."

Suave Prospect ran well early and along the backside past the barn once home to Julie Krone. He still had a chance as the nineteen horses came to the last quarter-mile.

"But when I pointed him to the outside, to the daylight," she said, meaning she needed a way around a wall of horses, "he didn't give me anything. I hit him with the stick, just to make sure he wasn't bluffing. But nothing." Eighth entering the stretch, Suave Prospect finished thirteenth, a five-dollar cab ride behind the winner, Thunder Gulch.

Mud on her face, Julie Krone walked back to the jockeys' room. Fans called out. "Julie, you're beautiful." "When you gettin' married, Julie?" "Julie, my boy wants his picture with you." Julie Krone hugged a small boy with big brown eyes and smiled for a mother's camera. In the jocks' room, she watched a replay of the race and said, "Such a sweet trip. Darn."

To see Julie Krone up close is to see improbability made

real. Even among the littlest, bravest athletes in sports, she is small. Both ankles were wrapped and padded; her upper arms were bruised, and under her silks she wore the flak jacket that became standard issue for riders after Krone's terrifying fall two years ago put her under hooves. On the jacket, these words: "Julie Krone: Live to Ride."

She brushed mud from her rosy cheeks and watched it fall onto a shelf. Then she arranged the dustings into a small pile and told a friend, "Kentucky Derby mud. Real Derby mud. Put it in your pocket and keep it. You'll want it because I'm going to win this race someday."

Dave Kindred

[EDITORS' NOTE: *On August 7, 2000, Julie Krone became the first woman included in the National Racing Hall of Fame.*]

A Championship from the Sky

To be a champion, you have to believe in yourself when nobody else will.

Sugar Ray Robinson

Our Pony League season whizzed overhead, encapsulated in a fist-sized chunk of horsehide and hurtling toward right field like the bully's punch you see coming but just can't dodge. I turned from my position at second base to face the outfield fence and brace for the blow—there was Chris, head cocked sideways, glove hand extended, dancing a timid tango with a deep fly off the bat of the Southern Bank's best hitter.

No way Chris catches this ball. No way we win this game if he doesn't.

It was a shame, too, because until now, Coach had done a masterful job of hiding Chris in right field, working him into the game when no left-handed pull hitters were due or sending him to the plate when a Hilton Lawnmower victory was no longer in doubt. Chris was a weak link, you see. He never missed a practice, never loafed through a drill, never sassed a coach . . . and never showed a scintilla of improvement. He played the requisite two innings each game—maybe three if we were way ahead. By age fourteen, every other kid as awkward and unathletic as Chris had long given up baseball, perhaps for a musical instrument or a seat in front of a computer—wherever it is pubescent males flee when the herd that roams schoolboy athletic fields is thinned.

It wasn't just a triple-naught batting average that betrayed Chris's meager talents. Nothing in his physical appearance recommended competence, either. He was tall, but not as tall as his long, spindly legs should have made him. In fact, all of his limbs seemed too wispy to control and conspired to produce a snarled gait that traveled in several directions at once. But Chris never heeded his genes. He kept showing up for practice, kept taking a seat after three futile waves of the bat, kept chasing after singles until they became doubles.

Not that his teammates minded. Chris was a nice guy from what we could tell, though he never said much to the kids who earned more playing time. Come to think of it, we didn't say much to him, either. Maybe we'd ask him to fetch us some gum from the concession stand if he wasn't in the game. Or maybe we'd pass him in the hall at school and exchange a quick nod and a smile. On a good day, Chris might even rate a "hello," though we certainly wouldn't have thought to join him at the lunch table or invite him along for a trip to the video arcade. Chris simply wasn't one of the jocks—just a ubiquitous, occasionally amusing sideshow to a team that treated baseball as religion.

As inept as Chris was, he was even more inconsequential. No matter what Chris did to deter the cause, Hilton Lawnmower won every time it took the field, except two games near the end of the summer when Coach mixed up the lineup and let the position players pitch. We were

18–2 in the regular season, and we had managed to push it to 20–2 after the first two rounds of the postseason tournament.

Yes, this was a team of Swiss machination.

I was the magnetic glove with just enough speed to make a decent lead-off hitter. Stephen was the bat that never wilted in the clutch. Brad was the future major-league lefty with command of three pitches by age fourteen. Sam was the power stick, Reggie the dependable backstop, Bryan the blanket that covered center field. Even the bit players contributed—Robbie couldn't hit a lick, but he was a good outfielder and a decent left-handed pitcher; Woodrow was good for a hit every once in a while; Jeff played a dependable third base. Each player was a cog with its own vital function and place.

Except Chris.

Now, irony of ironies, this well-tuned engine stood to backfire because of a twenty-five-cent gasket. Hilton Lawnmower led by a puny run with runners at second and third in the top of the sixth inning of the tournament semifinals. If that ball fell, we'd trail by a run with Southern Bank's ace pitcher ready to trot from the bullpen to snuff any comeback. So as the ball flew over my head leaving a contrail of blur, I consoled myself for a season snipped a game too early. For what other outcome could there be with our summer of weighty accomplishment resting on the narrowest of shoulders?

As I mourned, I got the feeling you get on a slow cruise past an interstate pile-up—you know something terrible is at hand, yet you can't resist a glimpse at the ruination. So I enjoyed the best seat in the house as that ball fell from an orange dusk toward Chris's unsure hand. His pursuit ended, and he camped underneath the descending orb, eyes clamped shut, glove raised in a posture meant more for protecting than catching. My knees crimped and my heart fluttered as the ball completed the final feet of its dastardly route.

And I stood there in slack-jawed silence as Chris plucked a championship from the sky. The ball fell directly into his glove pocket and stuck there. Chris had never caught a fly ball in his life, and I'm fairly certain he never caught one again. But his one-play dalliance with hand-eye coordination coincided with the most critical juncture of our season. Chris returned to the dugout clutching that third out, had a seat on the bench and wept as grateful teammates huddled around to cheer his good work. As I looked toward the other end of the dugout and saw Coach standing there, his eyes welling up a little bit, I realized Chris was a cog, after all.

He was the part of a championship season none of us would ever forget.

Jeff Kidd

Although the glove was tough to maneuver, Mark hadn't missed a fly ball since his sophomore year.

When Baseball Grew Up

One man with courage makes a majority.

President Andrew Jackson

[EDITORS' NOTE: *The following story took place over fifty-five years ago, as World War II was coming to an end. Many changes were taking place in the country and it was apparent that the racial barrier in major league baseball would be changing as well. The key question: Who would have the courage to take the first step? In the story below, the author quotes baseball scout Clyde Sukeforth in the pivotal encounter between Branch Rickey, the president and general manager of the then Brooklyn Dodgers, and a young African-American ballplayer named Jackie Robinson.*]

In August 1945, Mr. Rickey sent me out on an assignment, which I guess you might describe as memorable. He called me into his office one day and told me to have a seat.

"The Kansas City Monarchs are playing the Lincoln Giants in Chicago on Friday night," he said. "I want you to see that game. I want you to see that fellow Robinson on Kansas City. Talk to him before the game. Tell him I want to know if he's got a shortstop's arm, if he can throw from the hole. Ask Robinson to have his coach hit him some balls in the hole."

Mr. Rickey had been talking about establishing a Negro club in New York called the Brooklyn Brown Dodgers and we had been scouting the Negro leagues for more than a year. But you know there was always something strange about it. He told us that nobody was supposed to know what we were doing. So, instead of showing our credentials and walking into a ballpark, as we normally would have done, we always bought a ticket and made ourselves as inconspicuous as possible.

"Now, Clyde," the old man went on, "if you like this fellow's arm, bring him in. And if his schedule won't permit it, if he can't come in, then make an appointment for me and I'll go out there."

Mr. Rickey go out there? To see if some guy named Robinson was good enough to play shortstop for the Brooklyn Brown Dodgers? Well, I'm not the smartest guy in the world, but I said to myself: *This could be the real thing.*

So I went to Chicago and out to Comiskey Park. I seemed to remember that this fellow Robinson's number was 8. A few fellows came out, and one of them had number 8 on him. I stood up and said, "Hey, Robinson." He walked over. I introduced myself and told him just what I was supposed to tell him.

He listened carefully, and when I was through he spoke right up—Jackie was never shy, you know.

"Why is Mr. Rickey interested in my arm?" he asked. "Why is he interested in me?"

And I said, "That is a good question. And I wish I had the answer for you. But I don't have it."

"Well," he said, "I'd be happy to show you what arm I have, but I'm not playing today. I've got a bad shoulder, and I can't throw the ball across the infield."

I talked to the guy for a while, and I thought to myself:

Mr. Rickey has had this fellow scouted. The only thing he's concerned about is his arm. Is it a shortstop's arm? Well, I had heard reports that he was outstanding in every way. A great athlete. So I thought: *Supposing he doesn't have a shortstop's arm? There's always second base, third base, outfield.* I liked this fellow.

"Look," I said, "you're not in the lineup. If you could get away for two or three days, it won't arouse anybody's suspicions. Tell your manager that you'll be back in a few days. We'll go into New York. I think the old man would like to talk to you." I asked Robinson to meet me down at the Stevens Hotel after the game, and we would talk some more.

Later, it occurred to me that they might not let him in. This was 1945, remember. So when I got to the hotel, I saw the bellman out front, and I gave him a couple of bucks and I said, "There's going to be a colored fellow coming along here, and I want you to show him to the elevator." He said he would do that.

Evidently Jackie had no trouble getting in, because he came up to the room later on. And he starts right off. "Why is Mr. Rickey interested in my arm? Why does he want to see me?"

"Jack," I said, "I can't answer that. I don't know."

"You can't blame me for being curious, can you?"

"I can't blame you," I said, "because I'm just as curious as you are."

You could feel it boiling inside of him. *Why is Mr. Rickey interested in my arm?*

"Look, Jack," I said, "you know that the old man has originated a lot of things, he's revolutionized things, and I'm hopeful it's something along those lines . . . but I just don't know."

But he wouldn't let up. He kept pressing me.

"Tell me what he said."

"I told you," I said.

"Tell me again."

"He told me to come out and see if you've got a short-stop's arm. He also said that if you couldn't come to Brooklyn to see him, he would come to you."

The significance of that last part wasn't lost on him. I could see that. He was no fool, this fellow. No, sir! The more we talked, the better I liked him. There was something about that man that just gripped you. He was tough, he was intelligent and he was *proud*.

"Mr. Sukeforth," he said, "what do *you* think?"

I was honest. I'd learned in a short time that that was the way you had to deal with Robinson.

"Jack," I said, "this could be the real thing."

It evidently sat well with him. It pleased him. Was he afraid of the idea? He was never afraid of anything, that fellow.

Now this is Friday night, and on Sunday I have to see a second baseman in Toledo. So I asked Robinson if he would meet me in Toledo, and meantime I would make transportation arrangements in New York.

"I'll meet you," he said.

"You got money?" I asked.

"I've got money," he said.

Well, he did meet me in Toledo and we boarded the sleeper for New York that night. When I got up the next morning, he was already up.

"Jack," I said, "let's go get some breakfast."

"No," he said, "I'll eat with the boys." He meant the porters.

I didn't make an issue of it. I went and got breakfast and came back, and we sat and talked on the way in. When we got to New York, I took him straight out to the Brooklyn Dodgers' office, at 215 Montague Street.

I brought him into Mr. Rickey's office and made the

introductions. Then I said "Mr. Rickey, I haven't seen this fellow's arm. I just brought him in for you to interview." But the old man was so engrossed in Robinson by that time that he didn't hear a damn word I said. When he met somebody he was interested in, he studied him in the most profound way. He just stared and stared. And that's what he did with Robinson—stared at him as if he were trying to get inside the man. And Jack stared right back at him. Oh, they were a pair, those two! I tell you, the air in that office was electric.

Listen, Mr. Rickey knew he would come under a lot of pressure for signing Robinson. He would be criticized by a lot of people, including some of the big wheels in the Brooklyn organization. But he was always that much ahead of everybody else. He knew this thing was coming. He knew that with the war over, things were going to change, that they were going to *have* to change.

When you look back on it, it's almost unbelievable, isn't it? I mean, here you've had fellows going overseas to fight for their country, putting their lives on the line, and when they come back home again, there are places they're not allowed to go, things they're not allowed to do. It was going to change, all right, but not by itself. Somewhere along the line you needed a coming together.

Do you know for how long the idea was in Mr. Rickey's head? More than forty years. For more than forty years he was waiting for the right moment, the right man. And that's what he told Robinson.

"For a great many years," he said, "I have been looking for a great colored ballplayer. I have reason to believe you're that man. But what I'm looking for is *more* than a great player. I'm looking for a man that will take insults, take abuse—and have the guts *not to fight back!* If some guy slides into second base and calls you a black son of a bitch, you're coming up swinging. And I wouldn't blame you. You're justified.

"But," Mr. Rickey said, "that would set the cause back twenty years."

He went on along those lines, talking about turning the other cheek and things like that. He told Jack that he wanted to sign him for the Brooklyn organization, to play at Montreal. He described some of the things Robinson would have to face—the insults from fans, newspapermen, from other players, including some of his own teammates.

When the old man was through, Robinson just sat there, thinking about it. I'd say he sat there for the better part of five minutes. He didn't give a quick answer. This impressed Mr. Rickey.

Finally, Jackie spoke up. "Mr. Rickey," he said, "I think I can play ball in Montreal. I think I can play ball in Brooklyn. But you're a better judge of that than I am. If you want to take this gamble, I promise you there will be no incident."

Well, I thought the old man was going to kiss him.

Yes, that's about thirty years ago now, since those two came together. I guess you could say that history was made that day.

What was I doing while it was going on? Listen, I was pretty uneasy—remember I hadn't seen the guy's arm!

Donald Honig

3

HIGHLIGHTS
AT ELEVEN

*Far better it is to dare mighty things, to win
glorious triumphs, even though checkered
with failure, than to take rank with those
poor spirits who neither enjoy much nor
suffer much, because they live in the gray
twilight that knows not victory or defeat.*

Theodore Roosevelt
Speech before the Hamilton Club
April 10, 1899

Across Home Plate

The wind blew through John's curly red hair as he stood at bat. Crack! The baseball connected. It sailed high over the left outfield fence. The crowd stood and cheered as he ran across home plate. Then his daydream bubble burst . . . and young John limped away from the empty diamond dragging his polio-damaged leg.

In 1944, a poliomyelitis epidemic ravished the United States. This serious infectious virus hit children especially hard. It caused inflammation of the gray matter of the spinal cord and brought on fever, motor paralysis and muscular atrophy. John's concerned parents kept him away from swimming pools, from theaters, from crowds. But polio does not play fair. On a Sunday in September just after John's seventh birthday, he started walking across the living room at his home in Spokane, Washington. His legs collapsed. His stepfather carried him upstairs to bed. Three years later in 1947, Jonas Salk would develop a dead-virus vaccine that protected against poliomyelitis paralyzation, but it came too late to help John.

For six lonely months, John was in the contagious-patients ward at St. Luke's Hospital in Spokane. His mother could not even visit her little boy. Many tears flowed as the hospital attendants rolled his bed to the window so he could wave to his mother standing on the sidewalk.

Treatments at that time were consistent with the Sister Kenny philosophy—moist hot packs on the affected areas, bed rest and very little, if any, physical therapy. John graduated to leg braces. Subsequent follow-up orthopedic surgeries came a few years later.

As John was growing up, his parents, six younger siblings and friends never treated him as handicapped. Therefore, John never considered himself disabled. He lived in an atmosphere of encouragement. His interest in sports remained high, and he participated as much as he could. He just did, or tried to do, what the others were doing.

John realized that his having polio had turned him away from a career in sports. For an occupation, he knew he wanted to do something with his hands and help people. He enrolled in the University of Washington School of Dentistry, where he became president of his class and graduated in 1962.

As the years passed, John and his wife, Ginger, were blessed with five robust, sports-loving sons. Coaching the boys in soccer and in Little League allowed John to remain involved with sports while he watched his boys grow. On September 7, 1998, John's sixty-first birthday, he and Ginger were attending a baseball game. Their second-oldest son stepped up to the plate. He swung with powerful strength. His home run sailed over the left outfield fence and shattered the history books! Mark McGwire had hit his sixty-first home run of the season, tying Roger Maris's thirty-seven-year-old record.

"Happy birthday, Dad!" Mark yelled. He threw a kiss into the sky in Maris's memory. Then three generations of McGwires—Mark, Mark's son Matthew, and John— greeted the standing, cheering crowd. And John, leaning on his cane, crossed home plate.

Sharon Landeen

Truly a Baseball Immortal

I've always made a total effort, even when the odds seemed entirely against me. I never quit trying; I never felt that I didn't have a chance to win.

Arnold Palmer

On the morning Pete Rose broke Ty Cobb's hit record in Cincinnati, I was already sitting in my box at Riverfront Stadium. A cardboard box, that is. It was Wednesday, September 11, 1985, for you historians, and I was stacked in a storage closet. Suddenly, in midafternoon, I was rushed down to the umpires' room, where an attendant rubbed me up with Delaware River mud (a bit roughly, I might add) and tossed me in a canvas bag with five dozen other balls. Just like that I was on the cutting edge of history.

There was something portentous about that evening. I overheard Lee Weyer, who had umpired at third base the night Hank Aaron hit his 715th home run in Atlanta, saying that for the last three years he'd been promising Rose that he would be behind the plate for Pete's record-setting 4,192nd hit. Sure enough, Weyer was working the plate that night. Wednesday was also the fifty-seventh anniversary of Ty Cobb's last at bat. Even the weather, sweltering for several days, had turned autumnally cool, as if to invigorate the forty-four-year-old boy.

It was an electrifying, emotional evening. When we reached the field, there must have been four reporters for every ball. I couldn't imagine how Pete had been able to go through this every night for two weeks. I overheard one of the ballboys say that Rose had apologized to some of the reporters the night before, telling them that he hoped to get the record hit soon "so you guys can get on with the rest of your lives." That's Pete Rose for you.

Young Cincinnati players kept coming up to Rose during batting and infield practice, asking, "Is this what a World Series is like?" The air had that kind of shivery chill. Reds first-base coach Tommy Helms, anticipating the historic moment, put in a special request to Pete: "Don't you let Steve Garvey shake your hand before I do."

While I waited in the dugout with the other fifty-nine balls, we talked anxiously about the prospect of being hit number 4,192. If it happened tonight, one of us would be immortalized. Only two or three thousand balls have ever made the Baseball Hall of Fame, and only one other from Rose's career. That was his 3,631st hit, the one that broke Stan Musial's National League record. Life can be tough for baseballs that aren't historic. Balls last for maybe a batter or two, then get tossed in a bucket and pounded around in batting practice for a couple of days. Finally they're shipped off to some minor-league team for more batting practice and then hammered until their stitching starts to unravel.

On the other hand, Rose's trophy room—which is where I am for the moment, by the way—is the lap of luxury. Pete treats his milestone balls well. He's kept half a dozen to display at home and given away others to people who are near and dear to him. Third-base coach and hitting instructor Billy DeMars, for example, who has been with Pete in Philadelphia, Montreal and Cincinnati, received the baseballs from Rose's 3,500th and 4,000th hits. Mind you, many baseballs abhor Pete Rose. Rose has knocked us around pretty good. We get irritated when he slam-dribbled us on the AstroTurf. And when he painstakingly wipes the ball marks off his black bat with alcohol . . . well, it's as if we were *dirty* or something. Just before the game, I got to thinking about Ty Cobb's baseballs. I never met any and as you might understand, we don't particularly like to talk about the so-called dead-ball era. It's a touchy subject. But the truth is, the Hall of Fame doesn't have any of Cobb's balls, and the Tigers don't either. I hear that when Cobb became baseball's all-time hit leader, passing Honus Wagner (3,430) with a four-for-four day in Boston back in 1923, newspapers scarcely noticed. No one seems to know where that ball went.

As Wednesday's game began, Weyer carried me and half a dozen other balls out to home plate in his belt bag. I stayed there as the Padres went down one-two-three in the top of the first. With one out and no one on in the bottom of the first, Rose came to bat. He took a pitch high for ball one, then fouled the next delivery back. This was my big chance. Weyer grabbed me and tossed me out to Eric Show.

I was so excited I was nearly bursting at the seams. I was out in the open at last. My senses were sharp. I saw the entire crowd on its feet and counted at least twenty-two Pete Rose banners hung around the stadium. The fans—all 47,237 of them—were chanting his name while wearing, waving and carrying all sorts of Rose paraphernalia. To my great disappointment, however, I saw Kurt Bevacqua playing third base for the Padres. I was hoping for Graig Nettles, who just happens to be the author of my favorite book, *Balls*.

Show threw me slightly inside to Rose, who let me go by, raising the count to two and one. It was scary: the whole way in, Rose stared at me like a hungry man eyeing a piece of fruit. He didn't seem his usual chatty self at the plate, either. Pete was really concentrating. Show wanted me to curve into Rose on the next pitch, so he put me in his slider grip. But as I was about to cross the inside half of the plate, Pete jumped on me. I saw his black bat flash and *bam!* I was flying toward left center-field. I bet Pete knew it was a hit even before I did. That comes with experience. I could see the confetti and the streamers and the balloons flying from the upper decks even before I hit the ground. The noise from the crowd was absolutely astounding.

I came down about fifteen feet in front of left fielder Carmelo Martinez. I bounced off the AstroTurf and shot high in the air. Pete was watching me. I wanted to show him something. Martinez reached up to grab me—I mean, he *just* got me—and saw Rose already making the turn to second base. Martinez fired me in to shortstop Garry Templeton. I think Martinez is a little mad at me, though. If I hadn't bounced so high he would have run me back to the infield and handed me to Pete himself. But there was enough going on as it was. Fireworks began shooting off. A big 4,192! flashed on the scoreboard. And the other Reds were pouring out of their dugout, led by fifteen-year-old Pete Jr. Joining them in a swarm around baseball's new all-time hit leader were Show and the entire Padre infield. Young Petey reached his father just before forty-three-year-old Tony Perez got there. "'Bout time," Perez told his teammate. "I been waiting twenty-three years." Then came Garvey. "Thanks for the memories," he told Rose.

Templeton handed me to Pete, who in turn handed me to Petey. I didn't feel at all slighted. Rose was being hugged and slapped and buried in an avalanche of noise.

After a moment, Perez and shortstop Davey Concepcion even tried to hoist Rose onto their shoulders. They had it planned all along. After getting him partway up, though, Perez said to the 205-pound Rose, "You're heavy." The procession continued. Reds owner Marge Schott came out for a long embrace and a kiss. She signaled to the outfield. A door opened and out rolled a brand-new red Corvette with PR 4192 license plates.

Then everyone cleared away and Pete stood alone. The cheering went on and on and on. You could tell Pete didn't know what to do. So he raised his index finger and then looked up to the sky. He smiled as if he had recognized somebody up there. His father maybe. Or Cobb. Then he started to cry. He turned to Helms, his old friend and teammate from their minor-league days together, and buried his head on Tommy's left shoulder as if to hide his tears.

Petey came out again after five minutes and hugged his dad long and hard. "Don't worry about it, son, you'll beat my record," his dad told him. It was a poignant moment. Many of the Reds were by now crying, too. Only after seven solid minutes of applause did the crowd settle down and the game resume. I was taken down to the locker room for safekeeping and then forced to listen to the remainder of the ballgame over the radio.

Suffice it to say that Rose walked and tripled in his three remaining at bats, and scored both runs in a 2–0 Cincinnati victory.

Deep down, I'm a lot like Pete—tightly wound and lively to the core. But while he goes on playing, I'm going into retirement. I thought I'd be going to Cooperstown, but Pete's talking about giving me to his son to pay for his college education. It's nice to know I'm valuable, but like Pete, I'll always want to get back in the ball game. I know I have a few more hits left in me.

Craig Neff

Joe DiMaggio Made My Day

I'll never forget the local semiprofessional baseball league run by the Tucson Parks & Recreation Department in the summers during World War II. I was fourteen and working to save money for a car. I was one of the youngest hustlers at the ballpark, selling peanuts and soda. Sometimes I went to my boss's house to help roast peanuts for upcoming games.

One league team, the Mustangs, consisted of military personnel from Davis Monthan Air Force Base in Tucson. Their pitcher, Bill Clemson of the Pittsburgh Pirates, had joined the air force when the war started. He was one of many professional athletes serving in the armed forces who would return to their teams once the war ended.

One day I was helping my boss roast peanuts when he told me something wonderful. "It seems that the Mustangs have invited the Santa Ana Air Force baseball team in California to come and play an exhibition game here. The game is to raise money for one of the service auxiliaries in Tucson."

"Sounds good, Boss. It ought to fill the stands and we can do well hustling."

"Yeah, but do you know who's on that team?"

"No, Boss. I've never even heard of them."

He smiled at me and said, "Would you believe Joe DiMaggio?"

DiMaggio? My all-time hero! The game was sold out the first day. One night after work, I found a brand-new baseball that had been fouled out of the park. Now I was ready to get the Yankee Clipper's autograph!

Exhibition day arrived. My dad had bought tickets for the game, and we left for the ballpark early. On the way he told me that the paper had mentioned autographing would only be allowed before batting practice.

When we arrived, the parking lot was already half full. I got into my uniform and rushed into the stands, new baseball in my pocket. As I moved up and down the aisles I kept an eye peeled for my hero to make his entrance. I was high in the stands when all of a sudden a roar went up and everyone was clapping. Joe DiMaggio ran onto the field with his team.

Every fan rushed to the end of the stands with base-balls, autograph books and game programs.

Now what? I couldn't just quit hustling and go stand in line. As I reached the bottom of the aisle and made my way to where Joe was signing autographs, he was smiling and talking to the fans. Cameras flashed. My heart pounded as I watched him and wondered how I would ever get him to sign my ball.

An usher told me to move out of the way. He said I was blocking customers from the line. My boss had stepped out to see DiMaggio and spotted me. He came over and told me loudly, "Move it! . . . Get to work or I'll get some-one else to take your place."

Embarrassment and humiliation racked my body as I felt hot tears on my face. A couple of fans who knew me from previous games tried to encourage me; they saw I was hurting. I made my way up an aisle yelling with a broken voice as I tried to sell the peanuts. By the time I reached the top of the aisle I had regained my composure. Joe DiMaggio was moving into the batting cage. He had finished signing autographs. I made it to where Mom and Dad were seated and told them I wasn't going to be able to get Joe's autograph. Dad pointed to the visiting team's dugout.

"You do go over there and hustle, don't you? Give it a try, son."

DiMaggio entertained the fans by hitting one ball after another over the left field wall until he was finished with batting practice. Everyone clapped as he made his way to the dugout and the umpire yelled out, "Play ball!"

Joe hit a few home runs as the game progressed and his team was in a comfortable lead. I decided to make my move when DiMaggio returned to the dugout. I had seen him go in there after his last home run. With ball and fountain pen ready, I stepped to the edge of the dugout and peeked around the edge. My mouth was dry. I would probably lose my job but I had to take that risk.

Then I got cold feet. As I started to back away another player in the dugout called, "Hey kid, come here. I want peanuts. How much?" I stepped down, almost falling because I couldn't take my eyes off my hero. I handed the player a bag and said, "Ten cents, sir." He handed me a quarter and told me to keep the change. I thanked him and asked if he thought Mr. DiMaggio would like some peanuts. I didn't know how else to get to Joe and maybe get his autograph.

The player turned and yelled, "Hey, Joe, the kid here wants to know if you want some peanuts." Joe turned and said, "Yeah, send him over."

My legs were shaking. I walked over and reached in the case for a bag. Joe reached under the bench and pulled out a duffel bag to get some change. I reached in my pocket and pulled out the baseball and pen.

"Mr. DiMaggio, I'll make you a deal. A bag of peanuts for your autograph, please." He smiled and said, "You're a good hustler. You'd make lots of money in New York." He took the ball and pen. I was in heaven. I handed him the bag of peanuts and he put the cap back on the fountain pen after signing his name. Then, as he handed me the pen, the ink broke loose and ran all over his fingers. He cursed, shaking his head. I didn't know what to say except, "I'm sorry, Mr. DiMaggio. This has never happened." I felt tears running down my face. I wanted to die. My hero was mad as a hornet, so I turned to walk away. One of the other players said, "It's okay, kid. He'll get over it." The player threw a wet towel to Joe so he could wipe his hands. As I climbed out of the dugout I turned for one more look at my hero. He wiped his hands and returned my gaze. I'll never forget his smile and wink, as he called, "It's okay, kid. I'll live. Don't worry about it."

I made my way back to my parents and told them my story. Other folks overheard the story and laughed. One man who said I was making it up believed me after I took the ball out of my pocket and handed it to my mother for safekeeping.

Joe DiMaggio was to be the next batter. I stopped to watch. He was talking to the umpire and the Mustang catcher, showing them the ink stains on his fingers. I yelled as loud as I could, "Get your fresh roasted peanuts right here!" DiMaggio turned and pointed me out to the umpire and catcher. They laughed as he stepped into the batter's box.

Joe DiMaggio made another home run and, even better, he had made my day!

Walter W. Laos, D.D.S.

Give Me a Break!

One day at a local course, the first tee was loaded with players and spectators. Over the PA system we heard, "Would the man in the green slacks and white hat respect the tee markers? Please get behind them."

The player stopped his address and looked around in disgust, and then stepped up to the ball again. Again the PA-system announcer said, "Would the man in the green slacks and white hat please respect the markers!"

The player stopped his address, turned around and shouted, "Will someone please tell the jerk on the PA system that this is my second shot!"

Gene Doherty

Nowhere Else to Go

It may sound strange, but many champions are made champions by setbacks.

Bob Richards

It was late May 1964. Ken Venturi was watching the Indianapolis 500 from Gasoline Alley. It was a natural place for Venturi to be, for his golf career was on its last lap and his life was in the pits. His career had brought countless fulfilling moments, but now things were different.

Venturi was at the 500 to support a friend from California named Johnny Boyd, who was competing in the race. Two days earlier, Venturi had missed another cut. Some guy in the last group chipped in at the eighteenth to knock him out of the weekend. His once-promising career had taken a wrong turn three years earlier, when a courtesy-car driver racing to the Cleveland airport was involved in a wreck. Venturi was a passenger that day. The accident derailed his confidence and career, and now at Indy he was running on empty, headed for home all right, but not with any checkered flag. "I'd gone from Who's Who to Who's He," Venturi recalled. "It was an embarrassment; I was embarrassed. I'd gone from a promising player to just useless."

Venturi was at a watershed point in his life. Thoughts of quitting the tour were circling in his head faster than the magnificent racing machines going around the two-and-one-half-mile oval. The day before the 500, Venturi had placed a call to Bill Jennings in New York. Jennings was the owner of the New York Rangers and chairman of the following week's Westchester tournament. Venturi begged for a sponsor's exemption. "I really need this, my house is already up for sale, I'm broke." Venturi knew his only other option was "to go back to Hillsborough, California, and sell cars." Jennings's reply was hardly enthusiastic. There was only one spot open and he really wouldn't know until Sunday afternoon. "Call back tomorrow," he said.

On Sunday at the speedway, Venturi could hardly concentrate on the race. How could he when his life was operating under a yellow flag? Who could blame Jennings for saying no? The year before at Westchester, Venturi shot eighty, then the next day picked up and withdrew. As the race neared its conclusion, Venturi found a phone at the back of Boyd's garage. He dialed New York and then heard "the four most important words of my life: 'You've got the invite.'" Venturi remembers saying, "Mr. Jennings, I promise if I ever make it, I'll find a way to give it back."

About that time, Boyd pulled his car into the garage with a fourth-place finish and a horde of writers in tow. He looked Venturi's way and asked if he had gotten the green light. Thumbs up, signaled Venturi. Boyd addressed the media, "I finished fourth today, but you see that guy over there? He's Ken Venturi, and in a couple of weeks he's going to win the Open."

The next week at Westchester, he finished third and won $6,400 and "went to the back of the locker room and cried my eyes out. I couldn't believe I'd made that much money. I knew then that I wasn't backing off. I had my nerves back." Plus his confidence. Venturi was on his way to making Boyd's prediction prophetic.

Venturi had always heard one voice buried in his brain. It belonged to his father. His dad was a proud man of Italian heritage who never satisfied his son's insatiable desire for praise. At the 1964 U.S. Open at Congressional, the hidden voice was working overtime. On June 12, Venturi emerged as a serious threat to the Championship during the first leg of the thirty-six-hole, final-day competition. In the morning eighteen, Venturi had shot a remarkable sixty-six, a round that had been somewhat compromised at the end by two closing bogeys, a result of the delirium-inducing heat. Temperatures were nearing 100 degrees with humidity to match. During the two-hour break between rounds, Venturi was advised to call it a day. The doctors feared possible heat stroke. They said it could be fatal. Venturi heard the voice. It was saying, "Quitting is for losers. The easiest thing in the world to do is quit." Venturi told the medical crew that he was going back out there. "I have nowhere else to go."

Venturi forged ahead, playing the last eighteen in a fog, and by day's end unable to recall a single shot struck by his twenty-one-year-old playing companion, Ray Floyd. At the last hole, Venturi sank a ten-foot putt to secure his victory. Sapped of energy, he watched, dazed, as Floyd took the ball out of the hole. Floyd, a future Open champion himself, was misty-eyed as Venturi mumbled his now-famous line, "My God, I've won the Open." It was one of the most unexpected and meaningful triumphs in golf history.

In '64, Venturi not only won the Open, but later showed it was no fluke by taking Hartford and the American Golf Classic at Firestone. In three months, he'd gone from possible Car Salesman of the Year in California to *Sports Illustrated's* Sportsman of the Year. The golf glory would last only two more years. By 1966 he was diagnosed with carpal tunnel syndrome, a debilitating affliction to the hands. He was no longer able to grip a club in competition without overriding pain. When he told his father that his all-too-brief career was now over, the reluctant praiser gave his boy the most important compliment of his lifetime: "Son, you were the best I ever saw."

As for his promise to Bill Jennings that "if I ever make it, I'll find a way to give it back," Venturi has returned to Westchester for over two decades to spearhead two charities that collectively have raised over $7 million for worthy causes. Ken Venturi proves that a man's word and his intestinal fortitude are two of the most honorable virtues known to mankind. They make Ken Venturi a Sportsman for All Time.

Jim Nantz

He's Gonna Do What?

When you're not practicing, remember that someone somewhere is practicing, and when you meet him he will win.

Ed Macauley

Before the Saints had their Superdome, they played at Tulane Stadium, the old Sugar Bowl. The New Orleans fans were so excited in 1967 about having a team at last that they would start stomping their feet so fast those old metal bleachers would begin to sway. Several times, I thought it was an accident about to happen.

A great Saints game happened on November 8, 1970, at Tulane Stadium, against the Detroit Lions. The Lions scored the go-ahead touchdown to make it 16–14, with eight seconds to go. They figured they had the game won.

On the kickoff, New Orleans caught the ball in the end zone and did not advance it, thereby taking possession on the twenty-yard line with eight seconds still on the clock. Billy Kilmer threw a sideline pass to Al Dodd, who stepped out of bounds, stopping the clock with three seconds to play. The Saints called their last time-out.

Kilmer went to the sideline to get the play. It was decision time for rookie Saints coach, J. D. Roberts. (Tom Fears, coach since 1967, had been fired earlier that week, and Roberts had assumed command.) "Just throw a 'Hail Mary,'" Roberts said. "No," said assistant coach Don Heinrich, "let's kick it." Roberts frowned, then smiled. "Okay, let's go for it."

He called, "Field goal, team!" North was sending Tom Dempsey in to try a sixty-three-yard field goal. I had seen some great kickers in the NFL—guys like Lou Groza and George Blanda. Back then, more than forty yards was exceptional, and the record was only about fifty-four. I wasn't alone in thinking Roberts didn't have a clue what he was doing.

Lions defensive tackle Alex Karras asked me, "What's he doing?"

I told him, "The Saints are going to try a field goal."

"You've got to be kidding me," Karras said. "They're going to be kicking from their own territory."

I shrugged. "I don't make these decisions, Alex."

Dempsey had a deformed right foot. His foot ended about where the arch is. He wore a piece of leather over the stub of that foot. Some opponents complained because he didn't wear a standard shoe. I figured he didn't wear a standard shoe because he didn't have a standard foot. Officials look for instances of unfair advantage, but I couldn't see any here.

Dempsey looked as surprised as the rest of us but trotted out on the field with full confidence. Center Jerry Sturm's snap was perfect. Holder Joe Scarpetti set it down right on the mark. Dempsey took his normal step and booted it. Straight as could be, the ball split the uprights as time went to zero. I gave the touchdown signal and ran off the field as the Saints cleared the bench to congratulate Dempsey. The Lions hardly moved, stunned and immobile. It was beyond amazing.

The New Orleans *Times-Picayune* played it up the next day: "It's Dempsey–Tunney again. Dempsey kicks a wonder; Tunney calls it good." A picture showed Dempsey just finishing his kick and my touchdown signal behind him.

Dempsey's amazing feat held solo as the longest field goal on record for twenty-eight years (until October 25, 1998, when Denver Broncos kicker Jason Elam tied the record as time expired in the first half of a game against Jacksonville).

Jim Tunney

The Ultimate Passport

Don't just learn the tricks of the trade. Learn the trade!

James Bennis

My family moved quite a bit when I was growing up, and sports was the one connective tissue in every town. We lived in Maryland, people followed the Colts. In Cincinnati, it was the Reds, in Boston the Celtics. I always wanted to be a sportswriter and I was blessed that my parents never said, "You can't do that, girls don't do that." And I was determined. My family had to weather this passion. When other girls dressed up as Cinderella on Halloween, I went as Sam Jones, the legendary backcourt player for the Celtics! I became one of the first women sportswriters, for the *Boston Globe*, in the early 1970s. It was a true frontier then, and there were many rough, even humiliating moments. At a Pittsburgh Steelers game in 1976, I waited for quarterback Terry Bradshaw in the parking lot for an interview (there were no provisions for equal access back then). When Terry finally came out and saw me with my notepad and a pen, he signed an autograph and hurried away. Mortified, I had to yell, "No, I'm a reporter, I have questions for you!" Pat Riley, the NBA coach, once sent me a note, and I always carried the thought with me. He wrote, "In every adversity is a seed of equivalent benefit; it's up to you to find it." I have learned that persistence, knowledge and a healthy dose of humor can make the difference.

The great thing about sports is that it is the ultimate passport—the cab driver or the king can talk about the Chicago Bulls or the Dallas Cowboys or the New York Yankees. It transcends all races and creeds, even nationalities. My favorite memory in all my years of covering sports came in the mid-1980s, when Martina Navratilova went home to Czechoslovakia for the first time since defecting to the United States in 1976. When she left, she became a nonperson behind the Iron Curtain. No one wrote of her wondrous Wimbledon titles or her great achievements. She was officially ignored—even her parents couldn't read about her success. On that rainy day in 1986, she returned as a member of the US Federation Cup, and I was lucky enough to be there to cover it. Word spread throughout Prague that the great Martina was coming home. When she landed and emerged to walk down the steps of the plane to the tarmac, she saw thousands of people who'd defied the government and had come to see her arrival—parents holding their children above a chain-link fence to catch a glimpse of the great Czech champion. She was moved to tears, and so was everyone else. It was a moment when sports was at its deepest, most satisfying best.

Lesley Visser

The Champion

Friendship is a single soul dwelling in two bodies.

Aristotle

He dozed in a fuguelike state. The blue-and-white striped wallpaper merged with the blue directional stripe on the white linoleum floor, ending at his closet. His Dodger Blue shirt hung next to his autographed Dodger hat.

I stood watching twelve-year-old John asleep in his hospital bed. His ghost like visage was covered with large and small areas of bruising. His skin was shriveled and had excoriated patches. John was dying—diagnosis: acute myelogenous leukemia. He had undergone three courses of chemotherapy; all were unsuccessful. There were no further treatments. My fellow interns suggested the most merciful approach was to keep him pain-free and let him die in his sleep. But they had not talked to John. He had not shared his dream to see his Dodgers win the pennant and then the World Series.

John's father had died when he was two. I was touched

he had chosen me as his surrogate father, sharing his baseball dreams with me.

I gently woke John so we could watch the last regular-season Dodger game. Both his Dodgers and my Yankees had already clinched the pennant. "Hey champ," I kidded him. "Your Dodgers were lucky to win the pennant. They will surely lose to my Yankees in the World Series." When the Dodgers won the game, John shrieked with happiness.

He said, "I really wanna see my Dodgers play and beat the pants off your Yankees. I wanna see them become champions of the world."

I vowed I'd do everything in my power to keep John alive so we could watch the World Series together. We could at least share our love for baseball since I had no more healing skills to share with him. "See you for the series, champ," I said. "We'll watch my Yankees murder those Dodgers."

The next evening I was sitting at home sipping a glass of wine, listening to Beethoven's Violin Concerto. I was just beginning to enjoy my first leisurely evening in three days when the phone rang. I dreaded this sound because it might bring news that would limit my precious free time.

I answered the phone. The ward nurse apologized. "Doctor, I know you're not on call, but you left instructions to be notified if anything happened to John. He looks terrible. He's pale and sweaty. His heart rate is extremely rapid. He's having difficulty breathing, grunting with each respiration."

"Please do a stat hemoglobin and hematocrit and type and cross John for three units of blood," I told the nurse. "Until the blood is available hang Ringers Lactate in his IV. I'll be right over, but if anything happens before I get there call a code." I remembered the vow I had made and was even more determined to do everything possible to keep John alive so he could watch the World Series.

The blood and I reached the ward at the same time. John looked so tired—so terminal. I knew that unless I could give him the blood rapidly he would not survive the night. I made a surgical incision into John's ankle and threaded a large-bore catheter into the exposed saphenous vein. I attached the blood to the catheter and hand-pumped the life-saving fluid into his body. By sunrise John had received all the blood. The GI bleeding had stopped. He was no longer in congestive heart failure.

John opened his eyes, smiled and said, "Hey Doc, I hope we're on for the World Series tonight." We watched all the games in his room.

We were experiencing the thrill of a potential last game together, wearing our team caps, drinking Coke and eating pizza. "Hey champ, my Yankees will easily win this last game," I kidded.

He said, "Ain't gonna happen, Doc. The Dodgers will be world champions." I must admit that I, a rabid Yankees fan all my life, who had reveled in the antics of Joe DiMaggio, was secretly rooting for the Dodgers.

The Dodgers won the world championship that night. John fell asleep with a smile on his face. Eyes filling with tears, I held John's hand and quietly bid him a silent good-bye. Like his beloved Dodgers, he too was a champion.

Paul Winick, M.D.

Chicken Soup to the Rescue

January 1, 1979. The Cotton Bowl. Notre Dame and Houston. Twenty degrees Fahrenheit, winds gusting at twenty miles per hour, with a wind chill of minus six degrees. Dallas had been turned into a giant skating rink by the worst ice storm in thirty years. Even so, Notre Dame's Fighting Irish started hot, with quarterback Joe Montana guiding them to a 12-0 lead. Then, it turned Houston's way, 20-12 by halftime. What was happening to Joe and his Fighting Irish?

As the teams trotted out for the second half, a groan migrated through the crowd as the Irish faithful noticed that Joe hadn't come out with the team. Soon the announcement came that Montana was in the locker room . . . with the team doctor.

Dr. Les Bodnar had been the team doctor for Notre Dame for thirty years. Joe's problem wasn't a difficult diagnosis. Joe's pale, clammy skin was clue enough. "But I'm not sick," Joe insisted, "I just have the shakes."

There wasn't any medicine in Doc Bodnar's black bag better than a cup of hot chicken soup for what was ailing Joe. Thanks to a Christmas stocking present from his daughter, Bethy, the doc had the right thing at the right time. As Joe sat under a pile of coats feeding himself chicken soup, the crowd noise filtering down to the locker room told everyone how it was going—not good. Coach Dan Devine sent graduate assistant Rick Slager down to see how Joe was doing. Slager raced back with the news, trying to sound optimistic. "His temperature's up to ninety-seven!"

Joe didn't join the team until late in the third quarter, still feeling punk, but with his temperature back to normal. It wasn't a good start, though: three and out. The third ended with Houston ahead 34–12.

That's the way it stood until 7:37 to go, when Notre Dame's Tony Belden blocked a Houston punt and the ball shot up in the air and came down in the arms of Steve Cichy, who burst through a crowd and sprinted thirty-three yards for the Irish touchdown. Montana threw for a two-point conversion and it was 34–20. Was the tide turning? Had the warmth and curative powers of the chicken soup kicked in?

In its next possession, Houston was three and out. Montana marched the Irish sixty-one yards to the end zone, again. The Cougar twenty-two-point advantage had been trimmed to six, with 4:15 left to play.

In two minutes, Notre Dame was threatening again. Montana ripped sixteen yards for an apparent first down, but the ball was stripped and Houston took over. The clock was at 1:50. Gambling on fourth and one at its twenty-nine-yard line, Houston called a dive, but Notre Dame stopped them. The Fighting Irish had the ball, just twenty-nine yards away from the end zone and twenty-eight seconds to get there. Montana scrambled for eleven, then hit Kris Haines for ten more, putting the ball on the eight. Houston called timeout with six seconds to go.

Joe ran a 91, designed to find Haines again at the

sideline, but when Haines couldn't shake free, Joe gunned the ball out of bounds. Two seconds left. Joe asked Haines if he could beat him again. Haines said, "Yes." Joe smiled, "Let's do it." And that's what they did. As Joe said later, "It couldn't have been a more perfect pass. It looked low and outside, but that's where it's supposed to be. It was so clutch."

Haines made the catch in the corner of the end zone as the clock went to 0:00. The score was tied.

Dallas native Joe Unis came on for the extra point. He made it, but illegal procedure was called, backing up the Irish five yards and forcing Unis to try again. Win the game on his leg two times in a row! And Unis did it. 35-34, Notre Dame.

Was Doc Bodnar's daughter prescient, knowing that within a week of Christmas, her dad would need a package of Mrs. Grass's chicken soup to save Irish pride and cement the legend of "Comeback Joe"? Probably not. Maybe it was simply "luck of the Irish" and another instance of chicken soup being good for the body and soul.

Bernie Kish

She Dares to Race the Iditarod

Being the best that you can be is possible only if your desire to be a champion is greater than your fear of failure.

Sammy Lee

Tekla lies beside the sled, too tired to go on. I look down at my most experienced lead dog and curse my luck.

A wrong turn in a heavy snowstorm had taken me more than thirty kilometers out of my way. The four hours lost in regaining the trail have put me far behind the front-runners in the world's longest sled-dog race—the Iditarod—which crosses Alaska from Anchorage to Nome. More important, I have lost Tekla for the remainder of the course.

The grueling route, more than 1,600 kilometers long, has in past races taken from twelve to thirty-two days to complete. It approximates one blazed in the early 1900s between the gold-rush towns of Iditarod and Nome, and the ice-free port of Seward. This is the 1982 running of the Iditarod, held annually early in March since 1973.

I was born into a comfortable family life in Cambridge, Massachusetts. During childhood summers at the seashore,

I spent every waking hour outdoors. Of many pets, my favorite was my dog.

As I grew older, I yearned for a life that would combine dogs and the outdoors. And deep inside I had a feeling that there was a place where I could breathe more freely and where my own hard work would be the measure of my success.

I came to Alaska in 1975, hoping to find my dream. Today, from my cabin door 225 kilometers northwest of Fairbanks and 6 kilometers from my nearest neighbor, I look at my sled-dog team and know my dream is as real as Mount McKinley far beyond. And as challenging as the Iditarod.

For three years I lived in the wilderness, raising huskies and building and training a team for my first Iditarod in 1978. I finished nineteenth, barely in the money. Only the first twenty into Nome share in some $100,000 in cash prizes. I came in ninth the next year, then fifth in 1980 and '81.

Of the fifty dogs I own, I race only fifteen, but more are always being trained to keep this number at full strength. Good racers must be able to trot at nineteen kilometers an hour, lope at twenty-nine. Mine are Alaskan huskies, descended from Eskimo and Indian dogs, bred for stamina and feet that won't be cut by ice or form snowballs between the pads. The dogs average fifty pounds and have long legs and slim builds. They must have an inherent love of running and a never-say-die attitude.

However, each has a distinct personality. Every evening, after training runs of as much as 100 kilometers, I invite some into the cabin for a treat and a discussion of the day's workout. Copilot voices her opinion with a loud howl when I commend her performance. The others thump their tails as their names are mentioned. When it's time to check paws for possible injuries, Tekla and Daiquiri roll on their backs, feet in the air, begging for immediate attention.

February has arrived, and I must put together 700 kilograms of food and equipment to be stashed at twenty-four checkpoints along the course: seventy-five burlap sacks filled with lamb, beef liver, beaver meat, lard, commercial dog food, fish, booties to protect paws, and extra batteries for the head lamp I will use along the trail. Meat must be cut into chunks for easy feeding en route. Honey balls must be made of ground beef, honey, vegetable oil, and vitamin and mineral supplements.

The dogs and I arrive in Anchorage to join an eventual field of fifty-four mushers and 796 dogs. We hear talk of an icy trail with dangerous turns. This only adds to the severe butterflies I already have. Now there is just one day left before I am out on the trail alone with my dogs and the life I love.

There is so little snow in Anchorage this year that our start has been moved eighty-four kilometers northeast to Settlers Bay. The teams will go off at three-minute intervals; I have drawn the twenty-sixth starting position.

My dogs are so eager to get going that it takes ten people to hold them as the earlier starters move out. My friend Kathy Jones, who helped raise my expense money, tucks herself onto the sled amid the gear that every contestant must carry: snowshoes, ax and sleeping bag. The rules require each musher to carry a passenger for the first thirteen kilometers in case of early trouble.

My countdown begins, then we're off! A kilometer and a half out we go into a slide on an icy hill, hitting a downed tree. Kathy and I feel only a few aches and pains, but the team has suffered. Cracker, Ruff and Screamer are running off-pace. Even so, we pass two teams.

Kathy leaves us at Knik Lake, and I continue on alone. It begins to snow as darkness falls. One by one, I overtake twenty-two teams; only three are ahead of me now.

Cracker, Ruff and Screamer quit pulling and begin to

limp. As much as it will slow me, I load them onto the sled to prevent further injury.

Kilometer after kilometer I ride behind them on the runners; I should have seen Skwentna, the third checkpoint, by now. I sense something is wrong. At dawn a musher approaches from the opposite direction and hails me with, "We're at least sixteen kilometers off course."

I turn my team around. All year I have nurtured but one thought: to win. Now my hopes are dashed. With three injured dogs aboard I cannot possibly make up the lost time. Then Tekla starts to limp.

At 6:55 A.M. we straggle into Skwentna, four hours behind schedule. My dogs are played out. I feed them, then take Cracker, Ruff and Screamer to a drop area where they can be flown home. I massage Tekla's shoulder. I can't afford to lose her this early in the race.

We push on. Seventy-two kilometers farther, at Finger Lake, I know my limping Tekla has reached her limit. Tears roll down my cheeks. She, who led my team all the way in my first three Iditarods, who has saved my life more than once, who can even read my mind, now has to be left behind. Her sorrow seems as great as mine as I leave her to wait for a flight home.

With only eleven weary dogs left, I head out again for Nome, still more than 1,500 kilometers away. After just sixteen kilometers, I know we have to rest. I lie in the snow next to Ali and Copilot, now in the lead. They cuddle up against me, and I massage their shoulders and legs. Other teams flash past me. My resolve is shaken, but I'm not ready to give up yet.

On the move again, I think only of reaching Rohn checkpoint, where I will spend a twenty-four-hour layover that the race committee requires. In these first two days on the trail, I have had only four hours sleep.

As we climb into Rainy Pass to cross the Alaska Range,

my mind is not fully focused. I let go of the sled so the team can clamber up a steep bank unencumbered by my weight. I have badly misjudged the energy of my dogs; they shoot away and are out of sight before I reach its top.

For ten kilometers I pursue them. Around one more bend and there they are, the sled on its side but intact. They bark and wag their tails as if to say, "Where the hell have you been?"

I know this close call was the result of my defeatist attitude, and I resolve to have no more of that. We finally arrive at Rohn at 5:01 P.M.

After our twenty-four-hour rest and four hot meals my team is yowling and barking to be off, and my determination to stay in the race is firmer than ever. Even Jimmy is running hard despite sore feet, which I have been treating with medication.

As night falls, the snow grows heavier, wiping out the trail. But I manage to catch up with the leaders, who have lost their way and are waiting for daylight.

Up until this point we have raced as individuals, every musher for himself. But now we must work together, taking turns at trail breaking through the deep, soft snow. As soon as circumstances permit, we'll be off on our own again. We travel in this tedious, time-consuming way for four days and 568 kilometers.

At Ruby, the sky clears, but the temperature drops to minus forty-two degrees as I start out alone down the frozen Yukon River. If I stay too long on the sled, I risk frostbite. Too long jogging behind can impair my lungs. I alternate between running and riding. Jimmy's feet are worse; I'm forced to drop him at Galena. Then a raging storm buries the trail. Those of us in the lead take refuge in a trapper's tent for the night.

Another day's travel brings us to Unalakleet. Only 436 kilometers to Nome! The weather worsens; winds increase to ninety-five kilometers an hour. My eyelashes and those of the dogs freeze shut, and I stop often to clear their eyes and check their feet.

It's midnight. Even with my headlamp, I cannot see the driftwood tripods that mark the trail across this flat, featureless country. Groping from tripod to tripod, I finally reach Shaktoolik with a frostbitten face. Lucy Sockpealuk welcomes us to her home. Even the dogs. It is too cold outside for them to rest easy. And I can't feed them outdoors because their pans blow away. By morning, winds are gusting up to 130 kilometers an hour, piling up nine-meter drifts.

I wait fifty-two hours in the village. When the storm lets up, all the mushers resume the race with new spirit. Only 372 kilometers to go, but the going is tough. We push through the continuing storm, seven lead teams traveling close together.

Then Taboo, worn out from punching too long through heavy snow, must drop out, leaving me with nine dogs of my original fifteen. Emmitt Peters is now running ten, Rick Swenson twelve and Jerry Austin fourteen. Even so, I feel this is still a wide-open race. Thoughts of winning again consume my mind.

Sixty-five kilometers from the finish line, we run into winds as strong as those at Shaktoolik. By the time they have died away, Ali, my best command leader, is tired of taking orders. So I put Copilot up front with Stripe. Both dogs drive hard, and the team picks up its pace.

I am now in fifth place, only a short distance behind Rick, Jerry, Emmitt and Ernie Baumgartner. The final push is on; fifty kilometers to go. My adrenaline is pumping.

I pass Ernie and pull away. I pass Emmitt, but he stays right on my tail. Through the last checkpoint we dash; only thirty-five kilometers now. Someone yells that Rick and Jerry are just two minutes ahead of me. Emmitt remains close behind.

Stripe falters. The change is quick, only forty seconds to switch Ali and Stripe. Emmitt is halfway by me when I holler at Ali and Copilot:

"Go! Go! Go!" The instant I feel my dogs diving forward, I know I've done the trick. I soon outdistance Emmitt.

Ali has raced with me to Nome before and senses he's into the homestretch. He knows his job and gives it his full measure. The other dogs respond to his leadership. I chase hard for thirteen kilometers to pass Jerry. But there's still Rick, barely visible in the distance.

My dogs and I try with all the energy we can muster to overtake him, but he still beats us into Nome by three minutes, forty-three seconds, in a race that has lasted sixteen days. Cheers ring out around me. I gratefully accept $16,000 second-prize money. The last musher will not cross the finish line until ten days later.

The wilderness is my life now, and the Iditarod its ultimate experience. I have only one dream to go. To be number one.

Susan Butcher

[EDITORS' NOTE: *Susan Butcher went on to win the Iditarod in 1986, the first of four wins in the next five years.*]

$\overline{4}$

ON TEAMS AND SPORTSMANSHIP

My responsibility is to get my twenty-five guys playing for the name on the front of their uniform and not the one on the back.

Tommy Lasorda

Once a Cougar

People acting together as a group can accomplish things which no individual acting alone could ever hope to bring about.

Franklin D. Roosevelt

The Cougars were the Cinderella team of the town Little League, making it all the way to the championship game. The team's road to the title began just as one of its players was diagnosed with cancer. Jimmy was battling all the odds, as were his beloved Cougars. They were underdogs at the start of the season, but then a miracle happened. As Jimmy became more and more ill, the Cougars rallied, winning game after game, bringing smiles to Jimmy's face as he heard about the games from his parents while sitting in his hospital bed.

He wanted so badly to be on the ball field with them, but everybody understood that he couldn't. His days were filled with treatments, not practice drills, suiting up and playing. It was hard not to feel heartbroken, and, finally, embarrassed when the radiation treatments caused his hair to start falling out. He didn't want his family to see him, much less his friends and teammates.

As weeks went by, the Cougars kept winning, and Jimmy started winning his battle, too. He was still sad, though. It had been weeks since he'd seen any of his buddies. He missed them so much, but he knew how cruel kids can be, especially to a bald Little Leaguer, so he kept saying no to their offers to visit.

The doctor came to Jimmy's room one day with great news. "You're doing so well, Jimmy," he said. "You can finally go home!"

Although still too weak to play, Jimmy wanted to see his Cougars play for the championship, but he was embarrassed about being bald and refused to leave the house. His mom and dad kept encouraging him, but Jimmy stuck . . . until it was almost game time. His parents saw the yearning in his eyes and pleaded with him, and Jimmy finally let himself be convinced. He agreed to let his mom and dad take him to the ballpark. He wanted to cheer for the Cougars.

As they arrived, Jimmy pulled his Cougar cap deep onto his head and hoped no one would notice him. No such luck. Some of his buddies spotted him right away and ran over with high fives and cheers. "Down to the dugout, man," they said. "You're a Cougar!" What could Jimmy do but go and be thrilled himself?

Game time! One by one the players were introduced over the PA system, and each in turn trotted out to the field. Then Jimmy heard his name called. Surprised and thrilled, Jimmy pulled his cap even harder down onto his head and trotted out to line up with his teammates. His mom and dad saw the brightest smile they had seen in months.

Then came the first notes of the national anthem. Talk about a smile fading fast. Jimmy knew he had to take off his cap, and stand there, merely bald but feeling naked, in front of family, friends and strangers. As he slowly reached up to his cap, he saw that his teammates were making a show of taking off their caps, with wide sweeps of their arms and broad smiles. Every Cougar had shaved his head in tribute to Jimmy! Jimmy proudly removed his cap and placed it over his heart.

Once a Cougar, always a Cougar!

Tim Palesky

Little League chalk talks

The Day Lisa Lost

Don't get me wrong. I'm not talking about the many professional athletes of today who have developed a me-first attitude after being raised in a win-at-all-cost generation. A generation in which role models are severely lacking, and most of the headlines that capture our attention concern those athletes who are in trouble. No, I am talking about high-school sports, where lessons of life are still being learned, and where athletes still compete for the love of the game and their teammates.

I know some of you are thinking, "The high-school athletes of today are just as bad!" And you would be partially right. The me-first attitude is trickling down into the high-school and junior-high athletes.

But in the midst of all of this is a young lady from Wisconsin.

I first met Lisa Kincaid on the volleyball court as she played for a rival high school in the conference where I coach. Many times I was on the opposing sidelines and could only watch in awe at her athleticism. The speed of a cheetah, the mental toughness of a veteran and a thirty-two-inch vertical jump! (Unheard of

for a high-school girl. And she was only a sophomore!)
Starting her junior year, I was fortunate enough to
coach Lisa on a USA Junior Olympic Volleyball team, and
it was during those two years that my wife and I grew to
love and respect her—respect her not only for her many
athletic achievements, but for her unselfishness and
humility to those around her in the face of the many honors bestowed upon her. Besides being one of the most
coachable athletes I've ever had, she was the epitome of a
team player and went out of her way to be humble.
If anyone had a right to be cocky or proud of herself
it was Lisa. Besides being one of the best volleyball and
basketball players in the state, she became a track legend
in the Dairy State. How good was she? She went sixty-four
consecutive conference meets without losing any event.
She made trips to the state finals all four years she was in
high school, and she came away with six state titles. Many
times she was the lone representative at the state competition for her team, and would single-handedly place her
high school as high as third.
Never once did she brag about her accomplishments. In
fact, she felt uncomfortable talking about her achievements and would usually steer the conversation away
from her and to the performances of her younger sisters
or other teammates. Besides coaching her in volleyball, I
was able to see her at many track meets, as my video production company was hired to produce track videos for
other high schools in the conference. I saw many
instances where she would lend her shoes to someone
who'd forgotten her own, or slow down at the end of a
race to finish up stride for stride with her sister, both of
them smiling from ear to ear as they crossed the finish line
together. And I vividly remember Lisa going up to an athlete from a different team and wishing her a happy birthday. The young lady's face just beamed as she told Lisa of

her birthday plans for later that night. I was smiling as I walked away, because I happened to know that it was Lisa's birthday, too, but never once did she mention it to her competitor.

Even with all these accomplishments and displays of sportsmanship, one particular track meet during Lisa's junior year stands out for the way she impressed upon me what is still good about sports these days.

It was a nonconference meet late in the year, and Lisa's coach told her he needed her to run the mile. Lisa had never done so, but agreed to do what was best for the team.

Lisa easily outdistanced the competition, but on the last lap she seemed to grow tired. Two athletes from the other team passed her, and then so did Jane (not her real name), Lisa's teammate. Lisa managed to stay just behind her teammate and cross the finish line at her heels.

Lisa lost an event for the first time in her track career.

You see, athletes in Lisa's track program needed to earn a set amount of points to gain a varsity letter. Lisa knew that Jane, a senior, needed to finish at least third to earn a letter for the first time. Lisa also knew that the two athletes on the other team were most likely going to beat Jane, if they ran anywhere near the times they had been running all year, but that barring an injury during the race, Jane was a lock to finish third—until the coach entered Lisa in the event.

Lisa remembered all this as she lined up for the start of that race. I had wondered why she wore a slight smile on her face after having "lost" for the first time ever. After four years of working hard, Jane finally received her first varsity letter and helped her team win the meet.

And Lisa? On that day, the day she lost, she earned my respect and admiration, and solidified herself in my mind as the role model this generation sorely needs.

Michael T. Powers

Phil Esposito's Wild Ride

In the spring of 1973, the Boston Bruins were knocked out of the Stanley Cup play-offs by the New York Rangers. During the series, Bruins' star Phil Esposito was nailed by a Ron Harris check and taken to a Boston hospital, where doctors diagnosed torn knee ligaments. The star center-man's leg was encased in a cast to protect the injury.

When the Boston players decided to hold a postseason farewell party, one of them suggested that the affair "just wouldn't be the same without Esposito, our team leader." The others agreed. The NHL scoring champ had to be present, even if he made only a token appearance. So they went to the hospital to get him.

While two of the Bruins, posing as security men, dis-tracted hospital personnel, several other players stealthily wheeled Esposito, still in his hospital bed, along a corri-dor, down an elevator and through an exit. Unfortunately, in the haste of their daring departure, they broke a metal railing.

The bed and its famous occupant flew down the avenue while car horns honked and pedestrians gawked. The Bruins, led by Wayne Cashman and Bobby Orr, wheeled their leader to a restaurant not far from the hospital. At one busy corner, Orr yelled, "Signal a left, Phil," and Espo's arm shot out from under the sheets.

After the party, Espo was wheeled back to the hospital. But officials there were not amused at the kidnapping of their famous patient. The Bruins were not only chastised for their behavior, they were presented with a bill charging them four hundred dollars for damage to hospital property.

They dealt with the bill in a predictable manner. While Espo slept, his mates quietly slipped the invoice under his pillow.

Brian McFarlane

It's How You Play the Game

Things turn out best for those who make the best of the way things turn out.

Daniel Considine

When I was growing up, I remember hearing and reading many times, "It's not whether you win or lose, it's how you play the game." In spite of these constant positive affirmations, I didn't believe that. The real world taught me the importance of winning. Finishing first at whatever I was doing became a priority, and if that didn't happen, "how I played the game" was meaningless. In my mind, second place meant first loser.

I've since learned that this winner-take-all attitude ultimately leads an individual in any phase of life to frustration and misery. And it was the world of sports—specifically as a fan of competitive wrestling—that opened my eyes to the value of doing my best and taking pride in the results, regardless of the outcome.

My son Kevin loved wrestling when he was growing up. I remember taking him to his first practice when he was only ten years old. On that warm spring afternoon, we walked into the wrestling room at Father Ryan High School, and he immediately wanted to know what was on the back wall. As we walked closer, he could see that there were fifteen or twenty plaques, each bearing an individual's picture. I explained to him that everyone on the wall was a Father Ryan wrestler who had won a state championship.

Years later, when Kevin entered high school, it was clear he was blessed with a lot of athletic ability. Even as a freshman wrestler he showed promise, and he continued to improve each year. As a senior, he was captain of a team that compiled an incredible record, and he went into the state tournament ranked number one.

He won his first match . . . he won his second match . . . he won his third match . . . and he won his fourth match. Here we were, in the finals of the state tournament, ready to claim our championship. Unfortunately, the next match didn't go well. I don't know if it was the stress of the season, the level of competition or just plain bad luck, but Kevin fell behind early in the match and he never recovered. As I watched the clock wind down in the final period, it was obvious that he wasn't going to win.

His season had ended, his high-school career was over, and we didn't have a state championship. Oh, I was devastated. I felt horrible, and I knew I was going to hurt for a long time. I believe at that moment you could've smacked me across the head with a two-by-four and I wouldn't have noticed. I stood there in shock, unwilling to believe what had just happened, and unable to accept it.

I painfully watched Kevin as he slowly took off his head-gear, shook his opponent's hand, and stood calmly in the center of the mat as the referee raised his opponent's hand in victory. Then he quietly walked out of the gymnasium.

A few weeks later I received a newsletter in the mail from Holy Rosary Academy, where Kevin had attended grade school as a young boy. The school's principal wrote the following words:

> One of our more recent graduates has been the sub-
> ject of our daily newspaper's sports section. In two of
> the articles about Kevin Baltz, his prowess in the sport
> of wrestling was discussed. While Kevin enjoys an
> impressive reputation statewide in the sport of his
> dreams, it is his noble character that is the focus of the
> newspaper articles.
>
> We who knew Kevin as a boy at Holy Rosary are not
> surprised that he should be honored. We enjoyed that
> same quiet heroism in him here. The impeccable cour-
> tesy now described by sportswriters was a hallmark of
> Kevin Baltz five years ago. His self-sacrificing manner,
> his respectful approach to peers, his devotion to friends
> and his spirit of cooperation were all very evident.
>
> We are proud that Kevin's character has left its mark
> at Father Ryan High School, and in the sport of
> wrestling in Tennessee. We are grateful he was a part of
> our lives here. May his spirit continue to bless those he
> will touch in all his life's journeys.

When I read this, I sat down and cried. For Kevin, they were tears of joy. Wouldn't any parent be proud after hear-ing comments like these about his or her child? For myself, though, they were tears of gut-wrenching disappointment.

You see, I had watched every single match Kevin had wrestled in high school, yet I hadn't noticed all the out-standing qualities that the sportswriters and his principal recognized. I was focused on the wins, the victories, the championships. And when he didn't get that final win, I was especially hurt and disappointed. I'd failed to recog-nize that Kevin was diligently working to achieve victo-ries, but always performing with character regardless of whether he won or lost. In that moment, my eighteen-year-old son became my mentor. He taught me that the pursuit of victory is a noble goal, but that winners in life appreciate the pursuit more than the victory itself.

I wish my son had won that state championship and claimed his plaque on the wall in the Father Ryan wrestling room. It was his goal, and I know how badly he wanted it. But really, he got so much more by not winning. That's because his championship plaque would forever be nailed to that wall, visible only to the eyes that walked into that room. Now, every second of the day, regardless of where I am or whom I'm with, I carry a much bigger announcement across my chest, which I'm sure most people see. And it says: "I'm proud of my son."

I applaud my son's effort and accomplishments, and his fortitude to accept that he had done his best. He taught me a valuable lesson about the game of life that has had a profound effect on me, and I am only grateful for his wisdom. I have now achieved an inner peace by refusing to accept losing as an outcome, rather recognizing that it is only a step in the process of growing.

In reality, all of us face adversities throughout our life, some that can destroy us physically, emotionally and financially. Our challenge is to stay in the game and enjoy the competition, whatever the outcome. Yes, we will experience obstacles, we will experience setbacks, we will experience defeat. They are inevitable. But winning in life is not based on the final score. It is only measured by "how we play the game."

Larry Baltz

Making a Point

Energy and persistence conquer all things.

Benjamin Franklin

As a middle-school coach I quickly learned that the easiest way to make your first cut was to look for things a kid could not do. When you are the only coach and you have almost fifty boys trying out, a simple checklist is the best way to eliminate half of them, and it is best to do so during the first two or three days. If a kid could not, for example, handle the ball, shoot the ball or at least get a check in the "hustle/intangibles" box, he simply was not going to be any help. That is the cold, hard truth of coaching and making cuts.

This particular year one kid named Tim quickly had Xs in several areas. He was tall, but a bit awkward, and not a good ball handler. He did, however, get a check for hustle, and he was a surprisingly good shooter. So he made the first cut, even though he looked neither natural nor athletic in drills or scrimmages. There was one other thing that he could not do, and I had made sure to note that on my chart at the start: He could not hear. Tim was totally deaf, the first hearing-impaired student who had ever tried out for any team I coached.

First cut was always easy, but then it got more difficult. The best players always stand out so well that any casual fan could pick them out as keepers. But that year was not a very strong one for basketball, and only three or four players stood out. Choosing the rest of the twelve-man squad was going to be tough, and when I got down to the last couple of spots on the team, there was Tim. He always hustled, something every coach loves, and he simply never missed a shot under ten feet during shoot-arounds. In fact, if we had been playing H-O-R-S-E he might have been my first choice, but he could not get open for his shots during scrimmages. And I could not forget the fact that he could not hear. I did not hold that against him, but I had to be practical and think of the difficulties his handicap might cause in practice. In the end, after considering everything from absences to free-throw percentages, Tim made the team.

He always tried to stand facing me when I explained plays or defenses, and his lip-reading was good enough to keep up with the other players on anything that I taught the team. I forced my players to "talk" on defense, letting each other know where screens were coming, etc. That was a problem, but Tim was smart and constantly watched the floor so well that he improved a great deal on his defense. And his teammates usually did all they could to help him.

I think our record that year was 6–8. Tim managed to play a total of about ten minutes, usually in games that were pretty much decided one way or the other.

Two moments stand out from that season, and neither had to do with a win or a loss. In one game, our point guard made a steal near the opponent's foul line and quickly passed the ball to Tim. However, the referee blew a late whistle, calling a foul on the play. Everyone stopped—except Tim. He raced across midcourt figuring the other players were close behind him, and he headed in for a layup. The referee blew his whistle again but Tim kept going and laid the ball in. Not until the ball came through the net and Tim turned back toward us did he realize that everyone else was still up court. Some of the fans started laughing, but when Tim looked at me I just smiled, clapped my hands a few times, and mouthed the words, "Good shot!" A couple of our players jogged down to meet him, one of them giving him a "high-five" and exchanging grins. Tim was embarrassed, but he was okay.

The other moment was a few games later. We were down by quite a bit with only two minutes left, so I cleared the bench. Tim got several rebounds before the game was over, and with just a few seconds to go, he was fouled going after a loose ball. With the score forgotten (at least as much as middle-school kids can forget a score), our entire team jumped up and stood on the sidelines cheering. Tim was the only player who had not scored that year. I am sure the other fans wondered what was going on when our bench exploded as the ball swished through the net. After all, we were still twenty points behind. Tim just stepped back from the line and looked over at us, holding up one finger and smiling. In more ways than one, Tim had made his point—loud and clear.

J. Michael Key

One Morning in May

Even when I went to the playground, I never picked the best players. I picked the guys with less talent, but who were willing to work hard, who had the desire to be great.

Earvin "Magic" Johnson

"Rain, no game!" While that's an expression sports fans regret hearing, it's one that I welcomed. This was particularly so in junior high.

What "rain" meant was that the softball game for gym classes outdoors had been canceled for the day due to inclement weather, and that the gym teacher would substitute another, less competitive activity for us eighth-graders to play inside the gym.

I loved when it rained on gym days that spring because it would save me and a few others the humiliation of being the last girls picked when each captain (assigned by the teacher) selected her players to make up the teams.

Even then, as a thirteen-year-old, I couldn't believe there wasn't another way to decide teams. Why didn't the teacher have us count off one, two, one, two? All the "ones" could be a team, and all the "twos" the other. Or why couldn't teams be arranged alphabetically? Those whose names started with A–L could be a team, and those with M–Z the other. Wasn't there anything to save those of us who were not "athletically gifted"—who could not throw, catch or hit a ball very well—from being humiliated and left standing with one or two others as "the rejects"?

Imagine the scene: an array of the prized players who had been selected on one side of the field, and a dwindling dismal few remaining, hoping to be called. It was a terribly imbalanced display.

I dreamed of and wished for a new way, had recurring nightmares about the reality.

We girls without athletic ability felt like toys half broken and out of their boxes, on sale tables labeled "75 percent markdown" after Christmas. We felt like books in bins containing overruns or books that no decent reader would have chosen. We felt like the kitten at the pound left behind while others went off with families who lived in white houses with geraniums on the window sills and window seats for catnaps in late-afternoon sun. We felt like orphans in an orphanage whose suite mates had found a home.

However, those feelings changed one May morning.

Her name was Joan. The gym teacher almost always selected her as one of the captains because she was a good player. Taller and heavier than most, she had the power to hit a softball far. Stronger and more muscular than most, she had the endurance to pitch, to throw, to run fast. There was no doubt Joan was the star and, therefore, the captain.

But what Joan also demonstrated—at least on that May morning I remember—was that she had courage. When Joan won the toss that morning, it meant she was entitled to make the first selection for the team. That in turn meant Joan had the opportunity to select the best player. After a little delay in looking over her possible picks and the gym teacher's reminder that there wasn't much time to play, Joan made her first selection.

The first name Joan called out was mine. Joan chose me! And after me, she selected someone else who was also not a richly talented player.

Joan—perhaps spontaneously generous, perhaps consciously sensitive; it doesn't really matter—taught us all something about sportsmanship that day. She demonstrated a fairness, a generosity of spirit. And I'm sure Joan taught several of the girls how to be good losers, because while I don't remember the score at the end of class that May morning, I have little doubt that Joan's team lost.

But what each of us girls won that morning was a lesson to carry with us to our professions as well as to our day-to-day interactions. We learned how to make others feel better by making them feel connected. And isn't that a game every one of us can win?

Ellen E. Hyatt

Marty and Bill were sick and tired of getting picked last in gym class.

When Silence Is Golden

*In basketball, you can be the greatest player in
the world and lose every game, because a team
will always beat an individual.*

Bill Walton

All-American in basketball from Princeton; member
(starting forward) of the 1964 U.S. Olympic team; Rhodes
scholar; member of two world-championship teams during his ten-year pro career with the Knicks; former senator from New Jersey; one-time candidate for president.
That's Bill Bradley, or at least a little bit of the man.

As an NBA referee running up and down the court, I
recognized his talent and skill when he was with the
Knicks. He had a mighty finger-roll and was a leader—a
champion whose work ethic was matched by his ability to
handle victory and loss with equal class—but the incident
that marked him as special for me happened in the 1964
Tokyo Olympic Games.

The U.S. team was matched in a hard-fought gold-
medal game against the Soviet Union. At one point,
Bradley was backed out of the key by a big, bulky Russian

who threw him a sharp elbow to the solar plexus that sent the lanky six-foot, seven-inch Bradley to the floor. Bradley got up, stepped over to the guy and in perfect Russian said, "Please back off, big fella."

The Russian team had been calling their plays in Russian. After Bradley's fluent remark, they stopped communicating totally, afraid that Bradley could understand and would cue his teammates.

Bradley hadn't learned enough Russian to follow their crisp, shorthand calls across the floor. He'd learned just enough Russian to be courteous. When he said "back off," he included "please." That's Bradley's way. This time, though, his regular courtesy led to the Soviet team's unraveling. The U.S. won the gold.

Joey Crawford

Let's Keep a Date

Just before Arnold Palmer won The Masters in 1960, he had committed to play in a country club exhibition shortly after The Masters. On the Monday after winning The Masters, I received a call (as Arnie's agent) from the organizers of the outing, saying they assumed that either Arnold wouldn't be available or that his fee would have significantly risen now that he had won The Masters.

I went to Arnold to find out what he wanted to do.

"Mark," Arnold said, "remind them that they wanted me long before I had won a major championship. I will honor my commitment, and, to show that I appreciate their faith in me, I'll do another outing for them next year at the same price."

People say that Arnold Palmer hasn't changed as a person despite his enormous wealth and popularity. This early story shows what a firm foundation he started from. It's easier to stay steady when you start steady.

Mark H. McCormack

Teammates Are for Life

One of the things many high-school athletes don't real-ize until later in life is that the young men and young women they now call teammates will also be among the best friends they'll have throughout their lives.

I remain close with several teammates I had on the Macon (Missouri) High School football team back in the late 1970s, one of whom was a fellow named Greg Hyatt.

Hyatt, a linebacker, was one of those sorts who had to put a good lick on someone every play. If he couldn't get to the guy carrying the ball, then someone else had to go down. He and I were the only two players out of our class to letter all four years in high school.

I remember a game during our senior season against one of our arch rivals. It was also a heated battle, filled with emotion and a lot of pads popping. Early in the game, on a punt, an opposing player attempted to block me on punt coverage. I sidestepped him, but as I went by he slugged me in the side of the head. I have to admit it dazed me somewhat, but not to the point where I didn't get his number.

It took about two more quarters, but opportunity finally arrived to provide a good, clean hit on him, and I did. He sprawled into a pile of players and came up quite irritated. Suddenly, I was nose to nose with not only that player, but about two or three of his teammates. That didn't last long though, as Hyatt was right next to me in about a second.

When you need a friend, you can always count on your teammates.

Ten years later, I found myself in a different kind of confrontation, a confrontation with adversity. My first wife, a lifetime asthma sufferer, had been hit with her worst attack ever. She died in my car as I was driving her to the hospital. Emergency-room personnel were able to get her heart going again, but she was transferred to a trauma center in a deep coma.

I can remember standing there in a waiting room looking out the window at the city. Family members were there, but there are times when you just want to talk to a friend. About that time, I heard footsteps coming up the stairway. As I turned around, there stood my old friend Hyatt, tears filling his eyes.

Seeing him standing there, an eerie yet comforting and familiar feeling came over me. For a moment I was back on the football field in Macon. I was facing a tough situation, but I had backup.

Seeing him at the top of those steps meant the world to me that night, and still does today. That's something I tell high-school kids whenever I get the chance, that these guys you've gone to war with in high school will be some of the best friends you'll ever have.

There have been a lot of changes in my life since that October 1988 night, but one of the constants has been my friendship with Greg.

After all, we are teammates, and teammates are there for each other even after the noise of the crowd is gone.

Jim Brown

What Goes Around Comes Around

Never let yesterday take up too much of today.

Texas E. Schramm

A unique directive was initiated at a high school in northern Utah, in which students with a physical or mental challenge were fully integrated into the mainstream classes and curriculum. To make it work, the administration organized a mentor program that teamed up each special-needs student with a mainstream student who would help him or her along.

The athletic director presented the idea to the captain of the football team. John was a tall, strong, intense young man—not the patient, caring type needed for this kind of program. He made it clear this "wasn't his thing," and he didn't have time to be a mentor. But the athletic director knew it would be good for him and insisted that John "volunteer."

John was matched up with Randy, a young man with Down's syndrome. Reluctant and irritated at first, John literally tried to "lose" Randy, but soon John welcomed the constant company. Randy not only attended every one of

John's classes and ate with him at lunch, he also came to football practice. After a few days John asked the coach to make Randy the official manager responsible for the balls, tape and water bottles. At the end of the football season the team won the state championship, and John was awarded a gold medal as the most valuable player in the state. Randy was presented with a school letter jacket. The team cheered as Randy put it on. It was the coolest thing that had ever happened to him; from that day forward Randy never took it off. He slept in his jacket and wore it throughout each weekend.

Basketball season started, and John was also the captain and star of that team. At John's request, Randy was again named the manager. During the basketball season they were still inseparable. Not only did John take Randy to special occasions—like dances as a joint escort for his girlfriend—but he also took Randy to the library to tutor him. As he tutored Randy, John became a much better student and made the honor roll for the first time in more than a year. The mentor program was turning out to be the most rewarding year of John's life.

Then tragedy struck in the middle of the state basketball tournament. Randy caught a virus and suddenly died of pneumonia. The funeral was held the day before the final championship game. John was asked to be one of the speakers. In his talk John shared his abiding friendship with and respect for Randy. He told how Randy had been the one who had taught him about real courage, self-esteem, unconditional love and the importance of giving 100 percent in everything he did. John dedicated the upcoming state-finals game to Randy and concluded his remarks by stating that he was honored to have received the MVP award in football and the leadership plaque for being the captain of the basketball team.

"But," John added, "the real leader of both the football

and basketball teams was Randy, for he accomplished more with what he had than anyone I've ever met. Randy inspired all who knew him."

John walked from behind the podium, took off the irreplaceable twenty-four-karat-gold state football MVP medallion that hung around his neck, leaned into the open casket and placed it on Randy's chest. He placed his captain's plaque next to it.

Randy was buried in his letter jacket, surrounded by John's cherished awards as well as pictures and letters left by others who admired him.

The next day John's team won the championship and presented the game ball to Randy's family. John went to college on a full athletic scholarship and graduated with a master's degree in education. Today, John is a special-education teacher; he also volunteers ten hours a week for the Special Olympics.

Dan Clark

5

INSIDE
THE GAME

There'll be two buses leaving the hotel for the ballpark tomorrow. The 2 P.M. bus will be for those of you who need a little extra work. The empty bus will leave at 5 P.M.

Dave Bristol

My Life in Pro Ball

It's what you learn after you know it all that counts.

John Wooden

The phone rings. I roll over in bed and grab the receiver. The motel operator says, "Wake-up call. It's 9 A.M. Your bus leaves at ten." We are in Cleveland, where last night we—the New York Knicks—lost to the Cleveland Cavaliers. Outside, a cold drizzle soaks the city. I draw a hot bath and sit in it for five minutes to loosen my body's stiffness. My socks, shoes and Knicks uniform hang drying over the chairs, the room heater and the floor lamp. My mouth is dry and burning. My legs ache. I've slept poorly.

Next day, Tuesday, we play at home. Before the game, at Madison Square Garden, an avid fan tells me the Knicks give him something to look forward to after a day at work in the post office. I am his favorite player. He is similar to other fans who have identified with the team and me. They suffer with us when we lose and they are ecstatic when we win. They are the bedrock of our experience as professional players.

That night we win by twenty points. After the game I take a long shower. Then I stuff my wet socks, shoes and jock into the traveling bag with my road uniform for the bus ride to the airport.

We land in Atlanta at 1 A.M. It is twenty-one degrees outside and the frost makes the runway sparkle as if it were sprinkled with bits of glass. We wait forty minutes for our bags, which delays our arrival at the hotel until 3 A.M.

There is an overpowering loneliness on the road. A local acquaintance may show up during the day. There is chitchat with him of times past and of his job and my activities outside of basketball. After that exchange, there is nothing more to say, little common interest. Sometimes I take in an art exhibit or visit an unusual section of town. Or I sit in a hotel room reading books, listening to the radio.

Someday, I say to myself, *I won't be spending 100 days a year on the road. Someday I'll wake up in the same place every morning.* I miss that sense of sharing that comes from people living together in one place, over time. I miss permanence.

From Atlanta we fly to Chicago. I go to a luncheon put on by Chicago Bulls' boosters, where I am the principal speaker. About 200 men attend. Part of being a professional basketball player is speaking at shopping-center openings, charity fund-raisers, sports banquets, bar mitzvahs and annual company dinners. The audience laughs at my jokes. Even unfunny stories told by athletes make audiences roll in the aisles.

We lose to the Bulls by sixteen points. Our plane touches down in New York at 3:45 A.M. The doorman of my apartment building tells me he is sorry about the loss in Chicago, but he made $100 betting against us. I get into bed around 5:30 A.M. Just one more game this week, then we have two days off. We will have played five games in seven days in four different cities.

Saturday does not begin for me until 1 P.M. Whenever

we return from a road trip late, the next day is always a jumble. At 3 P.M. I have my usual pregame steak-and-salad meal (I will not eat again until midnight supper after the game). I sleep for an hour. The alarm goes off at six. I arrive at the Garden just one hour before the game.

The locker room has become a kind of home for me. I often enter tense and uneasy, disturbed by some event of the day. Slowly my worries fade as I see their importance to my male peers. I relax, my concerns lost among the constants of an athlete's life. Athletes may be crude and immature, but they are genuine when it comes to loyalty, responsibility and honesty. The members of my team have seen me, and I them, in more moods and predicaments than I care to remember. Our lives intertwine far beyond the court. It is a good life with congenial people. If victory and unity fuse on one team, life becomes a joy. It is a life that truly makes sense only while you're living it.

I tape my ankles and put on my uniform. Then I turn to the mail that has just been delivered. I usually get forty letters a week, almost none of them from people I know. There are a few autograph requests.

The last letter I open is from Kentucky. It is from the father of a boy whom I had met when he was a sophomore at the University of Kentucky. He came all the way from Kentucky to ask me to show him how to shoot a basketball. He just appeared at my apartment one day. We went up to Riverside Park, talked and shot baskets for about an hour. He thanked me for the help and boarded a bus back home. I saw him later that year in Cincinnati. He had been cut from the Kentucky team. He was down, and convinced that his sprained ankle had something to do with it.

I wrote him a letter two years later, after his sister had written that he had cancer. The boy's father thanks me for the letter but says that his son has died. I put the letter down. Coach Red Holzman begins his pregame conversation. I can't concentrate. I should have written sooner. I feel numbed with anger and sorrow.

From the middle of September until May, there is usually no longer than one day at a time without basketball. There are no long weekends or national holidays for players. It is impossible to take a trip to the mountains or fly to Florida even for two days. We are a part of show business, providing public entertainment. We work on Christmas night and New Year's Eve.

We arrive in Los Angeles for the first stop of a five-game western trip. My normal routine the day before a game in another town is to find a facility where I can get a steaming bath, whirlpool and massage. Games and practices bring injuries, and travel brings fatigue. Hot whirlpool baths, diathermy, ultrasound, ice packs, elastic wraps, aspirin, cold pills, vitamins and sleeping pills are all part of the life.

A professional basketball player must be able to run six miles in a game, 100 times a year, jumping and pivoting under continuous physical contact. The body is constantly battered and ground away. During this year alone I have had a jammed finger, inflamed fascia of the arch, a smashed nose cartilage, five split lips, an elbow in the throat that eliminated my voice for a week, a bruised right hip, a sprained ankle, a left hip joint out of socket and a contusion of the left wrist.

Every workout brings the fear of reinjury and every night brings the hope for tomorrow's improvement. I wake up in the middle of the night and flex my knee to see if there is pain, or knead my thigh to see if the charley horse has begun to heal.

I often ask myself why I continue to play. In 1967, when I first signed, I was convinced that I would play no more than four years, the length of my initial contract. I'm still playing in 1976. One reason is the money. The average salary in the National Basketball Association (NBA) at this time is close to $100,000. Many players make more than $150,000. There is no question that it gives me a sense of security, and a greater feeling of freedom, mobility and accomplishment. But money is not the sole reason I play. The answer lies much deeper in the workings of the game and in me.

I recall, for about the fiftieth time this season, how it was in 1970, the first time we won the NBA championship. I stood at midcourt in Madison Square Garden, two fists raised, chills coursing up and down my spine. Since I was nine years old I had played basketball to become the best. Individual honors were nice but insufficient. An Olympic gold medal gave satisfaction, but it was not top-flight basketball. The NBA was clearly the highest caliber in the world, and there I was: a part of the best team.

All those statements of team solidarity expressed since high school; all the hours of loneliness, dribbling and shooting a basketball in a gym somewhere in the world; all the near misses in the smaller championships—high school and college—of America's sports hierarchy; all the missed opportunities in other fields; all the denied personal enjoyment; all the conflicts suppressed and angers swallowed—everything seemed worth it for the feeling at center court on May 8, 1970.

I remember those few moments after victory, in the locker room with the team, when there was a total oneness with the world. Owners and politicians celebrate in the locker room of a champion. But only the players, the coach and perhaps the trainer can feel the special satisfaction of the achievement. They start nine months earlier in training camp. They play the games and endure the travel. They receive the public criticism and overcome their own personal ambitions. The high of the championship is unequaled. The possibility that it could happen again is a sufficient lure to continue. The money is important, but the chance to relive that moment outweighs dollars.

But how fast it is gone! On a flight to Phoenix, I open a magazine to a story about Mickey Mantle at his home in Dallas, Texas, after several years out of baseball.

"I loved it," the author quotes Mantle as saying, his voice throbbing with intensity. "Nobody could have loved playing ball as much as me, when I wasn't hurt. I must have fifty scrapbooks. Sometimes after breakfast, I sit by myself and take a scrapbook and just turn the pages. The hair comes up on the back of my neck. I get goose bumps. And I remember how it was and how I used to think that it would always be that way."

The words seem to jump off the page at me. There is terror behind the dream of being a professional ballplayer. It comes as a slow realization of finality and of the frightening unknowns which the end brings.

When the playing is over, one can sense that one's youth has been spent playing a game, and now both the game and youth are gone.

By age thirty-five any potential for developing skills outside of basketball is slim. The "good guy" syndrome ceases. What is left is the other side of the Faustian bargain: to live all one's days never able to recapture the feeling of those few years of intensified youth. The athlete approaches the end of his playing days the way old people approach death. He puts his finances in order. He reminisces easily. He offers advice to the young. But the athlete differs from an old person in that he must continue living. Behind all the years of practice and all the hours of glory waits that inexorable terror of living without the game.

Bill Bradley

A Chance to Say Thank You

When you drink the water, remember the spring.

Chinese Proverb

I played for Vince Lombardi for nine of my sixteen years in pro football. I know well his coaching accomplishments with the Green Bay Packers and his skill at teaching and motivating players. There are more stories about Coach's methods and results than any other person associated with the National Football League, in that era or any time.

One sign of the respect and affection Lombardi inspired is that *everyone* called him simply "Coach"—all the players, the trainers, the grounds crew, everyone associated with the Packers organization; the sportswriters and media; avid Green Bay fans. Even people on the street who had never attended a game at Lambeau Field called Lombardi simply "Coach," with pride and thanks in their voice.

His reputation is deserved, even today, nearly three decades after his death, for he was a true original—a colorful, always passionate man who loved the game and those who loved it. He did not abide loose play and nonchalance. He expected and respected commitment. However, my most cherished memory of Coach is far more personal.

Coach left the Packers in 1969 to become head coach and general manager of the Washington Redskins. In May 1970 he returned to Green Bay for a visit and some time with his golfing buddies. My wife Cherry and I were surprised to receive a call from him on Saturday morning, asking if he could stop by to see our new home, which had recently been completed. Of course!

He greeted us warmly upon arriving and asked for a "walk-through" of the house. Afterward, we sat in the family room trading quips and reflecting on our great years together. Cherry and I were obviously pleased we could spend some time with him. Coach seemed relaxed, complimenting Cherry on details of how she had furnished the house and saying how happy he was for us.

"Coach," she said, "none of this would have been possible if you had not believed in Bart; if you had not given him the opportunity you did. We are very grateful to you."

I was surprised to see Coach's eyes fill with tears. He rose immediately, announcing he had to leave. He embraced both of us and walked out.

A short time later we learned Coach had been diagnosed with the cancer that would quickly take his life less than four months later, on September 3, 1970.

Cherry and I will always cherish that visit with Coach. We were blessed with a rare and timely opportunity to say "Thank you," to express our appreciation for what a truly great man had done to change our lives.

Bart Starr

The Good Side of Fear

I had the chance to sit down at Jack Murphy Stadium in San Diego with Joe Montana before he went onto the field with the San Francisco 49ers against Denver in Super Bowl XXIV (1989). We didn't know it then, but this would be Joe's last Super Bowl, his fourth championship and yet another high point in one of the most remarkable careers not just in pro football, but in all of sports.

Joe seemed restless. He had already won everything there is in this game—the respect of teammates and opponents, coaches and owners, and especially the fans—plus all the awards: multiple League Most Valuable Player awards (MVPs), Super Bowls and Super Bowl MVPs.

I said, "Joe, you can't possibly be scared."

What he said to me is, I believe, the key to his success and the reason I consider him the greatest quarterback of all time. He said, "If you're not afraid of losing, then losing means nothing."

Every time Joe Montana stepped on the field, he was scared. That element of fear kept him sharp through his entire career. If we want to be at our best, we need that same element of fear burning inside of us. It sharpens the focus, keeps the edge.

Joe Theismann

Playing the Cart Man

I learned to play golf at Tennyson Park Golf Links in Dallas, Texas. I worked hard at my game, and I got good at it. I used to hustle all the boys and got to the point where I couldn't find a game because I was shooting in the mid-sixties.

Then in 1965 I got a call to go out to El Paso to play Fred Hawkins, and met Martin Lettage. I beat Fred in two rounds, and they said, "Why don't you move out here? You've out-hustled everybody in Dallas, come on out here. Nobody really knows you." So I did.

A few months later I was working in the pro shop at Horizon Hills Country Club when a guy I hadn't seen in a year said, "I hear all the guys around here have a lot of money and like to bet on you."

I said, "Well, generally they'll back me against anybody I'll play." He said, "Do you think they would bet if you played a touring pro?" And I said, "I don't see why not." He said, "How about Raymond Floyd?" Floyd was only twenty-two years old and already had his first PGA victory.

So they brought Floyd out. I didn't know Raymond Floyd; Raymond Floyd didn't know Lee Trevino, but here he came, driving up in a new, white, shiny Cadillac. We didn't even have pavement on our parking lot, just crushed white rock. I drove a cart out to meet him. I took Raymond Floyd's big Wilson bag, with all the shoes and all the extra clubs, and carried it into the locker room. I shined his shoes and brought them back to him. He looked up at me and said, "By the way, who am I playing today?" I said, "Me."

Raymond looked at me and said, "You gotta be joking." One of the fellows walked into the locker room. "Hey, Raymond," he said, "you want to go look at the golf course before you play this guy?" "No," Floyd replied. "I'm a professional golfer. I'm playing the shoeshine boy. I don't need to go out there and look at the golf course." So he had breakfast, and I went out to the practice tee.

To make a long story short, I shot sixty-five and I beat Raymond pretty bad. He wanted to play an emergency nine, but I said, "Mr. Floyd, I can't play another nine holes. I have to put the carts up." He said, "That's about right. I'm playing the cart man."

The next day, I beat Floyd again. Then the third day, Floyd doubled up and pressed and we tied the front nine, then Floyd eagled the last hole to beat me one up. I'll never forget what he said when he pulled the ball out of the hole. He looked at his backers, and said, "Boys, I can find an easier game on the tour."

When Raymond went back out on tour, he told the pros, "I just played a little Mexican boy in El Paso, Texas, and you all are going to have to make some room for him when he gets out here." Raymond and I have been great friends ever since.

Lee Trevino
As told to Charlie Jones

Crucial Simplicity

Concentration is the ability to think about absolutely nothin' when it is absolutely necessary.

                                        Ray Knight

I remember one of the first times I went to the sideline for that "end of the first half, two-minute-warning talk" with the coaching staff. It was Don Coryell's first year as head coach of the San Diego Chargers. He had an impressive staff, as well as some great receivers for me to work with. On the phone was assistant coach Jim Hanifan, connected upstairs to the other assistants Joe Gibbs and Ernie Zampese.

So I'm at the sideline, expecting to hear Coryell tell me exactly what he wants me to do. But I don't hear a word from Coryell; Hanifan's doing all the talking. Gibbs is relaying to him, and Zampese is relaying to Gibbs, and the three of them are going back and forth, funneling all this information into a bewildered young quarterback.

Hanifan is saying, "Now, on the next play, we're going to run eight-forty-four wide. You want to look at the weak safety, and if the weak safety stays in the middle, try to hit

Charlie Joiner on the post. Now, if the weak safety hangs to the weak side, then try to hit Kellan Winslow over the middle, and then there's J. J. (John Jefferson), who's running a corner. Now, if the linebackers drop back too far," Hanifan's telling me, "then dump it off to Chuck Muncie underneath. Now you got that, Dan? You got that?"

The coaches are all talking at once: "Okay, go over it one more time." "Now you got that? Joiner, Winslow, Jefferson, and then down to Muncie. Joiner, Winslow, Jefferson, Muncie."

This is a crucial situation in the ballgame, and they're giving me all this information, but not a word from Coryell.

I was restrapping my helmet, thinking, *Here's the most innovative offensive coach in football, and I haven't heard a word from him . . . all I've done is hear from the assistants . . .* when I feel a tug on my jersey. I turn around, and there's Coryell. I think, *Finally, he's going to tell me exactly what to do.*

"Ah, heck," Coryell said. "Just throw it to J. J."

Dan Fouts
As told to Charlie Jones

I Did Not Know That

Bristol, Connecticut. 1991. The dead of winter. The dead of night. Inside ESPN headquarters, only a skeleton staff remained: the 2:30 A.M. *SportsCenter* producer Tim Kiley, coordinating producer Barry Sacks, and a handful of production assistants helping with the wire copy, highlights and scripts for the program. Monitors that earlier blared out programs in progress all around the country were now silent. My partner for the 2:30 A.M. broadcast, Mike Tirico, was tossing out facts about the games and information we were about to deliver to the audience. It wasn't enough. We reviewed the video, scanned the box scores and gathered the research—we always want to know more.

At the end of the broadcast that night, we had time to fill. Mike Tirico came up with a gem of a fact, the kind of pertinent, resonant piece of information that totally satisfied the hunger for more. My delighted on-air response? "I did not know that." That is how one of my heroes outside the sports world, former king of late-night television Johnny Carson, used to respond to a great anecdote from a guest.

As soon as we went off the air, we huddled in the conference room, knowing we were onto something. Let's face it, sports fans are as competitive as the athletes they admire. Even if you're just talking about sports, you want the edge. You want to know more than the other guy.

Barry Sacks said we should throw out a great nugget every night on the 2:30 A.M. show. Production Assistant Edwin Van Duesen said we should make up a special graphic. Someone else suggested naming the segment *I Did Not Know That.* Rather than using Carson's exact phrase, I proposed *Did You Know?* And a little piece of *SportsCenter* history was made.

The response was overwhelming. Whatever the top sports story that day, we'd compete to offer the best bonus piece of information. It wasn't that we were trying to outsmart the viewer. We *were* the viewer: ready to be surprised, eager to be informed, generous with what we knew. Viewers would send mail or call to give us their own items for *Did You Know?*—one of the first tangible links between the people who work at ESPN and our audience. Where else but *SportsCenter* could you learn that the only major-league pitcher to match his age in strike-outs in a single game was Bob Feller, who at age seventeen struck out seventeen batters in 1936? Or that the NFL record for fewest rushing touchdowns in one season was set by the Brooklyn Dodgers—the football Dodgers—in 1934?

I finally met Johnny Carson a few years ago, at a celebrity tennis tournament at UCLA. When there was a break in Andre Agassi's match, I approached the Hollywood legend and told him about his role in the creation of one of America's most beloved sports slogans. Without missing a beat, he smiled and said, "I did not know that."

Chris Myers

When Your Back Is Against the Wall

Great occasions do not make heroes or cowards; they simply unveil them to the eyes of men. Silently and imperceptibly, as we wake or sleep, we grow strong or weak; and at last some crisis shows what we have become.

Brooke Foss Westcott

The Los Angeles Lakers were dominating the Boston Celtics in the final round of the 1984 National Basketball Association championship. We thrashed the Celtics in game one, on their home floor. We beat them by thirty-three points in game three. We were ahead by ten points in game four and cruising. Then it all changed.

Two days after losing the deciding seventh game, we were back in Los Angeles for our last team meeting. I looked at the young faces and said, "Even though we lost, they can't take away our pride or our dignity; we own those. We are not chokers or losers. We are champions who simply lost a championship."

We came back for the '84–'85 season sharply focused. All year long, we heard about how we were the "showtime" team that folded as soon as things got tough. The Celtics and their fans referred to us as the L.A. Fakers. Abuse and sarcasm were heaped on, and we had to take it.

But we achieved a tremendous season, and ripped through the play-offs. On May 27, we got to face our tormentor, the Celtics, in Boston Garden.

The next day's headlines called game one of the 1985 finals *The Memorial Day Massacre*. The 148–114 humiliation was the most embarrassing game in the history of the Laker franchise. We saw ourselves become exactly what we had been called: choke artists, underachievers. *Why is it,* I wondered, *that every time we play the Celtics, we become paralyzed with fear?*

Before we went out on the floor for game two, we gathered in the dingy locker room of Boston Garden. The players were sitting there, ready to listen and to believe.

Every now and then, you have your back pushed up against a wall. It seems there's nobody you can depend on but yourself. That's how the Lakers felt. If we lost, the choke reputation would be chiseled into stone, a permanent verdict. If we won, we had the opportunity to prove that we could keep on winning. It was a do-or-die situation.

I faced Kareem Abdul-Jabbar, our star center, and said, "When I saw you and your father on the bus today, it made me realize what this whole moment is about. You spent a lot of time with Big Al today. Maybe you needed that voice. Maybe everyone in this room needs to hear that kind of voice right now—the voice of your dad, the voice of a teacher, the voice of somebody in the past who was there when you didn't think you could get the job done.

"A lot of you probably don't think you can win today. A lot of you don't think you can beat the Celtics. I want each of you to close your eyes and listen." And they did.

"When I was nine years old," I said to the players, "my dad told my brothers, Lee and Lenny, to take me down to Lincoln Heights and get me involved in the basketball games. They would throw me into a game and I would get pushed and shoved. Day after day, I ran home crying and hid in the garage. I didn't want anything to do with basketball.

"This went on for two or three weeks. One night, I didn't come to the dinner table, so my dad got up and walked out to the garage, where he found me hunkered down in a corner. He picked me up, put his arm around me and walked me into the kitchen. My brother Lee was upset with him. 'Why do you make us take him down there? He doesn't want to play. He's too young.'

"My father stood up and staring at Lee said, 'I want you to take him there because I want you to teach him not to be afraid, that there should be no fear. Teach him that competition brings out the very best and the very worst in us. Right now, it's bringing out the worst, but if he sticks with it, it's going to bring out the best.' He then looked at his nine-year-old, teary-eyed son and said, 'Pat, you have to go back there.'"

And I told the players, "I thought I was never going to be able to get over being hurt and afraid, but I eventually did get over it."

As I was talking, I was slowly pacing back and forth, staring at the ceiling, locked into the image of my father's face. Looking at the players, I saw that Michael Cooper, one of our stars, was crying. A couple of other guys looked as if they were about to start.

"I don't know what it's going to take for us to win tonight," I said. "But I do believe that we're going to go out there like warriors, and that would make our fathers proud."

We won the game. I never had any fears about losing. We also won three of the next four games. And the 1985 championship became ours. Seven times in Laker history, the NBA finals had been lost to those adversaries. Now the Celtic Myth was slain and the choke image with it.

During the off-season, Michael Cooper told me that the pregame message had gone so deep for him that the score was already 5–0 before the game started.

As a boy, Cooper had a grievous leg wound, an ugly cut through muscle. Doctors didn't think he'd ever walk right again, let alone become an athlete. He was sustained through those times by a wonderful mother and devoted uncles. So he heard voices from his most profound inner reaches.

All of us have at least one great voice deep inside. People are products of their environments. A lucky few are born into situations in which positive messages abound. Others grow up hearing messages of fear and failure, which they must block out so the positive can be heard. But the positive and courageous voice will always emerge, somewhere, sometime, for all of us. Listen for it, and your breakthroughs will come.

All great breakthrough messages deny the crippling power of fear. Fear of failure will lead you toward despair, wrong decisions and incomplete performance. It's one of the last hurdles between any person, or any team, and greatness. Listening to the voice that counsels courage, that affirms your life and your ability, will position you to do your best.

Pat Riley
Originally appeared in A 4th Course
of Chicken Soup for the Soul

An Important Phone Call

Speedy Morris, men's basketball coach for La Salle University, tells this story: "When I first got the job at La Salle, the phone rang and my wife told me it was *Sports Illustrated*. I cut myself shaving and fell down the steps in my rush to get to the phone. When I got there, a voice on the other end said, 'For just seventy-five cents an issue . . .'."

M. G. Misanelli

The Concession Stand

The sign on the door read, "No Admittance to the Concession Stand Unless You Are Scheduled to Help." I smiled. That was me—volunteer parent—contributing to the good of Little League baseball worldwide. I knocked. The door opened narrowly.

"Yeah?"

"I am a concession-stand volunteer," I said proudly.

"Where's your wife?"

"She couldn't make it," I said. "I'm filling in for her."

The door opened just wide enough for me to slip through. It took a moment for my eyes to adjust. As they did, three women in aprons—Rose, Juanita and Theresa—came into focus.

"Hi," I said cheerily. I grabbed a French fry from the infrared warming machine and popped it into my mouth. "So this is the concession stand," I said. "It looks bigger from outside." I swung my arms in a grandiose gesture, knocking over a rack and sending bags of potato chips skidding across the linoleum floor.

"You've never done this before, have you?" Rose asked.

"Well . . . no . . . But hey. How hard can it be?"

"Can you make change?" Juanita asked.

"Change? Sure."

"You're on window duty," Rose said.

"Window duty, huh?" I grabbed another French fry. "Don't need me to cook?"

"No," they said in unison.

They scurried about the small building, preparing for a big evening. Rose skillfully pushed hot dogs onto a rotating rotisserie. Juanita filled cups with soda. Theresa started the popcorn machine and poured purple and green syrup into the slushy maker. There was a knock on the window. I slid it open.

"Hot dog, Coke, fries, and Reese's Pieces."

I looked into a smiling retainer, surrounded by round rosy cheeks and the beginning of a second chin.

I shut the window. "How do I know how much to charge?"

"Candy's a buck. Popcorn's fifty cents. Hot dogs and drinks are seventy-five. Fries are fifty cents. Slushies are a quarter." Rose took a breath.

"Chips are seventy-five and coffee is fifty. Refills on coffee are free," said Juanita. Frantically I looked for a pen.

"And we do not allow any credit," said Rose.

"So how much?"

"Three bucks," they sang out.

"Of course," I said.

Faces came and French fries left. I got into a rhythm—repeating the orders loudly and waiting for the magical amount to sound out from behind me. I had several minor mishaps, including two hot dogs that now rolled about beneath my feet and an order of fries that I was sharing with a group of ambitious ants.

The fat kid with the retainer returned for a third time.

"More Reese's Pieces." He slid a couple of sticky dollar bills through the window.

"I'm out of Reese's Pieces."

"No way. What else ya got?"

I scanned the candy rack for inspiration. "Got some imitation-strawberry-flavored taffy."

"Cool. Gimme two."

I beamed with salesmanship. But the others did not seem pleased. I shrugged, skillfully sliding two sodas to a small girl and a hot dog to her friend. Then I served a party of three, but I slid one Coke a little too hard, right off the counter onto the ground. I rebounded, though, with two trouble-free slushies.

A woman appeared.

I bent down and displayed my smiling face. She grabbed me by my shirt collar and pulled me halfway through the small window.

"You ever buy a retainer?"

"Ahhh . . . no . . ."

"I've bought two of them in the last six months. They ain't cheap."

"I'm sure they're not. . . ."

"You know what kills retainers?"

"Ahhh . . . no . . ."

"Taffy kills retainers."

Suddenly I saw the resemblance. Before I could comment another mother appeared.

"This the guy?" she asked a small girl with one very large cheek. I remembered her. Only had a quarter. I gave her a deal on jawbreakers.

"You a dentist?" the second mother asked.

"No, I . . ."

"Fronting for a dentist?"

"Of course not. I just. . . ."

Behind me I heard a knock on the door.

"We once caught a dentist giving out all-day suckers at the mall. We ran him out of town."

The first mother let go of my throat.

"I was only doing my duty as a concession-stand volunteer. . . ." I felt a familiar hand on my shoulder.

"What are you doing here?" I asked my wife. "I thought you were sick."

"They . . ." She lowered her voice. "They called me at home."

"But . . ."

"It's okay, honey. I'm feeling much better. Besides, it turns out they need an umpire for the seven o'clock game."

I bent over and took one more look at the angry women at the window. I hugged my wife. Then I quickly made my way to the back door, released the bolt and grabbed the doorknob.

"You ever umpired before?" Rose asked.

I smiled. "Well, no . . . But hey. How hard can it be?"

Ernie Witham

IN THE BLEACHERS By Steve Moore

"Look, I told you at the start of the season: We win, I treat you to ice cream; we lose, I bring you here. . . ."

Steal What?

This story took place several years ago, when our boys were about eight years old. It was the first game of the season, and the first game in which the boys began pitching. I went out to discuss ground rules with the umpire and realized that this was also the first year that the boys could steal bases. Unfortunately, we had not gone over this in practice. So I hurried back to the dugout, gathered my players and proceeded to go over the rules. As I got to the subject of stealing bases, I announced enthusiastically, "And this year we get to steal!" The news caused the boys to erupt into yelling and cheering. Their response left me thinking positively that this might all work out okay after all. Then the cheers died down, and as our team was about to take the field, one player loudly exclaimed, "Steal what?!" I let out a groan as I realized that the question had come from my son!

Cary McMahon

A Classy Guy

If there is no wind, row.

Latin Proverb

My dad was a college and high-school football referee in southern California. I started tagging along to games with Dad at about age four, as soon as I was big enough to carry his equipment bag. Things really got exciting when I was eight—when I met Jackie Robinson. Because we lived just five miles from the Rose Bowl, where Pasadena Junior College played its games, I went with my dad for most of their games. Jackie Robinson was their star running back.

I sat on the bench with Jackie. I watched him play and do all those amazing feats on the field. How could a pigeon-toed, knock-kneed, gangly kid run so fast and evade so deftly? He was fun to watch. I just tried to soak up his magic.

I lost personal touch with him after I went on to college, but followed his career, which turned from college football at UCLA to pro baseball. I was thrilled when Branch Rickey brought him from the Dodgers' top farm team, the

Montreal Royals, to Brooklyn in 1947. Jackie crossed home plate *and* the color barrier with equal skill and grace.

After the 1952 World Series, in which the New York Yankees won a thrilling seven-game seesaw battle, Robinson taught us how to lose. Mickey Mantle was just a young kid then, in his first or second year with the Yankees. Years later, the memory of what Robinson had taught him about losing was fresh in his mind:

> *Jackie Robinson came into our clubhouse after the game and shook my hand. He said, "You're a helluva ballplayer and you've got a great future." I thought that was a classy gesture, one I wasn't capable of making. I was a bad loser. What meant even more was what Jackie told the press: "Mantle beat us. He was the difference between the two teams. They didn't miss DiMaggio." I have to admit, I became a Jackie Robinson fan on the spot. And when I think of that World Series, his gesture is what comes to mind. Here was a player who had without a doubt suffered more abuse, more taunts and more hatred than any player in the history of the game. Yet he made a special effort to compliment and encourage a young white kid from Oklahoma.*

That describes exactly the Jackie Robinson I watched when he was in junior college—growing his skills, aching with ambition, but always courteous, even to a wide-eyed kid who got to sit on the bench because his dad was the ref. Dad and I both knew Robinson would be great one day.

Jim Tunney

Unforgettable Jim Valvano

Jim Valvano was one of those rare people who lit up a room. I first met him when we were both coaching college basketball. I ended up broadcasting games on television. So did Jimmy, but along the way he achieved honors I could only dream about.

He was the most brilliant, energetic and inspirational man I've ever known. Good-natured teasing had always been part of our friendship. In 1988, I was "guest of honor" at a roast. Jimmy, then head coach at North Carolina State, was doing a good job of roasting me. But he hadn't touched my deepest secret, one I thought I'd kept from him for years: I, too, had applied for the North Carolina State job—and lost out to him.

Now, just as it appeared that Jim had finished his light-hearted put-downs, he pulled a letter from his pocket. "I have something I want to display here about your man Dickie V.," he told the crowd. "Dear Dick, We are sorry to inform you that we have named Jim Valvano head coach at North Carolina State. . . . "

I thought nobody knew about that letter. Jimmy had apparently saved it for years, just waiting. The crowd's laughter became so loud that Jimmy couldn't even finish.

In the short but wonderfully rich history of "Jimmy V." capers, this was a classic.

Jimmy's first love was basketball. Early on, he decided he would become a coach. He started as an assistant coach the year he graduated from Rutgers, and by age twenty-three was head coach at Johns Hopkins, which hadn't had a winning season in twenty-five years. In Jimmy's first year, they won ten and lost nine. He went on to Bucknell, and then to Iona—a small Catholic school in the New York City suburbs. With each team, he brought the players to life, giving them a love of the game and a hunger for victory. In five years he led the Iona Gaels to a 95–46 record and two National Collegiate Athletic Association (NCAA) tournament appearances.

In 1980, when Jim was only thirty-four, North Carolina State beckoned. Against all odds, North Carolina State beat North Carolina and Virginia to reach the 1983 NCAA tournament. All through the playoffs, Jimmy kept telling his players: "We belong here. We can win this thing. Don't give up!"

The Wolfpack advanced all the way to Albuquerque, N.M., for the finals against the University of Houston. Reporters thought the game was a real M&Mer—a mismatch. "Rain would make it perfect," wrote one. "It always rains at executions."

At halftime, the Wolfpack led by eight. Jimmy addressed his team: "You will never, ever, for the rest of your life in whatever field you go into, have the emotion and feeling you will have when the final buzzer goes off and we win."

But Houston came out strong, and the second half saw the score tied. State hit a shot at the final buzzer. The Wolfpack had won 54–52. National champs! Jimmy went on to guide his teams to two conference titles and seven NCAA tournament appearances. But in 1989 a dark cloud appeared on the horizon—a book alleged that the North Carolina State program had violated a number of NCAA rules.

A grueling investigation cleared Jimmy of any personal wrongdoing and found only three team violations. Still, North Carolina State was placed on two years' probation, and it was time for Valvano to move on.

After reaching a settlement with the school, he received lucrative coaching offers but decided to go into television instead. There was another reason, too. Going all out to be the best at his profession, he had become so occupied with wins and losses that he didn't have time at home. "I remember one Father's Day when I happened to be home and nobody had planned anything," he told a reporter once. "How could they? I'd probably never been home on Father's Day before. I might've been in Atlanta giving a Father's Day speech or in Chicago receiving a Father of the Year award, but you can bet I wasn't home."

That would change now. Jim suddenly had time for dinners alone with his wife, Pam, and time to spend with his daughters, Lee Ann, Jamie and Nicole. And so Jim and I became partners, broadcasting games for ESPN and ABC. Our fans called us "V and V."

As college basketball surged in popularity, our national exposure increased dramatically. Again Jimmy was riding high on life, but the wave didn't last.

One day in June 1992, when I called Jimmy at home, he said he was awaiting a call from the doctor.

"Coach," the doctor broke the news, "I'm 90 percent sure this is cancer." The test results confirmed bone cancer. Jimmy was forty-six years old. He attacked the disease the only way he knew how—with all his energy. While receiving chemotherapy, he read every cancer book he could find. He'd spent a career telling players never to give up. Now he said it to himself every day.

He made his battle public, too, and wanted to keep working despite his illness. In our hotel room the night before an ESPN preseason planning meeting that October, he was taking painkillers to relieve what he described as a toothache running through his entire body. But the next day, he bore his pain so gracefully that it was easy for those around him to forget it. I once complained to him about my hectic schedule the next day.

"Do you want to come with me tomorrow?" he replied. "You drive me to chemotherapy, watch me throw up and see people faced with real adversity."

That hit me like five thousand pounds. Finally, he said something I'll never forget: "You're missing the important stuff, Dickie. You're moving too fast. You gotta slow it down, baby." I have a picture of him in my office, and I think of that time whenever I look at it.

At the American Sports Awards in March 1993, I introduced Jimmy Valvano as winner of the Arthur Ashe Award for Courage. The cancer had advanced, and Jim thought he might not make the ceremony. But he came—in a wheelchair.

I was broken up as Duke University basketball coach Mike Krzyzewski, one of Jimmy's closest friends, and I helped him up for his acceptance speech.

"That's the lowest I've seen Dick Vitale since the Detroit Pistons' owner told him he should go into broadcasting!"

The place went nuts. Twenty-four hours earlier, he could barely talk and now he was cracking jokes. When the laughter subsided, Jimmy drew from some final reserve of energy, deep in his heart, as if his life wouldn't be complete without sending out his message one last time.

"To me, there are three things everyone should do every day. Number one is laugh. You should laugh every day. Number two is think—spend some time in thought.

Number three, let your emotions move you to tears. If you laugh, think and cry, that's a heck of a day."

He paused and announced that with ESPN's support a Jimmy V. Foundation for cancer research was being founded. Its motto is: "Don't give up. Don't ever give up."

Jimmy V. looked out at his audience and gave them one last thing to hold on to: "Cancer can take away all my physical abilities. It cannot touch my mind, it cannot touch my heart and it cannot touch my soul. And those three things are going to carry on forever."

On April 28, less than two months later, Jim Valvano died with his wife and family at his bedside. The speech he had given was played on a giant screen to the Opening Day crowd at Yankee Stadium, where Jimmy had hoped to throw out the first ball, and in other cities around the country.

In the months that followed, Jimmy's speech rallied support for cancer research and inspired thousands of cancer victims, who heard the message Jimmy Valvano had spent a career telling his players: *Don't give up. Don't ever give up.*

Dick Vitale

6

OVERCOMING OBSTACLES

Turn your wounds into wisdom. You will be wounded many times in your life. You'll make mistakes. Some . . . will call them failures, but I have learned that failure is really God's way of saying, "Excuse me, you're moving in the wrong direction."

Oprah Winfrey

Advantage: Courage

I've never known anybody to achieve anything
without overcoming adversity.

Lou Holtz

It was my second set in the quarterfinals of the Citizen
Cup Tournament on April 30, 1993. The late-spring
evening in Hamburg, Germany, was chilly. While the
stands were packed, my family wasn't among the spectators. The night before, my father had begun feeling sick,
and by noon he was too ill to leave the hotel. Mom and
my brother, Zoltan, planned to stay with him.

After a tough fight I took the first set from Magdalena
Maleeva, 6-4, and was leading in the second set, 4-3, when
I went to my chair for the sixty-second break. I wiped the
sweat from my neck, then put a towel over my face and
leaned forward so I wouldn't have any distractions.

Suddenly there was an incredible pain in my back—a
burning point on the left side. It radiated agony across my
back and down my right side. I heard a scream that was
more animal than human, an anguished cry that I hardly
recognized as my own, even as it echoed in my ears.

Looking over my shoulder, I saw a man in a baseball cap holding a bloody knife in both hands. His arms were raised over his head to strike again. In that split second I recognized him as someone I'd seen earlier, loitering around my hotel and watching in the stadium as I practiced. A security man grabbed him from behind.

I stood up and stumbled toward the net. Feeling dizzy, I collapsed onto the red clay. The pain in my back was agonizing. I reached around to touch the spot. When I withdrew my hand, it was slick with blood.

Everything was happening too fast. Dimly I saw my brother, Zoltan, race onto the court. *He came after all,* I thought, and felt a great relief. He would take care of me.

"It's going to be all right, Monica," he said, rubbing my legs. "Keep moving. Keep moving." Then he cried out, "Somebody help her!"

I was gasping. Paramedics laid me on a stretcher and rushed me to the hospital. My parents were there when I was wheeled into the emergency room. They were both crying, too frightened to attempt to look strong.

Doctors used an MRI to determine the extent of the injury. The assailant's knife had penetrated just millimeters from my spine.

I didn't even know who he was or why he had struck me. *What if he comes back?* I thought. I was terrified that he would find me in the hospital and try to finish the job.

Zoltan came back from talking to a police officer. "The man who did this is in custody," he said. "You're safe. You can rest now."

I started to shake. Mom crawled into my hospital bed and held me. The nurse wheeled in extra cots for Zoltan and Dad. That night we all slept in my room. As always, we dealt with the situation as a family.

Two days later Steffi Graf came to see me. She was my toughest opponent, and I'd taken the number-one ranking away from her. When she walked in, we both started crying.

"I'm so sorry that this happened in my country," Steffi said. We spoke, and then she had to leave for a match. Numbly I wished her good luck. After she went, my tears kept flowing.

In the days that followed, I learned that my attacker, Gunter Parche, was a fan of Steffi's. He stabbed me because I stood between her and the number-one spot. *He got what he wanted,* I thought obsessively. *I'm out of the game, and Steffi Graf will be number one.*

I was transported by medical plane back to the United States, where my family and I had lived for six years since leaving Yugoslavia. We did not fly home to Florida, however, but to Colorado, so I could be treated at the Steadman Hawkins Clinic, a sports medicine and rehabilitation center.

In the ambulance on the way to the clinic, I tried to let go of my thoughts about Gunter Parche—tried not to see his face or hear my scream again. *They're going to lock him up,* I reassured myself. I had to focus on recovering.

The next day Dad went with me to see Dr. Richard Steadman. The doctor noticed that Dad's face was pale and that he was sweating. He insisted Dad see an internist. After an examination, the diagnosis was prostate cancer. They caught it early, but Dad would need surgery right away.

My father flew to the Mayo Clinic. The operation was a success, but doctors followed up with chemotherapy treatments just to be sure.

As I continued my own physical therapy, I sank deep into depression. Life wasn't what I'd bargained for as a child. Back then there were no monsters except in my dreams. My father was healthy and strong; he was my coach and best friend.

My brother, Zoltan, was the one who had seen Bjorn Borg on television at our home in Novi Sad, Yugoslavia, and told my father he wanted to play tennis. There were no tennis stores in our hometown, so my dad drove ten hours to Italy to buy a racket.

Zoltan was fourteen, I was six, and I wanted to be just like my big brother. Soon I announced, "I want to play tennis, too." So my father drove to Italy again and picked up a tiny wooden racket for me.

There were few tennis courts in our town, so my father, brother and I played in the parking lot of our apartment building. We strung a net between rows of cars and hit down the narrow court.

My father is an artist. To help me play better, he would draw "little Mo," a cartoon rabbit, on a thick booklet of paper. When I flipped the pages quickly, Mo came to life. Dad used Mo to demonstrate things like serving technique. If I was leaning too far back or my behind was sticking out, he'd draw Mo serving that way. Then he'd draw a correct version so I could see the difference.

Today when I hear people say that you can't make it in tennis if you don't have a lot of money, I know they're wrong. We lived in a socialist country and were not at all affluent. But I loved the sport, and my dad was inventive and capable. That was enough.

By the time I was eight, I was the top junior player in Yugoslavia and loving every minute. At age fourteen, I got a scholarship to Nick Bollettieri's tennis academy in Bradenton, Florida. Lost in a country where I couldn't understand the language, I desperately missed my parents.

"You must come here, or I'm coming home," I said, finally breaking down and crying on the phone to Mom and Dad. I was just an unhappy kid. I didn't understand that I was asking them to quit their jobs and leave their homeland and friends.

After much deliberation they decided to come. It was for the sake of my career, yet they never pressured me. Win or lose, I was always their Monica.

Now struggling to recover at the Steadman Hawkins Clinic, I didn't know if I would ever play again.

The assailant's knife had damaged the soft tissues and muscles by my shoulder blade, and I was finding it difficult to maintain Dr. Richard Hawkins's physical-therapy regimen. Most athletes stick to their training, desperate to get back to their sport. I'd go to the gym, but I just could not seem to concentrate. I kept breaking into tears at odd moments. At night, bad dreams disturbed my sleep.

Drs. Steadman and Hawkins tried to help me. But they'd never worked with an athlete who'd been attacked, one for whom getting back to her sport raised a host of terrifying associations.

Then came another shock. On October 13, 1993, my mother and I were shopping near our home in Florida when we saw Zoltan running toward us. "He's free!" my brother called.

Zoltan didn't need to say a name. I sat down on the curb as the news sank in. "Tell me how," I said.

Parche had been found guilty of "inflicting grievous bodily injury" and given two years' probation. And so I would spend the next two years in the jail my assailant was supposed to inhabit. Two years of hiding in my house, afraid to play professional tennis, afraid even to go out in public. Yet the man with a "serious personality disorder" would be free.

In March 1994 I admitted that I needed more help than even my devoted family could give. My depression and nightmares were not going away. I went to see Jerry May, a psychologist Dr. Steadman had recommended.

I told May about a recurring dream in which I was back on the court in Hamburg, stepping out to play. Each time that I looked into the stands, there was Parche's face. I called to the umpire, "Please make that man leave—he hurt me." The umpire would turn away to look, and when he turned back, he had Parche's face, smiling an evil smile.

Night after night I woke up in a sweat with my mother standing over me. I would ask her to sleep in my bed, to hold me like a baby.

To help me fight the fear, May taught me mind-control techniques. And through our sessions I realized it was from tennis that I got my greatest joy. Whether or not I ever played competitively again, I loved the game. I needed to play.

Zoltan and I began practicing on our backyard court. Sometimes Dad, now recovered and feeling well, hit with me, too.

In February 1995 Martina Navratilova called. She was flying down to Florida to play in a tournament. "Would you mind if I came to visit?" she asked. "Maybe we could hit a few balls for a while."

Martina and I had a great time. At lunch she said, "You know, Monica, we'd all love to have you back on the tour. It must be your decision, but I want you to know that everyone would welcome you with open arms."

When it was time for her to leave, she unclasped a gold bracelet from her wrist. "I want you to have this," she said. "It has brought me a lot of luck." She hooked it on my wrist.

"Martina, I can't accept it," I said.

"When you come back, you can return it to me," she said, smiling.

Whenever I looked at the bracelet, I was warmed by the thought of Martina's generosity. I began to think about a comeback. Before long, I was practicing regularly.

In April 1995 the German appellate judge upheld Parche's suspended sentence. I told myself, *Monica, you are not going to get justice. You have two choices—return to tennis or do something else. Regardless, you have to move on.*

I made plans for an exhibition match in Atlantic City, New Jersey, in July. Although officially retired from singles competition, Martina agreed to play against me.

On the day of the match I was nervous. My father gave me some last-minute advice—the advice of a dad, not a coach. "Go out there and have fun," he said. "It's time."

The crowd gave Martina and me thunderous ovations. I hit some great shots and some really bad ones. But in the end, after a tough fight, I won the match.

I looked over at my beaming parents. Then I ran to the net and hugged Martina. "You're back, girl," she said with a smile. Later I returned her bracelet. She was right—it had brought me luck.

After Atlantic City nothing could stop me. I rejoined the professional women's tour at the Canadian Open held in Toronto in mid-August.

I made it to the quarterfinals, then to the semis. At last I faced Amanda Coetzer of South Africa in the finals. I'd played her before and had a hard time. As always, Dad put things in perspective. "This is a beginning, Monica," he said. "You're playing great tennis. But most important, you're back in the game." When the match ended, I had won. In the stands my father was crying.

As waves of applause rolled down from the crowd, I thought about the time it had taken for me to reach that moment. None of us were the same people we had been twenty-eight months before. I truly understood the depth of my family's love and the value of friends.

No matter what might happen in future matches, I knew I'd already won.

Monica Seles with Nancy Ann Richardson

You Make the Difference

Being told by the *second* doctor that my career in professional baseball was over was a mule-kick in the gut. I was coming off my best year in AAA ball, one step from the "big show." I led the league in most appearances (fifty-two) and had an ERA of 3.30 for the season. There was talk that I would be called up before the end of the season. Every day was a day of anticipation and happiness . . . except for the time I spent with the team doctor and orthopedic specialists. In those visits, the talk was about "hanging it up." Two surgeries hadn't fixed the problem in my throwing arm. I was dependent on more frequent and bigger doses of cortisone. My twenty-year dream was ending in a blaze of disappointment and self-pity.

I returned home to Fresno, California, morose and petulant. Linda, my wife of two and one-half years, wasn't fazed by the end of baseball; she only wanted me to be happy again. She reminded me that God was in charge of our lives, that we had lived wonderful lives thus far by trusting him and we should continue to trust that something better was ahead. She suggested I apply for a teaching job, asking the question, "Why don't you devote your life to helping young people develop theirs?"

Noble idea, certainly, but it didn't strike me as equivalent to the excitement of pro ball. Feeling forced to do *something*, I applied for the job and got it.

Still chafing from self-inflicted brooding, I reported to work and, not surprisingly, was asked to coach three sports—football and baseball, in which I was experienced and felt confident, and wrestling, about which I knew zero, zip, zilch. I might have been able to plead my way out of the wrestling assignment, but I didn't even try. Feeling glum, I chose to view it as fate twisting on me again, forcing me to "take my medicine." Only later would I see that God's hand was guiding.

I knew I couldn't fool the young kids who turned out for the wrestling team. The greenest one of them knew *a ton* more about wrestling than I did. So I told the truth: the school didn't have the money to hire a bona fide wrestling coach; I was it, and I would need their help.

The boys accepted their plight better than I expected. They instituted a system in which the better wrestlers taught the newer guys the moves. My contribution was rounding up a nationally ranked talent, Ed Davies, from a nearby university to assist me, promising him half my pay.

Between telling them the truth at the start and being willing to split my pay to bring in some help, the team right away showed their appreciation. We formed a good group—energetic, focused, learning at every turn—but only one wrestler, Alan Katuin, qualified for the biggest match of the season.

Alan's opponent was Major Edwards, an undefeated, more experienced wrestler from a larger school. Both were known for their outstanding physical conditioning and overall ability, but Edwards was favored to win by a pin; he was simply more experienced.

Alan was motivated, intelligent and focused. Quiet by nature, he seldom spoke during the prematch preparations in the locker room. Thus, I was surprised when he came to me before the Edwards match. "Where is Coach Davies?" he asked.

"He had an emergency," I said, "and won't be able to be here." Feeling insecure, I added, "But he believes in you, as I do."

An official poked his head in the locker room. "Ready?" he said. "You're up."

We were ushered into the gymnasium—packed to the rafters, dimly lit, a spotlight keyed on the mat. My guts turned to ice. I hadn't felt such a rush of adrenaline since pitching a four-hit shutout against the number-one-ranked USC Trojans in a NCAA regional championship. The fourteen strikeouts that day didn't mean more than Alan's match today.

Suddenly, Alan stopped, grabbed my forearm, and in his soft, calm manner said, "Coach, do you think I can win? Have you got any advice?"

I stood speechless for what seemed a long time. "Alan," I said, knowing now was no time to start lying, "you know more about wrestling than I do. You know that. But I know your heart. I believe in you. If you wrestle as you always have, you can win."

What ensued was the match of the tournament. The crowd was in it from the start, making a din, adding to the excitement. Alan lost three to two.

I was an emotional wreck. I felt, as did most of the audience, that the referee had failed to award points to Alan because Edwards, after gaining the lead, wisely employed a tactic known as "stalling." I felt I should have been able to give Alan some tactical advice that would have helped, but I couldn't.

As the referee closed the match with the traditional raising of the victor's arm, I felt another mule-kick in the gut. It didn't subside as I watched Alan go over to Edwards and congratulate him. The loss could have made Alan bitter, but he showed no resentment, no sour grapes.

He then walked over to me and said, "Thank you, Coach." No apology, no excuse; just a firm handshake and the look of a winner in his eyes. I felt tears welling in mine. I became afraid I would embarrass him if I showed such strong emotion.

This was Alan's only defeat of the season. In the days to come, I watched him closely. He never brooded. He was a role model for everyone on the team, including his rookie coach.

Alan continued to gain both strength and "mat smarts," and became the dominant wrestler in the central section in his senior year. He went on to Fresno State University, where he continued to impress his opponents and coaches with his exemplary character and superb skills.

What Alan did that night—extending his hand to me with a sincere "Thank you, Coach," even in a loss—lit a fire in my belly that still burns today, thirty-three years later. His example inspired me to commit to coaching, to accept the challenges, as well as the rewards, of making a difference in people's lives.

The experience transformed my life by showing me the direct impact one can make. There have been low times, sure, mostly when I let the memory of a lost dream rise up like foul smoke, clouding the view of what I can do to make a difference. These lapses are short-lived, never close to blowing the flame out. I just remember Alan Katuin's grace and maturity.

God brought to me a young man of character whose unerring sense of what is important guided me to healthy living again—a life of *giving,* of making a difference.

All I can say, and do say every day, is "Thank you, Linda. Thank you, Alan. Thank you, Lord."

Jack Hannah

Lyle's Second Go

In 1982, when I was coaching the Raiders, we were approached by Cleveland on a possible trade for Lyle Alzado. After watching him on tape, I was not very impressed, but Raiders owner Al Davis felt we could pump some life into Lyle by surrounding him with the right atmosphere. We made the deal.

That summer at training camp, preparing for our first year in Los Angeles, Lyle was having a tough time mentally. He had that look in his eyes that many rookies and some old veterans get when things aren't going well. It's a scared, glazed look that isn't pretty to a coach.

One morning Lyle came into my office and closed the door. He looked like he hadn't slept. Here was a huge hulk of a man, with his head about as low as it could go. We talked, or rather, I listened. The bottom line was that Lyle felt his career was over and it would be best for him and for the team if he retired. He apologized for disappointing us since we had just traded for him, but. . . .

Lyle was always an emotional guy. This is one of the reasons he was a good defensive end. He carried all that emotional energy with him constantly, ready to fire out at the snap of the ball. Now he was in front of me, on the verge of tears.

I thought for a moment, realizing we had to stoke that fire. Then, calmly, I went through my reasons why he should *not* retire. He was running with the second defensive line. I assured him that would change if he stepped it up, but that he couldn't reach that level in his present mental state. At the end of our talk, I said, "You go out and play like hell, and let us decide if you still have it. Personally, I think you do."

Jump now to January 1984. Tampa Bay Stadium. Super Bowl XVIII. I'm pacing the sidelines. With less than two minutes remaining, we're leading 38–9. It's over! We're the world champions of professional football. My second Super Bowl win as a head coach. As I paced, I saw coaches and players ready to burst with joy, just trying to hold themselves on the sideline until the game was officially over. Then I saw Lyle, standing by the bench, crying like a baby. I had to turn away quickly or I would have joined him in tears.

I remembered that morning in my office, and what Lyle, and what the Raiders, had accomplished since he came to us: 8–1 in the 1982 strike year, and 12–4 in 1983, straight through the playoffs to the AFC title over Seattle, and now a win over Washington in Super Bowl XVIII to make us world champions. If Lyle hadn't kicked into gear and given his career another shot, he wouldn't have had this victory. Maybe the Raiders wouldn't have had this victory. During that moment, amid the almost-hysterical joy of the whole team organization, I felt one of the greatest satisfactions of my coaching career.

Lyle is gone now, the victim of an aggressive brain cancer that took him early, but not before he became a world champion.

Tom Flores

Race for Love

*Above all, challenge yourself. You may well sur-
prise yourself at what strengths you have, what
you can accomplish.*

Cecile M. Springer

One hundred and forty high-school runners fidgeted
nervously at the starting line, contemplating the grueling
three-mile cross-country race and the chance to finish in
the Michigan High School Cross-Country Championship.

This was Bill's last race. He looked pale and nervous. I
wondered if he really belonged here. Certainly the others
were endowed with greater strength and speed. But
nobody has ever invented a scale to assess the strength of
a young man's heart or the limits of his desire. Could Bill's
inner qualities carry him to his dream of being an "all-
state" runner? He would have to finish in the top fifteen
to earn that honor.

In theory, by comparing his qualifying time to the times
for the other runners, he should finish close to last. Defeat
seemed inevitable. In his eighteen years, Bill had already
suffered more than his share of setbacks.

Grade school had been a long nightmare for him. When it was decided that he should repeat first grade, he didn't complain; he simply tried harder. Over the years, his teachers called us in to discuss his academic struggles. When he was in sixth grade, another teacher called us in for a conference. "I'm sorry to have to tell you this," she said, "but Bill isn't trying anymore—he has given up completely." I was saddened by her words. And I was afraid that my son might have lost forever a good feeling about himself, that precious but fragile self-image that alone could tip the balance away from failure in later years.

At bedtime I told him about my own grade-school experiences, how I had been the dumbest kid in my class but that, with the love and understanding of my parents and teachers, I had somehow stumbled through those years and had ultimately gone on to law school. I also told him that it was easy to conclude that the achievements of others came simply and easily, but that life was not usually like that. Most triumphs grow out of the ashes of defeat. "Bill," I concluded, "I know that someday, in some way, you will overcome your defeats."

"You know, Dad," he replied, "I guess that not doing so good isn't all that bad if someone loves you and stands by you."

Crack! The starter's gun signaled the beginning of the race. My knees were weak, and a voice that sounded distant and husky left my throat on the chill November wind. "Go, Billy Blue!" I shouted to my son, who wore the blue of Royal Oak's Kimball High School. I hurried with the rest of the crowd to a flat stretch at the bottom of a hill where we could next see the runners, reaching it just as the first boy burst into view. Though I couldn't see his face, I could tell by his style that it wasn't Bill.

Finally, he came over the brow of the hill, very erect, his right shoulder lurching up and down with each pumping motion of his loosely swinging arms. The stride was unmistakable. There were thirty-nine runners ahead of him. Suddenly Bill moved to the outside and began to pass some runners.

It reminded me of how, in school, he kept trying despite all odds. It turned out that our son's puzzling academic problems were finally traced to a paralyzed eye muscle, which caused occasional double vision and severe perceptual difficulties. As junior high approached Bill began to work with an eye doctor and a reading tutor. Through sheer desire, he made so much progress that he earned a place on the honor roll.

In eighth grade, he went out for track, a sport where no one was ever cut and everyone got to run. During his first season, Bill lost every race. But with every defeat he grew more determined. The next fall he ran with the high-school freshman cross-country team. He finished poorly all year, but always ran hard. The team captain and top runner, Phil Ceeley, saw his determination and helped him. Soon our son became a familiar figure on the streets, running up to fifteen miles a day—every day. Those thousands of miles of hard work finally began to pay off in Bill's senior year. He became his cross-country team's fastest runner and his teammates selected him as one of their cocaptains. To achieve all-state he would have to beat literally thousands of runners.

I ran with the other spectators to the three-quarter-mile mark, where we would next see the runners. A lone runner burst over the crest of the hill—not Bill—and gracefully galloped down the grassy slope. Then a swarm of skinny, red-faced boys appeared. Ten . . . thirteen . . . sixteen . . . nineteen . . . There he was! My heart sank. He was running in 20th place and pinned to the inside. *You've got to make your move now! You can't do it later,* I thought. As if he had heard me, Bill suddenly swung to the outside and spurted from 20th to 6th place in less than one hundred yards.

"Go, Ba-ee," I yelled as he streaked past. "Ba-ee"—our sentimental nickname for Bill—had slipped out. When his younger brothers, Dave and Jim, had first started talking, "Ba-ee" was the closest they could come to "Billy."

My elation suddenly turned to fear as he headed for the trees. He had more than two miles to go. I could only wait, worry and wonder. He came out of the trees at the two-mile mark in a virtual tie for fourth place with a boy who had beaten him badly all year. My heart jumped into my throat—fourth place, even fifth place—either was good enough for all-state! Pain, anxiety and intense desire contorted Bill's slender face.

"Go, Billy Blue! Come on, Ba-ee!" Could he hear? Could he feel my love reaching out?

As I rushed along past the two-and-a-half-mile mark, I passed close to the finish line, where my wife stood waiting, hoping. "He's fourth," I choked, and turned quickly away as I felt tears welling.

Gasping for breath, I reached the finishing chute, two long ropes that narrowed to a "V" at the finish line. I had just got there when a smooth, confident runner from Grosse Pointe crossed the finish line to the spectators' cheers. Then the second and third runners streaked down the chute.

An eternity later came Bill, still matching his competitor stride for stumbling stride. Both exhausted runners crossed the finish line together. I looked closely at Bill's face. Agony twisted his boyish features as he staggered aimlessly on.

Thinking he was about to collapse, I instinctively ducked under the ropes, ran over, grabbed his arm and put it over my shoulder. He rasped and gasped uncontrollably for breath as he slumped lifelessly against me. In a few seconds, he straightened up. "I'm okay now, Dad," he said. And he jogged off to "warm down." He had recovered.

But I had not. I was overwhelmed. I tried to hold back the tears that welled in my eyes, but couldn't. I had to let them come. I tried to look at Bill, but could not see. I tried to talk, but no words came.

For a moment, I was ashamed. The everyday mask had been shattered unexpectedly, and for a second I wondered what others would think. But deep in my heart I knew that I wept in a manner that made weeping appropriate; yes, one might even say, majestic.

Judge Keith J. Leenhouts

A Perfect Skate

You've got to get up every morning with determination if you are going to go to bed with satisfaction.

George Horace Lorimer

She staggered off the practice ice supported by some of her skating-team friends. I hurried over to give Heidi her jacket and to brace her until we could find a seat. At fifteen, she had been living with cancer for a year. We'd learned the news just after returning from Chicago, where she'd won her first gold medal in an international competition.

Then came the tests, the invasive procedures and the surgery. Through it all, what mattered to her most was that she retain her ability to skate. Fortunately, her doctor agreed to let her skate as much as she was able.

Heidi's friend Greg helped me take off her skates. All of the children were initially frightened by Heidi's plight, but gradually pitched in to help keep her safe.

"Is she all right?" Greg asked.

"Yes, she just needs a nice nap before we can get her to the car," I explained.

Happy children swirled around me as Heidi slept away. They all tried to be quiet, but their exuberance for the upcoming Keystone State Games was evident. How I wished those days would return for Heidi.

Heidi had been working hard on her programs and was determined to compete, but now the deadline had passed. I woke her up and we began our journey to the car. "Mom, Coach Barb says I am skating my program well. I want to go to the State Games."

Pain shot through my heart. When I told her the registration deadline had passed, she said her coach could probably still get her in. "Mom," she pleaded. "I don't expect a medal. I just want to go there and be normal for a couple of days. Is that so bad?" A sob escaped her.

"Let's ask the doctor," I said, uncertain.

The next day at her checkup she filled the doctor in on all the details of the State Games.

"I'll tell you what," he responded. "It's okay with me if it is okay with your mom, but you'll have to get permission to miss your radiation treatments."

I added something else to the list: "You have to eat right, sleep right and take good care of yourself."

"I will, I promise!" she responded.

After getting permission from the oncologist and sending in a last-minute registration form, Heidi was set to go to the State Games. Now it was the big night and Heidi was about to alight on the ice for her freestyle routine. I prayed.

The speakers announced her name and I steadied my hand on the camera as she flowed across the ice gracefully, like her old self. Proudly, she took up her stance. *Steel Magnolias'* theme song filled the arena, and she took off for a full performance.

She picked her toe into the ice and lifted up into a jump. She was so high that a momentary look of fear crossed her face. I cringed, whispering, "Please God, don't let her break anything on the landing."

She landed perfectly, leg out behind her just like the pros. Her face bore a huge smile as if to say, "I did it!" She tore into her next move as the audience went wild. "Go Heidi!" echoed around the arena. She leaned into her ultimate move, the inside-outside eagle, perfectly done.

The stands erupted with joyful noise. None of us could believe it. Another huge jump! She was garnering points for the team. She glided into a lovely spiral, heavy boot held high like a flag of victory. Her cheeks were pink with effort and she was beaming with pride. Heidi had outskated her best!

She exited victoriously into her coach's arms. Barb grabbed her in a huge hug, crying as they savored this incredible moment. Then her joy turned to shock. Heidi lay lifeless in her arms.

The arena quieted. I ran.

I caught them as Heidi's weight began to overpower Barb. I backed to the bleachers and rested against them. Arms reached to help. I laid her carefully down and felt her neck for a pulse. She had one.

Everyone waited in shock as I checked her over.

The quiet was suddenly shattered by a snore! Bedlam erupted. Applause ripped through the rafters of the frigid arena. Parents of her rivals shared their blankets as Heidi took a well-deserved nap. She was still sound asleep when her teammates ran over to congratulate her. She had earned the gold medal in the freestyle division!

Nancy E. Myer

The Greatest Baseball Story Ever

A hero is someone who has given his or her life to something bigger than oneself.

Joseph Campbell

In 1937, Lou Gehrig, the outstanding first baseman of the New York Yankees, was asked to go to the Children's Hospital in Chicago, while there to play the White Sox, and visit a boy with polio. Tim, ten years old, had refused to try therapy to get well. Lou was his hero, and Tim's parents hoped that Lou would visit Tim and urge him to try the therapy.

Tim was amazed to meet his hero. Lou told Tim, "I want you to get well. Go to therapy and learn to walk again."

Tim said, "Lou, if you will knock a home run for me today, I will learn to walk again." Lou promised.

All the way to the ballpark, Lou felt a deep sense of obligation and even apprehension that he would not be able to deliver his promise that day. Lou didn't knock one home run that day. He knocked two.

Two years later, when Lou Gehrig was dying with the

dreaded muscular disease that to this day bears his name, on July 4, 1939, they celebrated Lou Gehrig Day at Yankee Stadium.

Eighty thousand fans, the governor, the mayor and many other celebrities paid their respects. Lou was one of America's great heroes.

Just before the mike was turned over to Lou to respond, Tim, by this time twelve years old, walked out of the dugout, dropped his crutches, and with leg braces walked to home plate to hug Lou around the waist.

That's what Lou Gehrig meant when he exclaimed those immortal words: "Today I consider myself the luckiest man on the face of the earth."

Mack R. Douglas

OVERCOMING OBSTACLES   201

A Simple Kindness

You can preach a better sermon with your life than with your lips.

Oliver Goldsmith

Vince Desmond took the call. It was one of hundreds he had fielded in his years as community-relations director for the Detroit Tigers—a dad asking if he could arrange for his son to meet a Detroit Tiger. But this request was special. The boy was dying, maybe a week to live. Vince told him he'd do his best and would call him back.

Vince went out to the field. The team was taking batting practice. He went up to one of the starters, told him about the youngster, and got the expected, "Okay, I'll meet with the kid."

Vince called the father. Could he bring the boy the next day about eleven o'clock? Sure thing.

Father and son arrived an hour early. When batting practice was finished, Vince went to the player to tell him the youngster was outside, waiting to meet him. "I don't have time," came the short reply. "I've got to work on fielding," and he trotted out to the infield. It is an unwritten, but strict, rule. Once a player crosses the white line, you can't go after him. Vince approached a couple other players. They were "too busy." Time was tight; it was close to game time.

Heading out of the dugout, Vince was fretting about how painful it would be to tell the kid he couldn't find anyone to take a moment to say hello. He walked by the clubhouse. There was only one player inside, who noticed Vince looking close to tears. "Hey, Vinnie, what's the matter?"

"You're starting today. I can't bother you," he said.

"Ask me."

Vince told him about the young boy. Could he, would he take a minute to say hello?

The pitcher smiled and was off to say hello. Twenty minutes later, the pitcher came back into the clubhouse, went to his locker, pulled out two twenties, went over to the equipment manager, bought a new Tigers team jacket and took it to the kid.

The pitcher won that day, after winning the heart of his newest fan.

The father called Vince the next day to tell him that his son had worn the team jacket to bed and had slept better than he had in a long time. And there was one last wish. "Please, is there any way the player would autograph a picture?"

Vince said he'd do his best. That's what Vince always said, and always did.

Photo in hand, Vince found the player, who saw him coming. "So, what now, Vinnie?" he said, laughing.

"Will you sign a photograph for that young boy you met yesterday?"

"Sure thing," was the simple reply. The pitcher signed it: "To my newfound friend forever. Jack Morris."

The young boy died less than a week later. His Tigers jacket and the autographed photo were in his casket.

John Gross

Albino Power

In the long run, you hit only what you aim at. Therefore, though you may fail, you had better aim at something high.

Henry David Thoreau

I was born an albino in Scranton, Pennsylvania, in 1945. No one in my family had ever known what an albino was, what it meant to be an albino, what had to be done differently because I was an albino.

My parents, relatives and friends treated me just like they treated everybody else. That was just about the best thing they could have done. It gave me a leg up on trusting myself, so when the annoyances came along, I could deal with them.

True, my schoolbook photo always looked like a snowball with two pieces of coal for eyes. Like most albinos, I had terrible eyesight, but the fact that I could barely see didn't bother me all that much.

Kids would tease me, asking if I was joining the circus and calling me "Whitey." My grades suffered until eventually I overcame being self-conscious and realized it was okay to ask to sit in the front of the classroom so I could see the blackboard better. People stared at me when I held reading material right at the tip of my nose so I could see it well enough to read. Even when I was eight or nine, movie-theater clerks started asking me to pay adult prices because I "looked older."

The worst part for me was that because my eyesight was so bad, I couldn't play sports very well. I didn't give up trying, though. I shot hoops every day and played whiffle ball (because whiffle-ball line drives can't kill you) in the summer. And I studied harder.

Eventually, I got better at school and loved it. By the time I got to college I was double majoring, going to summer school and immersing myself in every kind of extracurricular activity I could find. I had learned to be proud of being an albino. I did my darndest to make "albino" a positive word. And I decided to make my living with my eyes—and in *sports*.

I couldn't see well enough to play sports, but with a solid education and the drive to do it, I could make a living involved in the arena I loved. I've done it now for more than thirty years in print and in video, and now in cyberspace. People make jokes about how I'm the only "blind editor" they know, but the jokes are verbal smiles now, some of them signs of respect. And I make jokes about being an albino. I have even developed an all-white routine, if you could call it that.

I was just a proud albino kid from the coal country of Pennsylvania. I now realize that being born an albino helped me to overcome obstacles, gain confidence, and be proud of my personal achievement and humble about my professional accomplishments.

John A. Walsh

Heart of Gold

Her friends and family told her over and over that her time would come. She always responded with a half smile and a small nod, but she never seemed to really believe it. This was almost understandable because toward the peak of her career, she always seemed to be the one who narrowly missed the spotlight. The spotlight was almost always reserved for the marquee gymnasts of her era, such as Shannon Miller and Kim Zmeskal. But the shadow that hid her from the spotlight was also result-related. She was always one away from qualifying for something. In the 1992 Olympics, she narrowly missed the all-around finals by fourteen one-thousandths of a point. It would almost be an understatement to refer to Kerri Strug as an underdog for the 1996 Olympics.

After the 1992 Olympics, her coach Bela Karolyi retired, which left Kerri leaping from team to team looking for a suitable replacement. To add to the stress of searching for the right coach, she was plagued with injuries such as a torn stomach muscle and a severely sprained lower back. She refers to these years between Olympics as the "worst years of my life." The best thing that happened in those years was Karolyi's coming out of retirement in late 1994.

One year later, not many months before the Atlanta games, she returned to training under him and set her sights on the 1996 Olympics.

Going into the Olympics, the media focus was on the "sure-thing" names such as Dominique Dawes and Shannon Miller. Kerri's moment came when she was the last U.S. gymnast on the last apparatus on the last day of team competition. The gold medal for the team came down to her vault. An early landing on her first vault caused a serious injury to her ankle. The pressure was on. At the time, she and her teammates and coach thought that she needed the second vault to win. They were not aware that the first vault scored well enough for the victory.

Kerri went to Bela and told him that she couldn't feel her leg. Bela told her that they had to go one more time. "Do I have to do this again?" she asked. "Can you, can you?" Bela responded. She hesitated, "I don't know yet." Then she concluded, "I will do it, I will, I will." Kerri knew that this was her moment to prove to herself, her teammates and anyone else who doubted her will power that she was a champion. She was about to earn that title.

So she performed her second vault with a painful injury and won the competition. Strug's vault captured what *USA Today* proclaimed as the "greatest American team victory in the Olympics since the U.S. hockey team upset the Soviet Union in 1980."

For the medal ceremony, her coach, Bela, carried her to the podium, where her teammates supported her while she stood on one leg for the playing of the national anthem. It was the first time in history that the U.S. women's gymnastics team won gold. It was also the first time in history the spotlight shone on Kerri Strug.

Chris Tamborini

The Kid Who Would Be Coach

"Like a stack of dimes," is how his father described him. Skinny, too tall for his weight, and only one passion—anything that came with a ball, hoop, bat or glove.

His calendar had three seasons—football, basketball and baseball. Those more than covered the year for this kid.

Early one football season, when he was about twelve, he realized his body was not going to bulk up and give him the mass he needed to be a superstar athlete. He was way too light for football, even for quarterback. He was tall enough to do okay in basketball, for now, anyway, but he didn't see any sign he was going to get Empire-State-Building-tall.

For a while he thought about baseball. Certainly there wasn't anyone who loved the game more, who came earlier than he did to every practice or stayed as late, who always had questions, questions, questions, even *suggestions* for the coach.

Still, by age twelve, the kid knew, deep inside, in the same way he couldn't read a pitcher's nerves, he would never be a pro athlete. So, the question was, how was he gonna keep sports in his life?

He thought about it and thought about it. This went on for quite some time. Then the idea came, as simple and clear and sane as he expected it to be—he would coach!

The decision to abandon the idea of ever becoming the next Babe Ruth didn't stop him from playing all-out. No way. Having a goal that seemed realistic spurred him on even more. He now had more than his own performance to pay attention to—the mechanics of organization, the different ways coaches handled strategies and motivation. He started watching *everything*.

One lesson surprised him: He discovered he could learn as much from poor coaching as from great coaching. *Gee, I don't think I'd do it that way,* he'd say to himself, surprisingly often, and he'd think about why not and what he'd do instead. This was another whole level of the game!

For the next ten years, the *decision* stayed firm. He played as many sports as he could, winning some minor awards along the way, and steered his college courses toward a teaching credential so he could start coaching right out of college. And it worked. He got the offer, to be head coach for varsity basketball at an inner-city high school.

That first basketball season, they—he and his team of scrappy fighters who had more energy than discipline— were winning some, but losing more. He hated losing! The kids hated losing! They took it so hard, as if it were a disgrace.

One day he was admitting as much to one of the other coaches, who just laughed at him! He said, "No one likes to lose, but wise up! There are more lessons in losing than in winning. It shows you what to work on in the game and, besides, these kids need to learn how to lose, how to rebound. Sports is life training for them."

One Tuesday late in the season, the team was boarding a bus for the trip cross-town to play a team that had whooped them good last time. They were a better team now, but surely so was the rival team. The coach was thinking about game strategy and didn't notice right away that a commotion was building by the door of the bus. An Hispanic guy, too old to be a student, was pulling at Cheo, their star forward. The coach rushed to get to the front and as he did, he saw that the guy was reeling and unsteady, drunk as a skunk.

Cheo, a junior, was already their quickest and most accurate outside-shooter, averaging twenty points a game, and an exemplary player—on time for practice, worked hard, helped his teammates, unselfish in scoring, the best passer, the best dribbler and totally game-smart. He seemed afraid to pull away from the outsider, but with a silent signal from the coach, Cheo backed out of the guy's grasp and turned for the bus.

The coach put an arm around the guy so he could control him if he tried anything, and asked what was up. The guy was too drunk or didn't have enough English to answer. The coach walked him to the gym office and asked the athletic director to sort out the problem.

When the coach got back to the bus, Cheo was sitting in his usual seat at the rear of the bus. He seemed okay, so the coach plopped in his usual seat and turned his attention back to game strategy.

Later, as the players got off the bus, the team manager asked the coach, "What will happen to that guy?"

"Why do you ask?"

"Well," the manager said, "he's Cheo's older brother."

The coach was shocked. Cheo hadn't said a word.

After the team was changed into their uniforms and getting mentally ready, the coach called Cheo aside. What the coach sensed was true: Cheo was embarrassed by his brother's behavior. He was a proud kid, working hard to do well in school. His family lived in one of the low-income housing projects, the one the kids called "Dogtown." Kids can be tough on each other.

They talked about family loyalty and the restrictions in society Cheo called "fences." They talked about what made Cheo unique and why, even though his brother deserved compassion and help, that didn't put a taint on Cheo. The coach led Cheo's focus back to the game, back to what action he could take right then, in that moment. They discussed how he could help himself and his family, not by falling apart, but by staying strong and doing his usual great play.

Cheo scored twenty-nine points that game. And they won.

The coach never saw Cheo's brother again, but kept in touch with Cheo, whose full name is Eliseo Nino. He graduated as Player of the League in basketball, went on to play basketball in junior college and then at a state university. He graduated with solid grades, and became a teaching assistant and basketball coach at his junior college. A few years later he moved to another community college as head varsity basketball coach.

This story started out about a skinny kid who came to understand that coaching isn't a substitute for playing; it *is* the game on another level. But it's really Cheo's story, the story of one kid's determination to succeed against the odds of growing up in the barrio and an equal determination to give back.

Yes, the "stack of dimes" was me. I went on from teaching and coaching high school sports to officiating collegiate basketball and football, and ultimately to the National Football League as a referee for thirty-one years. Sports as a passion has never faded.

Jim Tunney

Rules of the Game

Sports. A six-letter word for failure. Maybe it wasn't so in your dictionary, but that was my definition. I was a skinny, gangly girl growing up in the seventies.

Sports at our Catholic grade school consisted of taking a walk around the parking lot during recess. As we got older, we would don mustard-colored gym suits and flat sneakers and do sit-ups on the cold gym floor. There were no dance classes, aerobics or swimming lessons.

Then came high school and sports got ugly. "Mr. Luther" was a swaggering little man who felt that teaching girls was his punishment for having been evil in his previous life.

First sport: baseball. Mr. Luther's practices all began the same: "Now listen up. These are the rules: you do what you are told. You goof off, you answer to me. Y'understand? Any questions?" Stony silence. "All right, you pansy girls, get running—NOW! If it's not too much trouble," he sneered.

Nowhere in "the rules" were there any directions on how to play the game. You were supposed to know that. If not, you were stupid. For all his years of teaching, he didn't know that children do not learn without being taught.

Mr. Luther put a bat in my hand and barked, "Don't you even know how to hold a bat?" I was too shy to explain that it was my first time. I held the bat out, hoping miraculously that it would hit his fastball and not the air. No miracle here. Mr. Luther shook his head in disgust. I didn't make his A team.

Catching practice was worse. I was finally relegated to right field. That was fine with me. I stayed out there and prayed that no balls would come my way. I squinted into the sun, checking my watch, just waiting for it to be over. And I waited throughout high school for gym class and all sports to be over.

Leaving high school meant leaving those memories of failure. Or so I thought.

Fast-forward twenty-some years, to another day, another town. My son was six and he wanted to play baseball.

Now whether you admit it or not, we all relive our past through our children. Their experiences trigger our own pain—things we thought we had buried years ago. I vowed my son would not suffer the same fate I had.

First day of practice and I was ready for the coach—whoever he was. No way would he destroy my son's confidence before it had a chance to grow. I was ready for battle. If you ever saw a mama bear with her cub, you'll know how I felt. The coach had no idea what he was in for if he messed with my kid's head.

The coach walked over and addressed the parents. "Now here's the team rules." My heart clutched. *Oh no, not again. Did all men have to say that?* The coach continued, "This is a noncompetitive league—we're not keeping score. Anyone who yells at the kids will be asked to leave. Remember, the purpose of this game is to let the kids have some fun."

I was stunned! What did he say? Did I hear right? Had

coaches really changed so much? Or was it just their line for the parents? I wasn't about to let down my guard just yet.

My son came up to bat, and I held my breath. The coach slowly pitched to him—right over the plate. He pitched, and pitched and pitched. After ten pitches with no hit, he handed the ball to the assistant coach. My heart froze as he walked over to my child. *Oh no, here comes the lecture,* I thought, willing myself to stay seated.

The coach walked behind my son and put his arms around him. He signaled for a pitch. Together, the coach and my son hit the ball. My kid let out a whoop and went flying to first base. Parents were cheering, and the coach was smiling from ear to ear. "ATTABOY!" he yelled.

By the end of the game, everyone who got a hit was allowed to run all the bases. With the coach's help, everyone did get a hit. Home runs for all! The kids were ecstatic. They went home that night pumped up with the thrill of playing baseball.

I came back for each practice, marveling at the patience and gentleness of the coach. Some moms were obviously frustrated with the league. One ex-cheerleader was frantically trying to keep score so she could prove her child had won and was the star. She was not happy. Someone had changed all the rules on her.

By the end of the season, all the kids had improved their skills. And the next year, they would learn more of the "official" rules. But for that first season, they learned how to love baseball.

For all the nostalgia for "the good old days," we forget that some things are better now. And therein lies the hope for our children.

Thank you, Coach, for giving my son—and me—the love of baseball.

Laura Ishler

Bad Hop

The ball pinged off the aluminum bat and headed toward the hole between shortstop and third base, the sort of one-hop screamer that the high-school junior shortstop, my son Chris, had backhanded a thousand times. Only this time, the ball hit a pebble and caromed weirdly toward his head. With a sickening crunch, the ball caught him flush in his left eye, and he went down in a heap. Bad hop, and a bad break.

The ambulance came onto the field, and he was taken away, something that just doesn't seem to happen in the pastoral world of high-school baseball. At the hospital, Chris was diagnosed with a blowout fracture of the bones in the orbit of his eye socket—a classic sports injury easily resolved by a simple surgical procedure.

Except that things went wrong, and when the surgeon finally screwed up his courage enough to tell my wife and me what happened—an undetected blood clot had cut off oxygen to the optic nerve—the long and short of it was that Chris would be blind in his left eye, probably for the rest of his life. In one instant, the college scholarships Chris had contemplated and the dreams of a professional baseball career vanished.

Chris was still groggy from the surgery when we went into his hospital room, his bandaged eye holding a secret we now had to share with him. We chatted about small things until he was alert enough to ask the inevitable, "Did everything go okay?"

My wife, Sue, gripped my hand as I told him that, no, it had not. That there had been complications. That the doctors had done their best, that medicine was still more art than science.

Halfway through my semiprepared speech, Chris interrupted me:

"Dad, am I blind?"

"Yeah, son. I'm afraid so."

"Will I be able to see out of it at all?"

"We don't know—the doctors don't know. Maybe a little. Someday. Not now." It was the toughest thing I've ever had to do.

Chris sort of nodded and looked away toward the window. Outside it was spring, and we listened for a time to a robin's territorial song from a nearby tree.

"Can I have a Coke?"

The duty nurse brought Chris a soft drink in a can with a cup and some ice. His mother poured the drink and he sat up and drank some of it through a straw, and then peered at the can on his bedside table.

"Dad, could you see if they have a pencil and paper I can use?"

I walked outside to the nurses' station and borrowed a notepad and a pencil and returned to Chris's room, where his mother was talking with him in hushed tones. I handed him the pad and pencil, and we elevated his bed. He raised his knees and propped the pad against them, looked at the soda can, and began to draw. Sue and I said nothing as long minutes passed. Finally, he tore off the sheet of paper and handed it to me. We looked at it—a photo-likeness of a Coca-Cola soft-drink can. Chris had always had an uncanny artistic ability: if his eyes could see it, his hand could draw it. We had thought of art as his second love—right behind baseball. In those brief moments, Chris took a bad hop, made a decision and changed forever the course of his life.

"I'm okay, you guys. I can still draw."

With that, he lowered his bed, turned onto his side and fell asleep.

That was eleven years ago. Since then, about 40 percent of the sight has returned to Chris's left eye. Even with this handicap, which severely affects depth perception, he went on to hit .385 and shortstop a state-championship baseball team the very next season, earning all-state honors in the process.

But his focus had changed. Chris took his college degree—with the help of an academic and not an athletic scholarship—in fisheries and wildlife management as a background for his career as a wildlife and sporting artist. Today, his paintings and pencil renderings grace the pages and covers of magazines and more than a dozen books, and they hang in galleries and museums in New York and Tennessee. The list of his clients awaiting oil and watercolor commissions is always at least a year long.

Human courage manifests itself in countless ways, countless times every day in every city and town and hamlet on every continent around the world. One bad hop, one routine ground ball, one instant of pain, and what could have been months of despair. But instead, that bad hop—and the courage to accept what could not be changed—altered the course of a life for the better.

In sports we call such things great comebacks. I suppose in Chris's case, there is no reason to call it anything else. Proving, I guess, that some bad hops can be fielded cleanly after all.

Steve Smith

7

FAMILY DAY

A life is not important except in the impact it has on other lives.

Jackie Robinson

Best Seats in the House

*It is not flesh and blood but the heart that
makes us fathers and sons.*

Friedrich von Schiller

The best thing I ever bought was the season ticket.
Actually, it was three season tickets.

I was thirteen years old at the time and a rabid fan of
the New York football Giants. They were called the football Giants in those days to distinguish them from the
baseball Giants, who had just moved to San Francisco.

How does a little thirteen-year-old boy gather enough
spare change to spring for three season tickets? With his
wits.

My bar mitzvah was looming, and everyone in my
rather large family was calling and asking what I wanted
for my present. I knew exactly what I wanted, but I also
knew that no one was going to give it to me. So I proposed the following deal to my father: I would buy as
many season tickets as I could with whatever money I got
as bar-mitzvah gifts if he would promise to renew the
tickets every year until I was old enough to hold down a

job. My father agreed. After all, he was a Giants fan, too. Then I told everyone in the family that I wanted cash.

When the big day was over and I totaled up the take, it came to three season tickets and about fifteen dollars left over. I half expected my father to make up the difference and purchase a fourth ticket to sort of round things out, but he didn't. A deal's a deal, I guess, and I suppose he thought he was teaching me something. Anyway, when the 1958 season came around, we had three seats in the upper deck on the five-yard line at the closed end of Yankee Stadium.

That was the year the Giants played the famous overtime championship game against the Baltimore Colts, the first sudden death in NFL history. Professional football exploded after that, and suddenly all the big-shot lawyers and account execs wanted tickets. But they couldn't get them anymore. The Giants were sold out, and season tickets would now become something like heirlooms, to be passed down from father to son. And I had three. Well, *we* had three.

For the first several years, the threesome was always me and my father and my best friend Richie, and then my best friend Bob, and then my best friend Philly, and then my best friend Richie again. But always, it was my father and I.

We wore Giants-blue sweaters before people sold such things. Grandma knitted them for us. We were boosters, my father and I, yelling ourselves hoarse on days at the stadium. I don't know if those were cold years or if I was just underdressed, but I remember shivering through those winter games even with the sweater. We tried everything. Hot coffee. Wool blankets. A can of Sterno burning at our feet. I had my first nip of brandy from a flask. I loved those games with my dad.

Then the war came—Vietnam—and I rolled off in a tank with the Third Armored Division. Guess what my dad did? He gave the three tickets to my cousin Bernie! Not to keep, just to hold until I came back. We never talked about this, my father and I, and so I don't know whether he was being superstitious or whether he just didn't want to go to a game if I wasn't there.

Not long after I came back, I got married. And we took the tickets back from Cousin Bernie. The Sunday gang became me and my father and my wife. Actually, my father, my wife and I coming along with a picnic basket and endless questions.

It wasn't the happiest of times for the three season tickets, because the Giants were in the midst of a long slump. In fact, they stunk. My wife couldn't understand why my father and I put ourselves through the agony of defeat week after week, especially when it was cold. My father couldn't understand how my wife couldn't understand.

Somehow we survived this. My father loved my wife, and although she didn't care much for the game, she loved us. She knitted a pair of Giants scarves, 100 percent wool with a snappy team logo that my late grandmother had never even attempted. People would actually stop by our seats and ask us where we got the scarves. We would point at my wife, and they would ask her if they could order one.

Then I had a son. Ivan came to his first football game when he was six years old. He spent half the game sitting on my father's lap and half the game sitting on mine. Without a doubt, this was the finest period for the season tickets, the three generations sitting in the upper deck— still on the five-yard line, but now we were in the Giants' new stadium in the Jersey Meadowlands, and the team was beginning its march toward two Super Bowls.

Every Sunday we gathered together, grandfather, father, and son, either at the stadium or in front of one of our TVs (if it was an away game). And we rooted. And we cheered. And we talked about the players.

What is it about men, men of six or thirty-six or sixty-six, that they find it easiest to share their intimacies not directly but through a protective shield of old stories and third-person assessments? By which member of the team we admired (the quarterback, the linebacker, the wide receiver), we told each other who we thought we were or, more likely, who we wished we were. By reacting to referees' calls that went against us, we spoke to each other about our sense of fairness, our belief that the world was just or unjust. By sticking with the team when they were playing badly, we informed each other, and ourselves, of the importance of loyalty and trust.

Once I remember booing a Giants player who had taken himself out of the game. I did this in order to communicate to Ivan (or maybe to my father) my belief that a real man always plays through the pain.

Another time, the three of us proved our power to stay with the team by remaining in our seats during a driving hailstorm. We were heroes after that one, boy, and when the Giants beat the Eagles that day we felt as much a part of the team as any cornerback.

Then there was my father's heart attack. Giants–Rams, 1984. It was bitter cold that afternoon, and in the second quarter I noticed that my father's lips had turned purple.

"Are you all right?" I asked.

Slowly, as if not to break something, he shook his head no. I turned to my nine-year-old son and said quietly, "Grandpa is having a heart attack. I want you to help me."

And Ivan did just that. As I helped my father to the men's room where he could get warm, Ivan went to the security staff. He returned with two burly guards and a wheelchair. "Will Doctor so-and-so please report to the ... ?"

We wheeled my father down to the training room, where a doctor was waiting. I was right, it was his heart. We put him in the ambulance that usually runs broken players to the hospital for X rays. I brought the car around to follow the ambulance. My son climbed in with my father. As they pulled out, Ivan flashed me the thumbs-up sign, and I smiled through my gathering tears.

My father pulled through, but he would never go to a game again. He was afraid of the cold. And he was afraid of the long climb we had to make to get to our seats.

For the next few years, whenever the Giants were on the road, we congregated at my father's house to watch the game on TV. At the stadium, the third seat was filled by my sister and a rotation of friends. But we all watched Super Bowl XXI together, my father and my son and I. When the Giants beat the Denver Broncos, we whooped and hollered and hopped around the room.

My father died soon after that—another heart attack. My son and I have shared the three tickets ever since, rooting and reminiscing and exchanging those protected intimacies across the past nine seasons.

Now my son is leaving for college, and it suddenly strikes me that for the past thirty-five years these three tickets, these magic tickets, have been a kind of special connection, first for my father and me; then for my father, me, and my son; and then for me and my son together. This year, for the very first time in the history of the three season tickets, there will be only me.

I find myself wondering what it was that made my father give the tickets to Cousin Bernie during the years when I was away at war. And I think I might give the tickets to my cousin Sam.

But then Ivan notices that he'll be home for one of the Giants home dates. He says, "I can go to that one, Dad!" And I think perhaps I'll just hold on to the tickets for maybe one more season. Maybe one more game. Maybe.

Barney Cohen

She Made a Memory

*Confidence is a lot of this game or any game.
If you don't think you can, you won't.*

Jerry West

Looking back, it's easy to get melodramatic about my one and only experience as an umpire.

The fact that it also was a wonderful parenting experience gives me an excuse to be just a little corny. If I embellish the facts, I apologize.

I'll blame it on pride.

My kids, Nikki and Dean, are aspiring baseball players in the Racine (Wisconsin) Youth Sports Association's Pee Wee League. Like most eight- and seven-year-olds, they also are aspiring skateboard stuntpersons, Lego engineers and video-game wizards. There's no need to rush specialization.

Nikki and Dean play for the Pirates. Their coach, a man of considerable patience, was not blessed with a roster full of future Sammy Sosas and Mark McGwires. We're talking about kids who can barely tie their shoes, let alone field ground balls in the hole or slap down-and-away sliders to the opposite field.

Nikki, in particular, has had problems at the plate. Even though the coaches pitch, and every batter gets five swings, Nikki has made her beleaguered, lob-tossing coach look like Sandy Koufax this summer.

Dean is the better hitter, but his fielding percentage is, I'm quite certain, some 300 points lower than his batting average. No matter. The Pee Wee League stresses participation and sportsmanship, and that's all that counts.

Still, when you lose 39–1, as the Pirates did earlier this season, it's hard to keep your chin up. Everybody likes to win once in a while. Or at least come close.

I guess that sets the stage for what happened recently: Pirates vs. Yankees and yours truly, home-plate umpire. I was pressed into service mainly because I was the first parent to arrive.

Thankfully, the game went smoothly. There were no close plays at the plate, in fact, there were no plays at the plate. There were no corked bats, no brushback pitches, no scuffed balls and no bench-clearing brawls.

The only tense moment occurred when I had to warn the catcher about drawing pictures in the dirt while the game was in progress.

Nikki, mired in a slump I would guesstimate at three-for-thirty or thereabouts, got a hit early in the game. But her exuberance quickly turned to tears of embarrassment when she became confused on the base path and was doubled up on a fly-out.

I wanted to console her, but feared the Yankees would think the Pirates had me in their back pocket. So I bit my tongue.

The Pirates trailed 16–12 going into their final at bats. This stirred cautious optimism on the bench because the team usually was ten to fifteen runs behind at this point.

Amazingly, they rallied.

They scored four runs to tie the score, the big blow a

twelve-hopper by Dean that eluded three or four gloves and bounced drunkenly into left field.

With the winning run at third and two out, Nikki stepped up to the plate. The game was on the line, but more important, so, too, was the fragile ego of an eight-year-old.

Forget Barbie dolls and pink blouses and hopscotch. This little girl was just dying to hang a rope into center field.

I called time and stepped to the plate, under the pretense of brushing it off. I glanced at Nikki and saw fear in her eyes.

"C'mon, honey," I whispered as I shooshed the imaginary dirt. "Watch the ball all the way to the bat and swing hard. You can do it."

My heart sank after two swinging strikes.

And then the coach delivered a waist-high lob ball, and Nikki put every ounce of her forty-eight pounds into the swing and made solid contact. The ball blooped toward the shortstop and bounced high over his glove for a clean hit.

I watched Nikki run to first base, ponytail bouncing under her helmet, and felt a surge of emotion I cannot begin to describe.

The winning run crossed the plate.

Nikki stood on the bag, grinning as the rest of the Pirates swarmed the field in victory. Our eyes met, and she started running toward me.

I figured I had fulfilled my duties as umpire, so I dropped the impartiality act and swept her up in a bear hug. She was laughing and crying at the same time.

"What's wrong, Nikki?" I asked.

"Daddy, I just can't believe I did that," she said through her tears. "I can't believe I made a hit!"

You made more than that, Nikki.

You made a memory.

Gary D'Amato

My Son, My Enemy

A while ago, shortly after a close encounter of the disciplinary kind, my then twelve-year-old son, Marlon, asked me if I was up for a game of one-on-one at the basketball hoop in the driveway. I had figured that I was in for a day of wrathful silence, but here was my son with an open grin and a friendly challenge. I was both surprised and pleased.

Which only goes to prove how naive a dad can be.

As soon as the kid stepped onto the driveway, a physical change came over him. His body grew taut; his eyes became lasers. In short order an outside jumper dropped soundlessly through the net. A layup floated over my outstretched hand and into the basket. He executed a twisting, crazy drive, climbing halfway up my chest to drop in a shot that I am sure violated the laws of physics.

Next thing I knew, I was sweating, breathless and down three baskets to zip, which is a fairly sizable hole when you're only playing to ten. Gripping my knees, struggling for air, I realized what I should've known all along: this was no friendly game.

This was a challenge.

There comes a time when sons test their fathers. A boy on the threshold of manhood wants to prove to himself how close he is, and the most convenient yardstick is Dad. The test may be physical, or it may be intellectual, but sooner or later the young lion has to take the old one's measure—to see if he's still got it.

I understood that perfectly as Marlon heaved the ball to me with a vaguely contemptuous air.

My son is all the things I'm not: quick and graceful, with a deadly shot and a killer crossover dribble. And I know that there will come a day when he will, on a regular basis, whip me like a recalcitrant mule.

Just not today, I told myself.

It was easier for me with Marlon's older brother, Markise. We all played board games, not basketball. But roughly after he turned thirteen, the games became a tug of war. Whether we were playing Monopoly or Risk, Markise would loudly question every move I made. He'd drag out the rule book, combing its contents in an effort to document my cheating. Not surprisingly, he is now studying to be a lawyer.

"Markise," I would say, "it's just a game." I didn't yet understand that it was anything but.

Frankly, part of me resents this testing between old blood and new. I've always considered myself the coolest of dads.

One's coolness isn't the issue, however. If you're a dad, and especially if this is your first time being tested, your reaction is—*huh?* And who can blame you? For eleven years the kid has regarded you as a sage on the order of Moses, a wise prophet and lawgiver. Then one day you find that you're the enemy.

I have one more son to go, eleven-year-old Bryan, and I suspect that the last may be the worst. He is, after all, the same child who at age two sized me up, gave me a gummy smile and announced, "One day I'm going to kill you so l can marry Mommy." For a year after that, I called him Oedipus. My wife had to make me stop.

Of course, I suppose we could be gracious and accept our limitations. Cede the pride to the younger lion. Be mature.

Heck, maybe we should even be flattered. The boy wants to gauge his manhood, and the best standard he can think of to measure himself against is Dad. Kind of makes you feel warm all over.

Yeah, right. I don't buy it either.

It's a man thing, I guess, like the way John Wayne might have said it. "Ya fight back till ya can't fight back no more. Ya don't give in till they shovel th' dirt in yer face, pilgrim."

Perhaps that's the lesson a father teaches an impatient son by refusing to give in on the driveway or at the game board or wherever. Toughness. Fortitude. Pride.

Marlon and I played a game for the ages that day in the driveway. A game they should write epic poetry about. Larry Bird versus Magic Johnson in game seven of the NBA Finals couldn't have been more intense. I backed him in, put up pump fakes and finger rolls, scrambled for loose balls, fought for rebounds. Marlon drove the lane, popped in outside shots, swatted the ball out of my hands.

When it was over, I had clawed my way to victory by the narrowest of margins: 10-9.

Afterward, wheezing like an asthmatic smoker, sweat rushing off my brow, I called him over so that I could impart a life lesson. I told him I knew why he had contested me with such feverish intensity.

"You played for the wrong reasons," I counseled. He nodded as if he understood.

A few weeks later Marlon challenged me to a friendly round of video-game boxing. Beat me soundly. And laughed while he did it.

And all the while my youngest, Bryan, watched me with a serene and knowing smile.

Leonard Pitts Jr.

Baseball Fever

For the parents of a Little Leaguer, a baseball game is simply a nervous breadkown divided into innings.

Earl Wilson

I've seen the highs and lows of baseball fever. During spring training, someone at work mentioned the upcoming season, and we realized that our kids would be playing each other in the same Little League. Soon after, my coworkers began bragging about their kids and bantering around some challenges.

I felt my stomach pitch (no pun intended) when I heard this. Last year, in T-ball, my son was less than athletically enthused. Don't get me wrong, he's coordinated. But, typically, when the other kids were paying attention to the baseball game, my son was throwing grass up in the air and trying to catch it in his mouth.

So, during the practice season, I had decided I wouldn't put pressure on my son or myself this year by trying to raise a super baseball player at home. And I wouldn't engage in the bragging and one-upmanship at work. But then, when I arrived for the first game, I saw John in marketing giving his son last-minute pointers. Suddenly, in a moment of insecurity, I, too, turned to my boy and whispered some game-playing advice: "Son, watch out for doggie doo-doo on the grass."

During the seventh inning, John wandered over to our side and shook my hand. "Great game, huh?" he said.

I nodded.

"Too bad about your son falling down on his way to third base, though," he continued. "Is he alright?"

"He's okay," I explained, my face turning red. "His stomach is bothering him—he had a big dinner."

"Really? I thought maybe he accidentally ate a rotten weed, or some bad thatch."

I knew word of that would spread through the office quickly.

"I don't want to go to work anymore," I told my wife.

"If you really want to do something," she said, "you should take Alasdair out to the park this weekend and practice."

I felt bad for expecting more from my son than he wished to give, but I took her advice nonetheless. I grabbed my son's hand and we walked around the infield. I pointed out the excitement of the game. We talked about each position. I explained how grass will give him worms.

Then, for the next several weeks, my son actually showed an interest in the game.

Once, he even caught the game-ending fly ball. As I stood and watched his teammates congratulate him, I silently patted myself on the back for encouraging him to try harder.

The next day, I even joined in the banter around the water cooler at work. It was fun bragging about my kid's final out. I had reached the inner circle. I felt a part of something greater than myself.

High on the moment, I even predicted that, later that evening, my son's team would "whoop" the team John's kid was on.

At the ballpark, I walked confidently over to John on the bleachers. "Great game," I remarked.

"You bet," he replied.

"Yep, I think we are going to win this one," I boasted, just as a fly ball landed two feet behind my son, who was hunched over on the grass spitting out a ladybug.

"See you at work tomorrow," John exclaimed as he rushed down to congratulate his son for hitting the game-winning home run.

My glory days as a sports dad were short-lived, but I'll always remember them fondly. (Sigh.)

Ken Swarner

THE FAMILY CIRCUS. **By Bil Keane**

©2000
BKI

"Bundt cake? No thanks. I'd rather have a piece
of home-run cake."

Encouraging Words

*In baseball you can't let losing carry over to the
next day. You've got to flip the page.*

Don Baylor

Someone said that encouragement is simply reminding
a person of the "shoulders" he's standing on, the heritage
he's been given. That's what happened when a young
man, the son of a star baseball player, was drafted by one
of the minor-league teams. As hard as he tried, his first
season was disappointing, and by midseason he expected
to be released any day.

The coaches were bewildered by his failure because he
possessed all the characteristics of a superb athlete, but he
couldn't seem to incorporate those advantages into a
coordinated effort. He seemed to have become discon-
nected from his potential.

His future seemed darkest one day when he had
already struck out his first time at bat. Then he stepped
up to the batter's box again and quickly ran up two
strikes. The catcher called a time-out and trotted to the
pitcher's mound for a conference. While they were busy,

the umpire, standing behind the plate, spoke casually to the boy.

Then play resumed, the next pitch was thrown—and the young man knocked it out of the park. That was the turning point. From then on, he played the game with a new confidence and power that quickly drew the attention of the parent team, and he was called up to the majors.

On the day he was leaving for the city, one of his coaches asked him what had caused such a turnaround. The young man replied that it was the encouraging remark the umpire had made that day when his baseball career had seemed doomed.

"He told me I reminded him of all the times he had stood behind my dad in the batter's box," the boy explained. "He said I was holding the bat just the way Dad had held it. And he told me, 'I can see his genes in you; you have your father's arms.' After that, whenever I swung the bat, I just imagined I was using Dad's arms instead of my own."

Barbara Johnson

A Lesson in Love

Life is a blend of laughter and tears, a combination of rain and sunshine.

Norman Vincent Peale

It was well past midnight and, after nearly eighteen hours of effort, Dick Hoyt was one hundred yards from the finish line. He tightened his grip on the racing wheelchair before him and broke into a rubbery-legged run toward the finish line.

Dick, forty-six, and son Rick (Richard Jr.), twenty-four, his ninety-two-pound wheelchair charioteer, had been competing in the Ironman Canada Triathlon Championship since 7 A.M. By the time they had finished the 2.4-mile swim, Dick was gray with fatigue from towing his son in an inflatable dinghy. During the grueling 112-mile bicycling event, Rick was strapped into a "racing basket" mounted on the front wheel assembly of Dick's bike. During the ordeal, Rick—who has cerebral palsy and is a virtual quadriplegic—withstood acute discomfort, while his father suffered through severe cramps that knotted his stomach and weakened his legs. In the last stretch of the 26.2-mile run, Dick slowed to a walk.

The race was officially over—David Kirk of Canada had won more than eight hours earlier—but spectators were four deep as the Hoyts sprinted down the main thoroughfare of Penticton. People knew about the Hoyts—knew that in the space of a half-dozen years the father had run with his brain-damaged son in some two hundred fifty road races, six Boston Marathons and fifteen previous triathlons of a less taxing nature.

Rick was born on Jan. 10, 1962. As Judy went into labor, a doctor phoned Dick, a National Guard career officer, with news of complications at the birth. At eight months old the baby was diagnosed with cerebral palsy. Dick remembers the pediatrician calling Rick a "vegetable." He had never heard that word applied to a person before. A stoic military man who has always held his feelings at bay, Dick says that driving home with Judy from the hospital that day was one of the few times in his life that he cried. Judy remembers the doctor telling them to put Rick into an institution and go on with their lives. "He said we were young and could have more children. We said, 'Damn it, we're going to parent this child.'"

Judy did not find much solace in her friends and neighbors. They believed Rick was retarded; Judy was certain he wasn't. As he got older she was able to teach him the alphabet, and she began to see in him the signal trait of a fully sentient human being: a sense of humor. When Judy said something funny, he would erupt into convulsive laughter. When the time came, Judy tried to put Rick in public school and was turned away. She responded with determination and a promise not only to get her son into a mainstream school, but also to devote her life to championing the handicapped. As Judy got more involved, Dick became more aloof. He stayed away from home as much as possible, working or playing in a local hockey league.

In 1970, when Rick was eight, the Hoyts found a way to communicate with him. Engineers from Tufts University built a computer and developed a software program that enabled Rick to type words through the use of a switch mounted near his head. If Rick, while viewing a pattern of letters, could tap his head against a narrow metal bar affixed to the right side of his wheelchair, the computer would register the chosen letter on the monitor. In this way Rick could put together complete sentences, although it might take several minutes to spell each word. The Hoyts began thinking of the computer as the "Hope Machine."

When he was a senior at Westfield High School, Rick composed an essay titled, "What It Is Like to Be a Nonvocal Person." "At first I felt cheated and angry," he wrote. "Even though my parents talked to and treated me the same as my brothers [Russell, now eighteen, and Robbie, twenty-two], I felt and knew I was different. I understand all the things said to me. Being a nonvocal person does not make one any less of a human being. I have the same feelings as anyone else. I feel sadness, joy, hunger, love, compassion and pain."

The young man still could not break through his father's reserve. In 1978 he heard that a nearby college was sponsoring a five-mile race to raise funds for a lacrosse player paralyzed in an auto accident. Rick told his father he wanted to enter and asked Dick if he'd push him. Dick said yes. The duo finished next to last. Total strangers were cheering for them. That night, after the race, Rick went straight to his computer and banged out, "Dad, when I'm out running I feel like I'm not even handicapped."

Dick, who was undemonstrative with Rick and his other two sons, was deeply moved. He began training. By

1980 the Hoyts were entering fifty to seventy-five races a year. That year they decided to run in the Boston Marathon. They managed to finish the race and in later years qualified to run. Since then the Hoyts have become a road-racing legend in New England.

Three years ago a Massachusetts-based sports promoter asked Dick to enter a triathlon. Dick said he'd participate only if he could do it with Rick. The promoter thought not. A year later the two men talked again and an agreement was struck. Fine. All Dick had to do was learn how to swim and bike competitively. "I got in the water one afternoon, and I couldn't swim a hundred feet," says Dick. "Well, I thought to myself, I started out running and I couldn't run. I can't swim, but I can learn. I had bought a home on a lake. Within two weeks I could swim pretty good." Their first triathlon was a one-mile swim, forty miles of bicycling and a ten-mile run.

These days Lieutenant Colonel Hoyt does what several years ago would have been unthinkable: He toilets Rick, feeds him and changes his clothes. Almost every night he cradles him in his beefy arms and carries him to his bedroom, laying him down gently on his waterbed.

After pushing themselves to their limits in last week's Ironman epic, nothing seemed beyond the reach of the Hoyts. They toasted one another in champagne at a private "victory" celebration, and Judy happily splashed some over Rick's freshly-styled Mohawk haircut. As they soaked in the hot tub, Dick turned to his son and said, "Congratulations, big man." Rick beamed with pleasure as his once-distant old man took one of his knotted hands and said, "You did real good out there, real good."

William Plummer

Two Dimes

A father is much more than a human being to his son.

Thomas William Simpson

During the 1966–67 football season, Green Bay quarterback Bart Starr had a little incentive scheme going with his oldest son. For every perfect paper that Bart Jr. brought home from school, his dad gave him ten cents. After one particularly rough game, in which Starr felt he had performed poorly, he returned home weary and battered late at night after a long plane ride. But he couldn't help feeling better when he went to his bedroom.

There, attached to his pillow, was a note: "Dear Dad, I thought you played a great game. Love, Bart." Taped to the note were two dimes.

The Christian Athlete

We Walked off the Field Together

It was a bright, hot Southern afternoon in June. Parents toting folding chairs and small coolers were beginning to gather along the foul line of the local Little League field. It was opening day!

My husband, Gil, and I were among the fans. It was our son Jason's first Little League game. Neither one of us admitted it to the other, but we were filled with anticipation—high hopes that our son would hit a homer or make the game-winning catch. Well, he walked once and struck out twice. As for fielding . . . in the bottom of the ninth, Jason stood in right field waiting for *his* moment. "CRACK." The ball was hit deep, *I mean deep,* into right field. I saw Jason look up and begin to position himself under the soaring projectile. I took a gasping breath and held it for what seemed like an eternity. As the ball dropped from the sky, I saw my son shift his cleated feet from side to side, readying himself.

Now, I know you think that I'm going to say he made the catch and won the game for his team, but no. The ball landed twenty feet behind him. The runners rounded the bases, and by the time Jason had reached the ball and made the throw, the game was over. They lost. The defeated outfielder walked off of the field with his head drooping. He approached us along the foul line with his arm outstretched to me. He was carrying something in his tiny hand. It was a daisy that he had plucked from underneath the outfield fence. We walked off the field together.

Two years later, on that same field, we once again sat in our folding chairs watching as Jason approached the plate. He stood confidently facing the pitcher. The first pitch flew past him—high and outside. The second pitch —a swing and a miss. I watched as he shifted his cleated feet from side to side, readying himself. The third pitch was high and inside, right into Jason's eye! Fighting tears, he picked himself up, took his base and finished the game. When it was over (I don't remember whether they won or lost) he approached us along the foul line with his arm outstretched to me. He was carrying something in his dusty hand. It was the ice pack that had been covering the most colorful black eye I had ever seen. We walked off the field together.

Through the rest of that season and the next one, Jason backed out of the batter's box with every pitch—terrified that the ball would once again make contact with his face. At every game, I perched myself behind the backstop fence as he neared the plate, coaxing him to take just one step closer. "Come on, you can do it! Just a little closer, stay in there."

His dad worked endlessly with him on his swing, his base running and his fielding. I even bought a mitt so that we could work on his skills after school. I would throw pop-ups and fast grounders to him in the cul-de-sac outside of our house.

Over the next several years Jason confronted his fears and fought his way back into the game. His love of baseball was so strong that he would not quit!

Just last year, I once again carried my folding chair to the ball field. It was a different field this time—we had moved to Vermont. Jason, a freshman in high school, was a starting varsity player. I watched as he made diving catches in right field and effortlessly sailed the ball in to the catcher to stop the run from coming in.

Without warning as my eyes filled with tears, I recalled the daisy picker in the Little League uniform and the ten-year-old with the shiner. I thought about the seasons of struggle that Jason had gone though to get to this point. I know that you're expecting me to say that my son became an All-American or a major-league player, but that chapter is yet to be written. I do know, however, that to one boy, the game of baseball has been a lot more than just a game. It has been a challenge, a test of physical as well as inner strength. It has served as a key to unlocking the door to acceptance and belonging in a new school. No matter how old Jason is, or where we live, the game of baseball has been a constant in all of our lives.

My daydreaming is interrupted by a distinct sound. "CRACK." I look up to see the outfielder charging for the back fence while fighting the glare of the sun to position himself under the soaring projectile, which drops twenty feet behind the fence. The crowd is cheering, and this time Jason is the runner trotting around the bases.

When the game was over, our team had won. A tall, confident and smiling young man approached along the foul line with his arm outstretched to me. As my son drew closer I noticed he was carrying something in his hand— a hand that now resembled his father's. It was the home-run ball. We walked off the field together.

Darlene Daniels Eisenhuth

My Favorite Baseball Card

Of all nature's gifts to the human race, what is sweeter to a man than his children?

Cicero

I had been an avid baseball-card collector as a youth, often collecting and selling drink bottles to pay for my packs. I remember sitting on the floor and arranging the cards for hours, putting the players in position on an imaginary field, stacking them in numerical order or by teams. As with many joys of youth, I set the hobby aside when it came time for college and jobs.

In 1990, I started reading about how the hobby was hot again, almost to the point of becoming a national fever. I was at a gas station in town when I noticed a box of base-ball cards by the cash register. I remembered how hard I had to work to buy my cards twenty years before. Now all I had to do was reach into my pocket and pull out some spare change. I bought a couple of packs and took them home.

The cards I bought, Topps, still included a piece of gum, unlike many of the newer brands. The smell of the gum, the cardboard, the ink and the wax paper brought the baseball memories of my youth rushing back as surely as did that first whiff of mown grass in the spring. I flipped through the cards, recognized a few of the players' names and then put them away.

The next time I was at the store, I bought a few more packs. I gave some of the cards to my eight-year-old son, who was also a baseball fan. We often played out in the yard, hitting a Nerf ball with an oversized plastic bat. Now we had an indoor "sport" that we could share as well.

I kept buying packs, and soon I was trying to put together a complete set of 792 cards. I gradually escalated to buying a box of cards at a time. My son and I would sit on the floor and separate the cards, going over the checklists to see which players we needed to finish the set. My son began his own collection with the doubles, the cards I already had.

Since the cards were randomly seeded within the packs, it was easy to get duplicates of certain players while others remained elusive. I must have had a half dozen Ozzie Smiths, and probably ten Steve Bedrosians. But I was unsuccessful in getting a Ken Griffey Jr. card. Griffey was far and away the most popular card among collectors that year.

I could have gone to the local card shop and bought one for the set by spending a couple of dollars, but I was determined to pull one out of a pack. Making my bad luck even worse was the fact that a replica of Griffey's card was on the box, advertising the Topps brand and the card design. It's almost as if that Griffey on the box was taunting me, daring me to buy another hundred packs.

The next time my son and I opened packs, I explained to him how badly I wanted a Ken Griffey Jr. His face set with determination, my son carefully opened pack after pack, almost apologetic when he failed to find one. Now my complete set was only lacking a few cards, Griffey being the most notable of them.

We opened the last of the packs I'd purchased that day, with no Griffey showing up. I sorted the cards, gave my son a stack of duplicates, and put the rest of my cards in a box. Then I forgot about them and became wrapped up in other pursuits.

Later that evening my son came up to me, his hand behind his back. "I have something for you, Daddy," he said.

He handed me a Griffey Jr. card. He'd taken a pair of scissors and cut one of the Griffey replicas off the box. "Now you don't have to look anymore," he said.

The hug I gave him was the best price I ever paid for a card.

I continued collecting and eventually ended up with some old and valuable cards. But there's one card I would never trade, not even for a Mickey Mantle rookie card. I still have that Ken Griffey Jr., the one with the uneven borders and the ragged corners, the one that has only plain gray pasteboard on the back instead of statistics.

That card, to me, is what baseball is all about. It's also what love is all about.

Scott Nicholson

Play Catch with Me, Dad

"Play catch with me, Dad?"
I hope you don't forget
about the small kid
with the baseball and the mitt.

I know that you are busy
with important things all day,
but it makes me feel so special
when you take some time to play.

Things like winning and losing
don't mean that much to me.
It's just being with you
that makes us family.

So, even if you are tired
from the day you've just had,
please don't forget
to play catch with me, Dad.

Tom Krause

I'll Get Another One

At his father's funeral, American Carl Lewis placed his one-hundred-meter gold medal from the 1984 Olympics in his father's hands. "Don't worry," he told his surprised mother. "I'll get another one."

A year later, in the one-hundred-meter final at the 1988 games, Lewis was competing against Canadian world-record-holder Ben Johnson. Halfway through the race, Johnson was five feet in front. Lewis was convinced he could catch him. But at eighty meters, he was still five feet behind. *It's over, Dad,* Lewis thought. As Johnson crossed the finish, he stared back at Lewis and thrust his right arm in the air, index finger extended.

Lewis was exasperated. He had noticed Johnson's bulging muscles and yellow-tinged eyes, both indications of steroid use. "I didn't have the medal, but I could still give to my father by acting with class and dignity," Lewis said later. He shook Johnson's hand and left the track.

But then came the announcement that Johnson had tested positive for anabolic steroids. He was stripped of his medal. The gold went to Lewis, a replacement for the medal he had given his father.

David Wallechinsky

Everything Counts

It's not necessarily the amount of time you spend at practice that counts; it's what you put into the practice.

Eric Lindros

In the scheme of life, YMCA football really doesn't matter much. Scores aren't reported in newspapers. Fans consist of mamas and daddies. And in my case, circa 1974, Saturday games were scheduled early in the mornings so the adults could get home in time to watch college football on TV.

But the fact that mamas and daddies did come to the games brings me to my one brief, shining moment of youth-football glory.

I played for the L. M. Smith Elementary School Cougars, and despite fine coaches and some talented players, we simply weren't very good. I played wide receiver on offense and safety on defense. I even served an inglorious, one-game stint at quarterback. But after finishing the battle with zero completions in a 14–0 loss, I was back to my accustomed spot at wideout when our winless Cougars faced the winless Warriors of Wright Elementary School.

When you're thirteen years old and have dreams of one day playing for Alabama or Auburn, then moving on to the NFL, then being elected to both the College Football and NFL halls of fame, then opening up a sports-theme restaurant, then becoming a TV analyst—winless seasons don't boost your confidence. But since we were winless and they were winless—and since I knew this was the game where I needed to make an impact—it was like playing in the Super Bowl.

My dad—Pop—showed up for every game, and every time I was on the field I would glance up into the rickety old bleachers and make sure he was there. Once I saw him, I knew that I was playing more than a game, I was doing what most all sons want to do—make Papa proud.

I was fortunate in that Pop was never the sort of youth-sports fan we've all come to loathe. He didn't second-guess the coach. He didn't scream at me when I dropped a pass. He didn't tell me what I did wrong when we lost—and believe me, we lost a lot.

What he did was smile and applaud, and he did it every single time I came off the field. Good play or bad, touchdown or turnover, Pop was always the understated cheerleader, clapping politely and remaining, for the most part, silent.

All that changed on a warm, fall night in Birmingham.

We kicked off to Wright, and after three straight rushing plays went for naught, the Warriors kicked it away.

The kid for Wright had a leg, and he sent a booming punt down to our twenty, where it took a hard chop and rolled out of bounds.

Our quarterback Keith and I were best friends, so invariably on first down he would throw the ball to me. Sometimes I caught it; sometimes I dropped it; sometimes

I turned to see Keith flat on his back while a couple of defensive linemen were on top of him.

But this time, the call was an end-around.

Since I was fast, I was placed at wide receiver. But because I was small, I never much had the chance to play running back. We had never run an end-around before, and the coach thought the call would catch the Warriors off guard.

He was right.

After Keith took the snap I backed off my spot on the right side of the line, and while Keith rolled to his right I went left, snatched the ball and took off for the sideline.

Ten players on the Wright defense bought the fake, and followed Keith in the other direction. But there was one cornerback who sniffed out the call, and as I ran laterally, he ran with me. Just before I reached the sideline I firmly planted my left foot and came to a sudden stop. The cornerback didn't expect this, and wound up tumbling out of bounds. That left nothing but blue skies and green grass in front of me, and I tucked the ball under my right arm and chugged untouched into the end zone.

I expected to hear a deafening roar of applause. Heck, I expected the cheerleaders to run onto the field and plant a big ol' kiss on my cheek.

But as I crossed the goal line and prepared to toss the ball to the official, I glanced backward at those who I left in my wake. While I saw them standing off in the distance, I also saw a yellow flag littering the ground.

There was no touchdown because we had been called for clipping, which explained why there was no deafening roar from the crowd.

I was crestfallen. I had scored a couple of two-point conversions during the season, but this would've been my first six-pointer. Instead of an eighty-yard scamper for six, I had to journey eighty yards back to my teammates, who had just watched me score a phantom touchdown.

As I began to trot toward a first-and-twenty-five dilemma I heard a faint noise from the bleachers. As I got closer, I could tell it was the rhythmic clap of one man.

That one man was Pop.

While the rest of the crowd either screamed at the officials or sat silently, my dad—my hero—was giving his son a one-man standing ovation.

I'll never forget that moment. Here was a kid who had a lot of desire but not a lot of ability, and his big moment had been ruined by a piece of yellow laundry. Yet, as disappointing as the play turned out to be, Pop made it one I'll never forget.

Six years ago, when Pop was near death from cancer, he and I talked about some of the great moments we spent together. I asked if he remembered the touchdown that never was, and he did.

"Pop, why were you clapping?" I asked. "It didn't count." He smiled and grabbed my hand.

"Everything counts," he said. "I knew how much that touchdown meant to you. Since it meant so much to you, it meant even more to me. And it was the prettiest run I've ever seen."

Scott Adamson

8

WISDOM OF THE GAME

The most important thing in the Olympic Games is not winning but taking part. . . . The essential thing in life is not conquering but fighting well.

Baron Pierre de Coubertin,
founder of the modern Olympic Games

The Wizard of Westwood

You cannot dream yourself into a character;
you must hammer and forge yourself one.

James A. Froude

As a student, I was there to see two of John Wooden's great years with UCLA basketball. I watched and cheered as the dynasty took off and soared for more than a decade in the '60s and '70s. Gail Goodrich, Lew Alcindor and Bill Walton called him "Coach." The sports media affectionately called him the "Wizard of Westwood" and honored him as "the architect of the greatest college-basketball program in the history of the game." His UCLA teams hold records few expect ever to be broken. Wooden led the Bruins to ten national titles in a twelve-year span. He won a record seven straight NCAA championships from 1966–73. From 1971–73, his teams won a record eighty-eight games in a row. Coach Wooden remains the only college coach to steer his teams through four undefeated seasons.

The man is an authentic legend. I daresay every college-basketball fan in America over fifteen years of age knows of Wooden's amazing success and lasting impact on the game.

Few of these same fans know anything about the private side of the man or of the loving woman who was his support through fifty-two years of marriage. Those who watched this humble man coach did know he was a man of values and a man of consistency. Before the start of every game, Wooden would roll up his program and turn his gaze toward the stands for an approving smile and a wave from his wife, Nell, who always sat in the same seat. There was love in their eyes that, even as a student, was comforting to see. For those who knew him, there was something more important to the Wizard of Westwood than winning basketball games, and her name was Nell Wooden.

Years later, I conducted a series of programs at St. Vincent's Hospital in Los Angeles. While discussing the importance of values in leadership, I mentioned some insights about Coach Wooden's Pyramid of Success, which was the cornerstone of his coaching philosophy at UCLA. Two nurse supervisors who were attending the program approached me during the break. They confided they knew little about UCLA basketball, but they did know a lot about John Wooden, the man.

Nell Wooden had been in an extended coma as a result of a heart attack she suffered following a hip-replacement operation in 1982. The nurses had seen him day after day as he came to Nell's bedside. He would spend ten-hour days just holding her hand. Other times he would be in prayer next to her bed. The doctors had told him to talk to her because her subconscious might be able to hear him. After three months in a coma, he squeezed her hand and felt a squeeze back. Nell was back!

In a few short months, she was again at death's door after having her gall bladder removed. Yet against the odds, Nell recovered enough to enjoy a few more months of life with family and friends.

Through it all, Coach Wooden was by her side just as

she had always been at his. His attitude, his courtesy, his faith and his enduring love for his wife showed to the end. On the first day of spring, March 21, 1985, his sweetheart of sixty years, Nell Wooden, passed away. The girl that had been with him most of his life would no longer be at his side.

Hearing about John Wooden's strength of character and gracious love didn't surprise me. It was but another testimony to the integrity of the man who always led by example. After all, as he used to say, "It's what you learn after you know it all that counts."

In 1998, I saw Coach Wooden at a UCLA basketball game. I went over to where he was seated and told him what the nurses at St. Vincent's had said. His eyes welled with tears, and he said, "That's the kindest compliment I've ever been given."

National championship trophies can lose their luster, but legacies of love have a way of enduring as memories that call us to do the same for those we love.

Terry Paulson, Ph.D.

There Should Be No Grimness

While reflecting on my life as I was writing *The Best That I Can Be*, one thing struck me hard, a simple lesson that goes to the heart of sportsmanship.

In the fall of 1954, America was bursting with hope and optimism. The full bloom of postwar prosperity was upon us. Jobs were plentiful. Automobiles were affordable, and a gallon of gas cost twenty-nine cents. Color television has just been introduced. The year before, the Korean War had been put to rest. Senator Joseph McCarthy was about to be condemned by the Senate, ending years of paranoia. In the famous *Brown vs. Board of Education* decision, the Supreme Court had just overturned the doctrine of "separate but equal" and ordered the states to integrate their educational facilities "with all deliberate speed." It was a time when people thought big thoughts and dreamed big dreams.

That fall I was thinking about the new life I was about to begin as a college student and dreaming about making the Olympic team in Melbourne, Australia, two years down the road.

As a star athlete and an A student in high school I had been recruited by colleges across the country—actually, more for football than for track. Early on I had decided that I would remain close to my family and friends in California. I narrowed the choice to three schools: the University of California at Berkeley, the University of Southern California and UCLA.

I was drawn to Cal Berkeley because of its academic reputation and the fact that its track coach and athletic director was Brutus Hamilton, a fine man who won the silver medal in the decathlon at the 1920 Olympics in Amsterdam and had coached the U.S. track team at the 1952 games.

Of the two Los Angeles schools, USC had more going for it athletically. Its track program was one of the best in the country and its football team was a perennial power-house. During my visit to the campus, the coaches painted a glorious picture of the Trojan tradition. It sounded great to me. Then I journeyed cross-town to Westwood and changed my mind.

The football coach, Red Sanders, wanted me badly, and he had a distinct advantage: he ran a single-wing offense, just like the one I had learned in high school.

UCLA also offered me the choice of an academic or an athletic scholarship. The academic one afforded more prestige and money, and would not bind me to any par-ticular sport. I wanted the option not to play football if I thought it might jeopardize my Olympic chances.

Importantly, UCLA had a proud and long-standing commitment to racial equality. Two of my all-time heroes, Ralph Bunche and Jackie Robinson, were alumni. In addi-tion to his greatness as a baseball player and a man, Jackie was—and remains—the only UCLA athlete to ever have earned letters in baseball, football, basketball and track. Mr. Bunche, who played basketball at UCLA, had been awarded the Nobel Peace Prize in 1950 for his diplomatic efforts on behalf of the United Nations Palestine

Commission. The clincher on the racial issue came when I walked into the student union and saw pictures of past student-body presidents. One of the faces was black.

Then I met Elvin "Ducky" Drake, the UCLA track coach. As we set out for a walk across the campus, I was still undecided. By the time I shook his hand to say good-bye, I knew I would be returning as a student.

Universally respected and admired, Ducky had been improving the Bruins' status in track since taking over as head coach eight years earlier. Under his tutelage, every school record had been either broken or tied. But the team had still never won a conference championship or an NCAA title, or beaten arch rival USC in a dual meet. Ducky wanted badly to accomplish those goals.

In the end, what really did the trick was when Ducky said the magic words: "You can make the next Olympic team." Implicit in that statement was a willingness to help me get there.

And so, that August, I sent letters to USC and Berkeley, thanking them for their courtesy and telling them I had chosen UCLA. I was not prepared for the wonderful response I received from Brutus Hamilton:

> *Dear Rafer:*
>
> *It gave me a kind of clean and noble feeling to get your kind and gracious letter of August 20. Only a fine sportsman and gentleman in the finest sense of that word could have written such a letter. I must admit that your letter also made me a little sad, because I know you are going to achieve great things in all phases of your university life and it is a source of regret to me that I shall play no part in directing you toward those successes. But I am glad that you have chosen a great university to attend, and I am pleased you are happy in your decision. . . .*

I know you will find Ducky Drake one of the grandest men you will ever meet in your journey through life. He not only knows his business, but he is a man of impeccable character and good influence. He takes an interest in his boys above and beyond their ability in sports, and I count it a great asset to the coaching profession that such a man is in it. If you have problems— and what university student does not?—I would advise you to go to Ducky and get his advice. He will not steer you wrong. . . .

I close this letter with a confession. I was never a good hater, and I never coached my boys to hate an opponent. Amateur sports should be friendly but spirited, and there should be no grimness characterizing the competitions. I shall try to get my boys to honor you with their very best performances against you, and I hope that you will honor us with your very best efforts. After the contests, we will walk down to the corner drugstore and have a malt and talk over the day's activities. . . . I hope I never become so embroiled in a winning complex that I can't appreciate fine performances and the splendid characters of the boys wearing the other-colored jerseys. I sincerely hope and believe that you and I will be such friends for many years to come.

I have kept that letter all these years because it epitomizes what an educator and sportsman should be. Brutus and I never got to stroll to a drugstore after a meet, but we spoke often and remained good friends until he passed away in the early 1960s.

Rafer Johnson

The All-Leather, NFL Regulation, 1963 Chicago Bears–Inscribed Football

The year was 1964. The place was Chicago. A man I worked with had acquired a couple of all-leather, NFL regulation, 1963 Chicago Bears–inscribed footballs and was selling them at a real good price. My first son was on the way. I bought the football. I had my son's "coming home from the hospital" gift, and it was something truly special.

Several years later, young Tom was rummaging around in the garage as only a five- or six-year-old can rummage when he came across the all-leather, NFL regulation, 1963 Chicago Bears–inscribed football. He asked if he could play with it. With as much logic as I felt he could understand, I explained to him that he was still a bit too young to play carefully with such a special ball. We had the same conversation several more times in the next few months, and soon the requests faded away.

The next fall, after watching a football game on television, Tom asked, "Dad, remember that football you have in the garage? Can I use it to play with the guys now?"

Eyes rolling up in my head, I replied, "Tom, you don't understand. You don't just go out and casually throw around an all-leather, NFL regulation, 1963 Chicago Bears–inscribed football. I told you before; it's special."

Eventually Tom stopped asking altogether. But he did remember, and a few years later he told his younger brother, Dave, about the all-leather, NFL regulation, 1963 Chicago Bears–inscribed football that was special and kept somewhere in the garage. Dave came to me one day and asked if he could take that special football and throw it around for awhile. It seemed like I'd been through this before, but I patiently explained, once again, that you don't just go out and throw around an all-leather, NFL regulation, 1963 Chicago Bears–inscribed football. Soon Dave, too, stopped asking.

A couple of months ago I was in the garage looking for some WD-40 when I noticed a large box that had "coveralls" written across it. I couldn't remember bringing along any coveralls when we moved from Chicago to Albuquerque, so I opened the box. And there, long forgotten, was the all-leather, NFL regulation, 1963 Chicago Bears–inscribed football.

But it wasn't special anymore.

I stood alone in the garage. The boys had long since moved away from home, and suddenly I realized that the football had never been so special at all. Children playing with it when it was their time to play is what would have made it special. I had blown those precious, present moments that can never be reclaimed, and I had saved a football. For what?

I took the football across the street and gave it to a family with young kids. A couple of hours later I looked out the window. They were throwing, catching, kicking and letting skid across the cement my all-leather, NFL regulation, 1963 Chicago Bears–inscribed football.

Now it was special!

Tom Payne

A Parent Talks to a Child
Before the First Game

This is your first game, my child. I hope you win.
I hope you win for your sake, not mine.
Because winning's nice.
It's a good feeling.
Like the whole world is yours.
But it passes, this feeling.
And what lasts is what you've learned.

And what you learn about is life.
That's what sports is all about. Life.
The whole thing is played out in an afternoon.
The happiness of life.
The miseries.
The joys.
The heartbreaks.

There's no telling what'll turn up.
There's no telling whether they'll toss you out in the first
   five minutes or whether you'll stay for the long haul.

There's no telling how you'll do.
You might be a hero or you might be absolutely nothing.
There's just no telling.
Too much depends on chance.
On how the ball bounces.

I'm not talking about the game, my child.
I'm talking about life.
But it's life that the game is all about.
Just as I said.

Because every game is life.
And life is a game.
A serious game
Dead serious.

But, that's what you do with serious things.
You do your best.
You take what comes.
You take what comes
And you run with it.

Winning is fun.
Sure.
But winning is not the point.

Wanting to win is the point.
Not giving up is the point.
Never being satisfied with what you've done is the point.
Never letting up is the point.
Never letting anyone down is the point.

Play to win.
Sure.
But lose like a champion.
Because it's not winning that counts.
What counts is trying.

Steve Jamison

Strike Out or Home Run?

It ain't over till it's over.

Yogi Berra

Everyone said the Yankees would lose this game. It was the fourth game of the 1996 World Series. Now the score was 6–0 with Atlanta winning. I lay in bed half awake.

Forget it, I thought, as I turned off the radio and fell asleep. But when I awoke, I immediately turned on the radio. It was the eighth inning now, the score 6–3, the Yankees making a comeback. *But what chance do they really have?* the realist in me asked.

What chance do I have? I thought as I lay there in the dark. When you have had cancer, you're always fighting the statistics, always hoping for complete recovery. When you're a widow, you're always fighting loneliness. I felt like the Yankees in the fourth game of the World Series. That night, I didn't think I had a chance, either.

And then the Yankees hit the home run with two men on base. I jumped out of bed. I ran into the kitchen and gulped a sandwich and had a drink. The dog thought it was time to go out and play. I let him into the backyard.

The cats thought it was morning. I fed them. All the lights blinked on in the house. I was fully awake. I was shouting. I was talking aloud, as if there were others in the room. "Come on, Yankees," I yelled.

And then they did it in the tenth inning. They put the game away. I was laughing, running around the house and jumping on the sofa, telling the dog and the cats, "They did it! They really did it!" Though I had not been a baseball fan before, I vowed I would be a Yankees fan forever, because now I understood about baseball.

My husband had been a passionate baseball fan. He would sit there, sometimes by the radio, sometimes by the television. He would talk to the radio, talk to his favorite team. If they were doing well, he smiled. If they were doing poorly, he cursed the set, cursed the players, threw the newspaper on the floor. He never went through the game alone. There were always friends to call, back and forth a dozen times, through all the innings. If it was a victory, they rejoiced together. If it was a defeat, they mourned. And, of course, they went to games with hoagies and sodas packed away, enough food for a week; fathers took sons and daughters, and mothers wondered what this excitement was all about.

I was envious of my husband's baseball passion when springtime came. There was nothing outside my home and family that possessed me so fully. My husband knew baseball better than he knew me. His mother told me he had loved baseball as a boy, and that love had continued into manhood.

I never understood about my husband and baseball, about his baseball cards, about his dream to attend just one spring-training camp in Florida, about the pride on his face when he wore his team's baseball cap.

"You're not watching baseball again," I would say to him.

I never understood about baseball until the Yankees won the fourth game of the 1996 World Series. The odds were against them. Nobody thought they had a chance, certainly not to come back from a 6–0 deficit.

There were times when the bases were loaded against them, and their pitcher threw the ball anyway. There were times when the batter was up at bat and it looked bleak, but it was his turn and that's all there was to it. There were times when the score turned sour, and there didn't seem to be a reason to even try, but try they did.

Many times I feel the bases are loaded in my life. The odds pile up against me. I just don't want to pitch that ball. It seems futile. But every day, I get the opportunity to pitch the ball again. The bat's in my hand, and it's my turn up at a new day. I can hit the home run if I believe it, and sometimes I do and sometimes I don't.

Those Yankees didn't care about the people who didn't believe in them, and I'm sure they didn't care about the statistics. They believed in themselves, in the game and in the unpredictability of life.

I thought about it that night, why I felt so good, so energized, why I was celebrating, why that good feeling remained with me. Now I understood why my husband loved baseball.

Life is just one big baseball game. That was the secret he knew. You never can tell what the outcome is going to be until the very last inning.

Perhaps tomorrow will be the day I hit my own home run.

Harriet May Savitz
Originally appeared in Chicken Soup
for the Golden Soul

A Letter to a Coach

Goodness is easier to recognize than to define.

W. H. Auden

Dear Coach,

Thanks for the special gifts that you have given to my child. You learned his name and spoke it often. You taught him the basics of the sport as well as special ways to improve and excel. Although you had a whole team of kids to mentor, you took time for individual instruction where needed.

Under your care I have watched him transform from a timid, doubting child to a strong, happy player willing to give all for the team. Throughout the season when he gave his best, even though it was not quite good enough to gain that extra point, you recognized his contribution with a pat on the back and encouraging words.

Your wise approach showed him that, although winning is a goal, there are other goals just as worthy. He learned the value of finishing what he started and the joy of personal accomplishment. These attributes carried him through a season that was full of hard work and fun, discouragement and resolve, defeat and victory.

And, at the very end, at that championship meet when he brought home the first-place medal, you were among those who were so very proud of how far he had come. It was a victory for all of us. What amazes me is you've done this year in and year out for so many kids. You've taught them skills that will last a lifetime. You've kindled in them a desire to excel. It may be that none of us can even comprehend the full extent of your contributions to these young individuals and the world they are shaping for themselves. But decades from now, I know my family will look back on these amazing, growing wonder years. We'll look at the ribbons, the trophies and the medals, and we'll see them as mere symbols of the real gifts. These most certainly have had to come straight from your heart.

With appreciation,
A parent

Anita Gogno

[AUTHOR'S NOTE: *Gabi Johnston, the coach who inspired this letter, died January 6, 2000, after a seven-year battle against cancer.*]

The Inspiration of the Football Huddle

*Here's my Golden Rule for a tarnished age: be
fair with others, but then keep after them until
they're fair with you.*

Alan Alda

I saw my first professional football game at age twelve,
when the Los Angeles Rams were playing in the Coliseum.
This experience fueled my dream of one day playing pro
football. I wanted to be like my heroes—quarterbacks Bob
Waterfield and Norm Van Brocklin and halfback Kenny
Washington, who became one of the first African
Americans to play in the NFL.

Playing sports taught me early that nothing great happens without discipline, perspiration and inspiration. My
inspiration came one day when, as a freshman at
Occidental College, Coach Payton Jordan called me into
his office. "Jack," he said, "I watched you play at Fairfax
(High School, Los Angeles) and now here at Occidental.
You've got great potential. You should know, confiden-
tially, that if you work hard, *real hard*, you can reach the
NFL someday." I walked out of his office on cloud nine,

promising myself I would work harder than ever. I wasn't going to let down Coach Jordan, or myself.

Years later, I learned that Coach Jordan had the same "confidential" talk with most of his players, but it didn't matter. He had inspired not only me; he inspired the whole team. We were *all* for playing under Coach Jordan, and because of that extra measure my dream came true: I was drafted out of Occidental by the Detroit Lions. I was a seventeenth-round pick, but it didn't matter. I had my chance to prove myself in pro football.

For me, I saw it as a case of putting in the effort and achieving my boyhood dream. I saw clearly, though, that it wasn't an even playing field. The American dream of equal opportunity didn't exist for everyone. My African-American teammates dealt with the ignorant, hateful attitudes of many people, which meant they were treated unfairly. This prejudice was at odds with what was good for our nation and our declaration of equity and freedom of opportunity.

In 1961, when I was quarterback and captain of the San Diego Chargers, we were scheduled to play the Oilers in Houston for the AFL Championship. Traditionally, the night before the game, Coach Sid Gilman took the entire team to a movie. Shortly after we sat down in our seats, I noticed that Paul Lowe, Ernie Wright, Ernie Ladd and Charlie McNeil were missing. I asked around and discovered they had been sent to the "blacks-only" balcony. When I told Coach Gilman, he stood immediately and said, "Gather the team. Get all the guys. We're out of here." In a silent, powerful demonstration of our belief in equality, living and working as a team, we walked out as a team. I was very proud of Coach Gilman, but so much more needed to be done.

Four years later, after I had joined the Buffalo Bills and been elected captain, we were at the 1965 AFL All-Star

Game in New Orleans. Our black teammates had trouble getting a taxi or even basic service at restaurants. Here again, the wisdom of team unity, and, admittedly, the popularity of pro football, gave us the leverage needed to combat discrimination. We discussed the situation at our team meeting and agreed to boycott the game as a statement against the racial climate in the city. As a result, the game was moved to Houston, which by that time had made progress toward more equal treatment in public accommodations. This was the first boycott of a city by any professional sporting event in history.

We didn't tolerate bigotry on the field, either. Any difference in race, creed and class immediately dissolved in the common aim of a team win. Divisiveness only weakens a team. It has no place in a huddle, on or off the field.

Every team requires unity. A team has to move as one unit, one force, with each person understanding and assisting the roles of his teammates. If the team doesn't do this, whatever the reason, it goes down in defeat. You win or lose as a team, as a family. A successful team walks onto the field with issues of race, religion and all societal pressures ratcheted down to inconsequential by the strength of common goals.

That became the case in 1947 when Branch Rickey, owner of the Brooklyn Dodgers, informed his team that he was bringing Jackie Robinson up from the minors—the first black man to play in the majors. Rickey wanted Robinson's talent at the plate and his speed on the base paths. Some players circulated a petition stating they would not take the field with a black man. Pee Wee Reese, the Dodgers shortstop and team captain, refused to sign and tore up the petition, effectively putting an end to a stupid and ignorant idea that was wrong, as well as bad for the team.

Reese showed his character many times that season. At

one point, he'd had enough of the fans heckling, spitting and throwing things at Robinson. During a game in Cincinnati, Pee Wee walked over to Jackie, put his arm around him and there they stood. They stared down the crowd until the stadium was near silent. Then the game resumed. Robinson may have been the first black man to play major-league baseball, but more important to Pee Wee was, "He's a Dodger, our teammate."

The power of one man or one woman doing the right thing for the right reason, and at the right time, is the greatest influence in our society. Individually, we may not be captains of our teams, but we are *always* captains of our own souls and collectively the soul of America. The soul of America rests in our hands, as we seek reconciliation and racial healing in America at the dawn of this exciting new century.

Jack Kemp

The Cure for Disappointment

In 1992, Jeff Sluman played in the AT&T Pebble Beach National Pro-Am. My seventeen-year-old son Derek and I were excited. In a conversation with Jeff the week before his arrival, we'd made arrangements to get together. In fact, Jeff had promised Derek he would spend some time with him and help him with his golf game.

The week of the tournament arrived, and, as things happen, circumstances multiplied and time didn't. Plans for Derek and Jeff to get together kept disappearing. On Friday, Jeff called Derek. "I'll tell you what," he said. "After the round on Sunday, we'll get together and I'll help you with your game." We left it at that.

On Sunday, the final round of the tournament, Jeff made an awesome twenty-two-foot birdie putt on the eighteenth, which tied him with Mark O'Meara for the lead. They went into sudden death, starting at the sixteenth.

Derek, my friend Bobby Rahal, and I were in Bobby's hotel room at The Lodge watching the drama unfold on television. We were sitting only a few hundred yards from the finishing green, but via television we were equally close to every hole, even the sixteenth, as Jeff and Mark went off to the start of sudden death.

Jeff and Mark both reached the fringe of the sixteenth green in two. Mark chipped his ball in for a birdie. Jeff's forty-foot putt died short. Mark won the AT&T on the first playoff hole.

Derek, Bobby and I groaned in sympathy for our friend Jeff. He hadn't won a tournament since he'd won the PGA some ten years before.

Bobby, winner of the Indy 500 in 1986, three times the CART PPG World Champion, knows the feeling of running out of gas one lap short of victory. No competitor ever greets loss as anything but the enemy.

"Derek," Bobby said, "it's been a tough day for Jeff. I don't think you guys are gonna be able to get together."

The three of us headed over to Cypress Point to play a few holes. We were putting out on fifteen when, down the path to the green, Jeff appears. "Hi, guys," he called. "I knew I'd find you here." I was amazed at his apparent ease, at the smile in his voice.

"Come on, Derek," he said, "grab your clubs. We're gonna play sixteen, seventeen and eighteen. I want to see your golf swing."

Bobby and I walked along with them. I proudly packed my son's bag as he took a lesson from Jeff Sluman! They played three holes, with Jeff assessing and critiquing every shot, every minor improvement in Derek's setup and swing mechanics.

Jeff had just finished nineteen holes of professional tournament play, had lost the AT&T by one shot in sudden death, and he was willing to spend time to help a young kid with his game. I remarked to Jeff later that everyone would have understood if he had passed on the golf lesson. "Ah, nah," he said. "Nothing's better for getting rid of disappointment than helping someone who loves the same thing you do."

Clay Larson

The $50,000 Baseball Cards

I stepped into All-Pro Sports Cards carrying a sack so heavy that I leaned as I walked. I felt like one of those old prospectors who staggers into a Western saloon to show the boys the nuggets he's found in the hills.

I laid my sack on the counter at the strip-mall shop and explained, "A long time ago, I took these to a friend who's a collector. He said they were worth $200. I found them again today. Are they worth anything?"

The next few minutes are still a blur. Within seconds, a crowd had gathered. Phone calls were made. Grown men began surrounding me, looking over my shoulder, handling my cards. They talked amazing nonsense. "Look, mint Mantles. God, there must be a dozen Mickeys. Mays, Koufax, Maris. He's got hundreds of stars," said one. The store owners, without consulting me, began inserting my cards into screw-down Lucite cases or individual plastic holders. They put each card into its protective sheath with the exaggerated care one might expect of a surgeon.

"Daddy, I need to go potty," said a voice.

"Not now, Russell," I said to my four-year-old son.

"Daddy, I really need to go."

We went potty in the back as unknown hands scooped up my cards (or Russ's freshman year tuition, whichever way you chose to think of them). When I got back, Vince Chick, the store's co-owner, was muttering to himself.

"What did you say?" I asked.

"Must be fifty here," he repeated.

"Fifty what?"

"Fifty thousand dollars."

I got a very cold feeling all over my body as the local experts began an impromptu pool, with $42,000 the lowest guess.

It all started when I was just trying to help a friend. He wanted to buy a box of cards for his friend's infant son—a gift that would combine fun for the kid someday with a little yuppie investment potential. After we found a card store, I asked casually, "What are old '50s cards worth now?"

"A beat-up Mantle—at least $180."

I went directly to my truck and drove in a straight line to my childhood home on Capitol Hill. "Hi, Dad," I said, and headed up to my old bedroom. My cards were in a brown paper bag in the bedroom closet, right where I had left them years before. Sports cards were the first material possession that I bought with my own earned money and then took care of with an adult level of concern.

I made a second trip back home after the $50,000 appraisal. My father is lucky that, before I left on that hot evening, I did not tear down his brick walls because, in our old row house, there were baseball cards everywhere. On the second manic visit, I found Mantle as a bookmark in a detective novel. I found Fleer cards of Hank Greenberg and Charlie Gehringer in the attic under a pile of tiny rubber toy soldiers. Hank Aaron, batting lefty due to a reversed photo negative, was under a stack of Nats bleacher stubs. The card had been carried in my wallet for so many years (imagine, a left-handed Aaron!) that Hank's face was worn away as well as all of his $240 "book" value.

To my horror, Willie Mays's four rounded corners had been clipped with scissors in 1957 for a neater look—at a 1991 cost of about fifty dollars a snip.

One '57 Roy Sievers was entirely encased in Scotch tape, presumably so that, had I been hit by a truck at age nine, I could have been buried with it.

By the time I finished my attic-to-cellar excavations, I was so filthy I looked as if I'd climbed out of a mine shaft. But the sense of relief—that there couldn't possibly be much more to find—was enormous. I could move on. I could make myself and my family miserable as I turned into the "Card Miser from Hell." For weeks I spent every spare minute studying the world of card commerce.

My son looked perplexed, as though to ask, *Who's the child?* My wife was mad. Inevitably, the estimated value of my cards went down, and my disappointment was much worse than it should have been. Within thirty-six hours (spent largely in the company of Vince Chick, a pocket calculator and the Beckett price-and-condition guide), I realized the $50,000 guess was gold-fever fantasy. No matter how I fiddled and gave myself the benefit of the doubt, the truth looked more like $25,000. And that's retail. Most card dealers will only give you about fifty cents on the dollar for the "common" cards and perhaps 67 percent for Hall of Famers.

In a blink, I had gone from $50,000 to $15,000. John McCarthy, All-Pro's other owner, advised me, "Sell 'em quick. Everybody who finds their old cards is just like you. It drives 'em crazy to sell to a dealer for half what they're worth. So they go to card shows, trying to sell to collectors for a decent price. Damned if they don't end up hooked on collecting themselves." The sign on All-Pro's door should be, "Abandon Hope, All Ye Who Enter Here."

My own house of cards began collapsing at the House of Cards. Everyone told me to go there. Everyone said Bill Huggins, the owner and a relative of the old Yankee manager Miller Huggins, was smart and fair about antique cards. He'd tell me what I was holding and maybe buy them, too.

"Sorry to hurt your feelings," said Huggins, watching my face fall. "These are nice cards. But they're not that nice. You played with them. Everything is, basically, a level lower than you thought. The '56s and '57s are good. The '58s very good. The '59s excellent and the '60s excellent-mint. Only the '61s and '62s are near mint—or 100 percent of book value."

How much difference could that make?

"They're worth about $15,000 retail," he said. "I'll give you $10,000."

I must've looked like my dog died. Maybe it was because, the day before, my wife had informed me that solving our most recent home disaster (a defunct heating-and-cooling system) would require $7,000. My low point came when I sat down with a respected dealer who found barely visible flaws in all but three of my three thousand cards. "Keep these," he said.

"They're 'blazers'"—meaning totally perfect and beyond criticism. Despite the differing opinions on their value, what really started to heal me was that, card by card, I found myself regaining misplaced parts of my childhood—parts I needed more than I knew.

I remembered how I used to be at Kendall's Market, a hundred yards from our house, as soon as it opened at 7 A.M., for my morning pack. In the afternoon, I'd walk across the park to another store for my evening pack. On weekends, I'd trek ten blocks to Tommy T.'s.

What patience my parents must have had. My mother actually kept track of which cards I wanted badly or needed to finish a series and would ask if I had gotten them yet. In a family where waste was abhorred and Depression tales were periodically invoked, I never heard the words, "That's enough baseball cards."

The first summer I went away to camp, my parents faithfully bought cards for me while I was gone. That's why, to this day, there is no six-week gap in the middle of my '60s set.

Finding the cards—and the old cigar box I'd kept them in, which turned up inside my camp trunk—helped me open some doors into the past. I'd never understood the degree to which my memories of growing up had been diminished in sweetness, in intensity, by all those necessary adult understandings and demythologizings. I hadn't realized that very little from my youth still felt as innocently rich as it had back then.

Until the cards.

Through them, I reconnected with some of my unalloyed pleasure as a kid—as well as the sincerity of my parents' flawed love. Just being around the cards, "playing" with them, made me feel secure, cared for and appreciated.

A touchstone like that is hard to find. And difficult, perhaps even stupid, to give up. Maybe that's why, one autumn day with the World Series approaching, I realized that I was glad my cards were not worth $50,000. If they were, I'd have to sell them.

Still, I couldn't decide whether to hold 'em for sentiment or fold 'em for a heating system that works. Then one day I was watching my son merrily abuse his cards, just like I'd taught him, as he prepared to trounce me again at flip.

"Show me some of your good players," he said. "Show me Willie Mays."

I did. "Daddy, are you going to sell all your baseball cards?" he asked.

"No," I decided. "I'm going to save all the good ones for you."

Thomas Boswell

Can I Have Your Autograph?

Tom Lasorda, manager of the Los Angeles Dodgers, grew up in Norristown, Pennsylvania, and became a serious baseball fan at an early age. When he was twelve or thirteen, he volunteered for duty as a crossing guard at his parochial school because he knew that the reward for this service was a free trip to a big-league ball game—an event he had yet to witness. The great day came at last, the sun shone and the party of nuns and junior fuzz repaired to Shibe Park, where the Phillies were playing the Giants. Young Tom Lasorda had a wonderful afternoon, and just before the game ended he and some of his colleagues forehandedly stationed themselves beside a runway under the stands. The game ended, the Giants came clattering by and Tom extended his scorecard to the first hulking, bespiked hero to come in out of the sunshine.

"Can I have your autograph, please, mister?" he asked.

"Outta my way, kid," the Giant said, brushing past the boy.

When Tom Lasorda tells the story now, the shock of this moment is still visible on his face. "I couldn't *believe* it," he says. "Here was the first big-league player I'd ever seen up close—the first one I ever dared speak to—and what he did was shove me up against the wall. I think tears came to my eyes. I watched the guy as he went away toward the clubhouse and I noticed the number on his back—you know, like taking the license of a hit-and-run car. Later on, I looked at my program and got his name. I never forgot it."

Seven or eight years went swiftly by, during which time Tom Lasorda grew up to become a promising young pitcher in the Dodger organization. In the spring of 1949, he was a star with the Dodger farm team in Greenville, South Carolina, and took the mound for the opening game of the season at Augusta, Georgia, facing the Augusta Yankees. Tom retired the first two batters, and then studied the third, a beefy right-handed veteran, as he stepped up to the box.

Lasorda was transfixed. "I looked," he says, "and it *was the same man!*"

The first pitch to the unsuspecting batter nearly removed the button from the top of his cap. The second behind his knees inspired a beautiful, sudden entrechat. The third, under his Adam's apple, confirmed the message, and he threw away his bat and charged the mound like a fighting bull entering the plaza in Seville. The squads spilled out onto the field and separated the two men, and only after a lengthy and disorderly interval was baseball resumed.

After the game, Lasorda was dressing in the visitors' locker room when he was told that he had a caller at the door. It was the former Giant, who now wore a peaceable but puzzled expression. "Listen, kid," he said to Lasorda, "did I ever meet you before?"

"Not exactly," Tom said.

"Well, why were you trying to take my head off out there?"

Lasorda spread his hands wide. "You didn't give me your autograph," he said.

Tom Lasorda would tell this story every spring to the new young players who make the Dodger club. "*Always* give an autograph when somebody asks you," he says gravely. "You never can tell. In baseball, anything can happen."

Roger Angell

Sensing a confrontation, the umpire steps into the relative safety of the new "Lasorda-proof booth."

50 Ways to Get the Most Out of Sports

1. Remember it's just a game.
2. Play full-out.
3. Put honor and sportsmanship above winning.
4. Suspend cynicism and experience the game like a kid again.
5. Remember to be amazed.
6. Appreciate excellence.
7. Introduce a child to your favorite sport.
8. Help a kid start a trading card collection.
9. Give your most cherished sports memento to a kid who will appreciate it.
10. Celebrate the heroic, but also appreciate the bit players and their contributions.
11. Do a silent play-by-play of your most memorable sports moment.
12. Spend an entire game or event just watching the crowd.
13. Clap for things that no one else does.
14. Make more noise than you ever have.
15. Take pride in occasionally looking foolish.
16. Respect other fans' experiences by keeping your own under control.

17. Cheer for the underdog.
18. Cheer for the overdog.
19. Become a Special Olympics volunteer.
20. Play catch with a kid.
21. Don't be an overbearing sports parent.
22. Be the most encouraging and supportive parent in your community.
23. Be there after a tough loss.
24. Play sports for as long as you can.
25. Make up the difference by being an avid fan.
26. Read the sports section first.
27. Write your local TV station and ask them to put sports first on the eleven o'clock news.
28. Call in to sports talk shows and say something interesting.
29. Become a student of sports; in doing so you'll become a student of life.
30. Read about and marvel at the players and records of yesteryear.
31. Spend all day watching your favorite sports movies.
32. Watch the Super Bowl game instead of the commercials.
33. Watch your least favorite sport and really enjoy it.
34. Start a Fantasy League team to bring your sports ego back to earth.
35. Thank God for sportswriters and sportscasters, and their ability to so eloquently turn motion into emotion.
36. Remember that athletes, whether professional or grade school, are just people playing a game they love.
37. Instead of looking to sports for role models, become one yourself.
38. Thank the umpire for a job well done—even if there were some questionable calls (and when aren't there?).
39. Imagine the world before instant replay.

40. When the game is over let it be—and move on.
41. Celebrate the small victories as well as the big wins.
42. Take the day off and go to a game.
43. Take the week off and go on a sports vacation.
44. If you mix sports and business, remember that sports isn't work.
45. Pass on your love of sports to someone you love.
46. Make sports a family affair.
47. Take a deserving child to the ball game.
48. Celebrate the universality of sport.
49. Think what a wonderful world it would be if life really were more like sports.
50. Remember it's just a game.

Mark and Chrissy Donnelly

We Remember Lombardi

Everyone has the will to win, but few have the will to prepare to win.

Bobby Knight

He lay in his bed at Georgetown University Hospital, looking so drawn and tired, the intravenous needles feeding his right arm and hand. He motioned for me to come up on the left side of the bed. I went up to him and squeezed his hand, trying to say without words all the things I wanted to say. How much I had learned from him, how grateful I was, how much I loved him.

"Ouch," he said. "Don't break my hand." And Vince Lombardi grinned, that grin that could lift you or warm you or dazzle you, that grin I had seen so many times in locker rooms and on sidelines. That grin didn't belong in a hospital room. If anyone had ever suggested to me that there was one indestructible man in this world, I would have thought it was Vince Lombardi.

"It's good to see you, Coach," I said. "I've been worrying about you. I've been praying for you. My mom asked me to tell you she's been praying for you."

"Jerry," he said, "I'm just so tired. I just can't talk to any-body—not till I get this thing licked."

"I know, Coach." I held his hand again, said good-night and walked out, wandering through the hospital, feeling depressed and vulnerable and lost. I wished I could fight the cancer with him. He'd taught me that there was so much we could lick together.

For a long time, I thought that Vince Lombardi was born at age forty-five, grinning and growling, demanding perfection, shouting, "Up . . . down . . . up . . . down . . . up . . . down." That was the only Vince Lombardi I knew—the man who built the Green Bay Packers, the man who turned us from an uninspired, losing football team into what I will always believe was the greatest football team there ever was.

No coach ever stamped himself so clearly upon a team. Even in the hottest days of summer, when he whipped us and prodded us and punished us, when he rode us so hard we all came together in our transient hatred for him, I knew I was his creation, and we were his creation, and the difference between being a good football team and a great football team was only him.

I am awed by the universal respect for him. "I owe my whole life to that man," insists Bart Starr, the Green Bay quarterback. Frank Gifford, a spectacular halfback for the New York Giants when Vince was their offensive coach, says that he played football for one reason: for Vince's approval. "When we played a game," Frank recalls, "I couldn't have cared less about the headlines on Monday. All I wanted was to be able to walk into the meeting on Tuesday morning and have Vinny give me that big grin." Sam Huff, a linebacker for the Washington Redskins, says, "Receiving a compliment from Coach Lombardi was like receiving the crown from the king."

Many of my Green Bay teammates flew into Washington

to visit with Vince in the hospital. Willie Davis, former all-pro defensive end for Green Bay, was in Los Angeles when he heard how sick Coach was. Willie got on a plane the same evening, flew all night, had a cup of coffee, went up and saw Vince for two minutes and then turned around and flew home to Los Angeles. "I had to go," Willie says. "I had to. That man made me feel like I was important."

This past year, I've been collecting stories about Vince Lombardi. Here are a few that I think capture the essence of the man who shaped my life and many dozens of others:

When Vince was coaching at St. Cecilia High School in New Jersey in the 1940s, his younger brother, Joe, played for him. Vince leaned over backward to avoid showing favoritism for Joe, so far backward, in fact, that many times during the football season Joe wouldn't speak to him.

Joe Lombardi won a scholarship to Fordham University, and not long before he was to start classses, the school named Vince Lombardi the freshman coach. Joe promptly switched to St. Bonaventure University. "I'm not gonna play another year for that mean sonofa-gun," said Joe.

Later, of course, the brothers became great friends once more.

During his years as an assistant coach at the U.S. Military Academy, Vince became a close friend of the head coach, Earl Blaik, the man he often credited with molding his own coaching methods. Colonel Blaik told me recently that he'd telephoned the hospital and spoken with Vince. "He holds the watch on the people who give him the cobalt treatments," Colonel Blaik said. "He counts off the two minutes they're supposed to give him."

One day, during the Giant years, Marie Lombardi was driving her husband to practice. A friend went along for the ride, and he sat in the front seat between Vince and Marie. Vince didn't say a word during the ride; he was deep in his football fog. When he reached his destination, he opened the car door, turned, said, "Thanks, honey," and kissed the guy sitting next to him.

Vince was always a terror at contract negotiations, and I don't know anyone who played for him who wasn't at one time or another sweet-talked out of a raise he was demanding. Willie Davis once walked into Vince's office with a speech all prepared about how much money he deserved and how he couldn't survive without it. Before Willie could get in a word, Vince was up and patting him and hugging him, and saying "Willie, Willie, Willie, it's so great to see you. We couldn't have won without you, Willie. You had a beautiful year. And, Willie, I need your help. You see, I've got this budget problem. . . ."

When Vince left the New York Giants and moved to Green Bay as head coach and general manager in 1959, he brought along one Giant player—Emlen Tunnell, a thirty-seven-year-old defensive halfback who had already served eleven seasons in the National Football League. "When I got there," Tunnell told me, "Nate Borden, the only black player in Green Bay before me, was living in a place where you wouldn't keep your dog. Vinny found out about it and made Nate move and gave hell to the people who rented him the place. He found Nate a decent place to live. Vinny didn't go for any kind of prejudice. I remember the first day of practice, he said, 'If I ever hear of anyone using any racial epithets around here, like nigger or dago or jew, you're gone. I don't care who you are.'"

Paul Hornung and Max McGee, former Green Bay stars, became famous for violating Vince's eleven o'clock curfew. Actually, they did it only a few times, or at least they got caught only a few times—and they were, in a way, Vince's favorites, his lovable scoundrels.

One weekend last year, after they'd retired from football, Paul and Max went to Washington to see Vince. They had dinner with him and Marie, and after dinner he invited them back to his house for a nightcap.

Max looked at his watch. Paul looked at his. It was almost eleven o'clock. "Thanks a lot, Coach," they said, "but we've got to meet some . . . ah . . . people in a little while."

Vince grinned. "You guys haven't changed at all," he bellowed. "You guys are still running out on me at eleven o'clock!"

A while ago Frank Gifford was talking about Vince's belief in the Spartan life, the total self-sacrifice. "You and me—we grew up believing in Lombardi's way of life," he said. "I'm not sure that it's the answer for everybody, but I wish my son could play for Vince Lombardi."

I do, too.

Jerry Kramer

9

ROAR OF THE CROWD

It is not the critic who counts; not the man who points out how the strong man stumbled, or where the doer of deeds could have done them better. The credit belongs to the man who is in the arena, whose face is marred by dust and sweat and blood; who strives valiantly; who errs and comes short again and again; who knows the great enthusiasms, the great devotions; who spends himself in a worthy cause; who, at the worst, if he fails, at least fails while daring greatly, so that his place shall never be with those timid souls who know neither victory nor defeat.

Theodore Roosevelt

The Perfect Day

From time to time that spring, postcards and packages would arrive at my house in Speedway, Indiana, first from Florida, then from various American League cities. They were sent to me by my second cousin, New York Yankees pitcher Don Larsen. I still have one card that bears a Chicago postmark dated May 17, 1956: "Here's luck on your baseball. I'm rooting for you. Don Larsen." On the other side was a black-and-white photo of my great-uncle Jim's mammoth son, who looked like he'd been shot and stuffed while in the act of pitching.

On May 31, my ninth birthday, I opened a present wrapped in brown paper. It was my cousin's Yankees cap. I brought it to school the next day. "Won't make you play any better," someone said. "Anyway, he's no good."

"You got a cousin on the Yankees?" I demanded.

"I don't need one," came the reply.

The truth was that Don Larsen and I were both in the middle of hard baseball times. The winter before, I had moved to Speedway from South Bend, Indiana. Nobody in my old school had played baseball. In Speedway, baseball was everything: A boy's caste was established by his performance in the recess games. I had never held a bat.

One swing gave me away as an Untouchable.

My dad bought me a bat and a ball, but he couldn't help me put the two together. Sensing my desperation, one morning he offered me the only advice he could think of. "Never stop running,"' he said firmly. Later, at recess, I hit a ball for the first time, causing it to roll back to the pitcher. With my dad's words pounding in my ears, I raced, head down, around the bases and slid into home as my schoolmates doubled up with laughter.

Larsen wasn't doing much better. With Baltimore in 1954, he won three games and lost twenty-one. It was the worst record I or any of my friends had ever seen on a baseball card. Privately, I had to agree that no one in his right mind would keep a Don Larsen card if he could get rid of it.

The strange thing was that after doing so poorly, Larsen had been traded to the Yankees, baseball's best team.

I first met my cousin in July 1956 when our family drove to Chicago to see the Yankees play the White Sox. Unfortunately, the game was rained out, and I stopped crying only after my dad sprinted back from a phone booth to tell us that we were going to meet Don at his hotel.

We entered through the revolving door, and there he was. He wore a loose-fitting brown suit with pants whose creases seemed to converge somewhere over my head. After he greeted my dad, I offered him my hand. Instead, he wrapped his arms around me and asked if I would like to meet a few of the Yankees.

That day remains one of the best of my life. Whitey Ford cautioned me against trying to throw curves too soon. Don spotted Yankee manager Casey Stengel holding court with a cluster of baseball writers and shoved me towards him. "Go over there by yourself," he said. "Tell him you're my cousin." I walked across the room, heart hammering. "You're Larsen's cousin?" asked Stengel. He

grabbed my arm, drawing me close, and signed my autograph book.

Mickey Mantle was standing alone, flipping through a
magazine. When I started towards him, Don held me
back. In mid-1956, Mantle was on pace to break Babe
Ruth's sixty-homer mark. He was among the most
hounded people in the world. "Give me your book and
wait here," said Don. They spoke, and without looking up
Mantle scribbled his name in my book. Yogi Berra walked
by and rubbed my head. Weeks later I washed it again.

October 8, 1956, was the day everything changed for
Don and me. I was now in grade four, still trying to hit a
baseball. Don had had a rocky spring, but he finished the
regular season with an 11–5 record, and was now playing
in the World Series against the Brooklyn Dodgers.

Our school had a fifty-minute lunch period, and I lived
one mile away. My mother did her best to make sure that
I could watch at least a half hour of each World Series
game. She prepared my lunch and placed it in front of the
TV set. Then she rode my bike halfway to school. When
the lunch bell rang, I sprinted to meet the bike and leaped
on, wheeling for home with Mom in pursuit on foot.

When I got home for the fifth game, Don was pitching
in the second inning with the score tied at zero. I watched
Mantle blast a home run in the fourth and make a wonderful running catch in the fifth. My cousin was pitching
well, but I had no idea how well.

I begged my mother to let me stay home, but she
refused. So I went back to school, unable to think of anything but the game. Most Series games ended after school
let out, so I would go down to the boiler room and listen
to the final innings with the janitors. But that day our
classroom door opened at three o'clock sharp, the principal, Mr. Lincoln C. Northcott, came in, and he asked our
teacher, Miss Hazelsmith, if he could speak to the class. I

remember his every word, and the hot feeling on my cheeks.

"Something special has happened," he said. "It is about the World Series. The Yankees won today." Groans and cheers. "But it's more than that. Phil's cousin has pitched the first perfect game in the history of the World Series. Who knows what a perfect game is?"

I knew, but I just couldn't move. Someone said, "It's a no-hitter."

"No," said the principal, "it's even better. No Dodger even got to first base. Don Larsen didn't give up a hit. He didn't walk anybody, and the Yankees didn't make any errors. Phil's cousin got every single batter out. They are saying it might be the best game anyone ever pitched. Congratulations, Phil."

As our teacher beamed, my classmates began to applaud. Then they gathered around my desk to pump my hand and pound my back. In the weeks that followed, glory was mine. I still have scrapbooks full of clippings: Don having a drink with Jackie Gleason; Don in his Series MVP Corvette; Don on a Bob Hope special.

I never made the big leagues. In fact, I topped out as a fourteen-year-old Pony Leaguer, wearing the enormous Spalding glove that my cousin sent me in 1957 for my birthday. In truth, the best day I ever had in baseball was October 8, 1956. I still have scrapbooks full of newspaper clippings about the perfect game and its aftermath. In one article, Don confides, "It's amazing . . . not long ago, I was a nobody, and now, everybody wants me."

In the fall of 1956, when I was having trouble hitting and the game of baseball was all the world to me, I knew exactly what he meant.

Phillip M. Hoose

Now!

For eight years I had the joy of coaching competitive swimming in San Fernando Valley, California, as a United States Swimming Coach. This meant that I worked with athletes not just for a season or a semester, but year-round. I coached some kids for eight straight years; these young people had become a real part of my life.

One of my greatest moments in coaching came with a swimmer named Allison. Although a part of our team for many years, she never achieved any great honors. She was short and slight of build, yet very big of heart, and she had bright red hair like Little Orphan Annie.

In local age-group swimming the major goal for the kids was to qualify for the Junior Olympics. Age-group swimming was like a roller coaster: Just as the kids reached the top of their age group, their birthdays would come, they'd move to an older age group, and they'd find themselves at the bottom all over again. Allison had been close to qualifying for the Junior Olympics a couple of times, but had always just missed before she "aged up." She never gave up trying, though!

Finally, Allison made it! In my last summer as a coach, she qualified for the Junior Olympics in the hundred-meter butterfly. She hit the time standard on the nose—one one-hundredth of a second slower and she would not have qualified. I was sure this was the pinnacle of her swimming career, but had no idea how much her achievement would impact my own coaching career.

Allison was a "drop-dead sprinter." She had good natural speed but would inevitably "tie up" toward the end of her races. Over and over again I would watch her burst to a great start, then struggle painfully as kids passed her in the final few strokes. Exhausted, she would struggle out of the pool and walk dejectedly over to see me.

"Allison," I'd say in my most inspirational coaching voice, "one of these days you're not going to die!" Great coaching, huh? Off she'd go, her body in knots and her mind filled with thoughts of "dying." Unwittingly, I was consistently directing both Allison and myself toward a belief she would die at the end of her races.

At the Junior Olympics, Allison's event turned out to be the first of the meet. With sixty-four girls in the one-hundred-meter butterfly, that meant she would be in heat one, lane eight, right next to the pool edge.

As Allison approached the starting block for her warm-up sprint, her excitement was evident. I signaled her to step up on the block and called out, "Ready, ho!" She exploded toward me with more speed and power than I had ever seen. I clicked my stopwatch as she plowed by me at the twenty-five-meter mark, and watched her grin when I read her sprint time to her. It was by far the best she had ever done.

I don't know if it was the shock of her terrific sprint time or the look of excitement in her eyes, but something shook loose in my brain and a new idea burst forth. There would be no more thoughts of dying in the water.

"Allison, when you dive into the water for your one-hundred-meter butterfly, I want you to remember just how you felt in that sprint. I'll be standing right here, at the seventy-five-meter mark. When you get to me with twenty-five meters to go, I'll yell, 'Now!' As soon as you hear me I want you to pretend that you just dove in to do that exact same sprint all over again. Can you see it?"

"Yes, Coach!"

"Can you feel it?"

"I got it, Coach!"

"Great!"

I sent Allison off to check in for her event and gathered the rest of the team together. Typically we'd send a contingent down to the end of the pool to cheer for their teammates as they approached the turn. This time I decided to do something special, though. I instructed half the kids to head down to the end of the pool to cheer Allison on. But then I gathered the other half of the kids around me and showed them the seventy-five-meter signal I had set up with Allison. I told them that when I gave the signal, I wanted them to let out the loudest "NOW" in history! I wanted that place to shake.

When the gun fired, she took off like a shot. By twenty-five meters she had opened up almost a full body-length's lead on the rest of the heat. As she closed in on the turn, every stroke seemed to pump up her teammates more. They went crazy, waving her on and cheering their lungs out.

She exploded out of the turn and headed home with fifty meters to go. As she approached the seventy-five-meter mark, she continued to move strongly. She had well over two body-lengths on the nearest competitor. Then, something magical happened. Spontaneously, without any coaching from me, the fifty or so kids who had been cheering for her at the turn sprinted around the edge of the pool and joined the other kids gathered around me at seventy-five meters. We had almost one hundred wildly excited kids squeezed together waiting for my signal: eighty meters . . . seventy-seven. . . . As she moved her head forward to breathe at seventy-five meters, I whipped my arm down.

Together, one hundred voices joined in a window-rattling "NOW!" I will always remember what happened next. This little girl, who had died in race after race, suddenly climbed up on top of the water like a hydroplane! She exploded toward the finish with more speed and strength than I thought possible. With eight strokes to go, she took her last breath. Head down and every muscle driving, she blasted to the finish.

I looked at my watch and froze. She had dropped her time more than ten seconds! For years I had watched her struggle out of the water, totally exhausted as she finished her races. Now, though, as she heard her time, she leaped out of the water like an Olympic gymnast.

Allison's father walked shakily toward me with a stunned look on his face. I had known him for years. A calm, soft-spoken man, he attended every event. He put his arms around me and hugged me tightly. Tears streamed down his cheeks.

I felt my eyes mist over as he looked at me with astonishment and gratitude. Allison's remarkable swim had taken place in the first of eight qualifying heats. The top sixteen girls would return that night for the consolations and the finals. When the last of the eight heats finished, Allison had moved from sixty-fourth to first!

That evening, Allison came back and swam a whale of a race. She improved her time another two-tenths of a second over her unbelievable morning performance. She was touched out on the very last stroke and finished second. But there has never been a truer winner.

Brian D. Biro

The Day the Goal Was Scored

Even today, no matter where I go, Canadians want to thank me for scoring The Goal. Almost everyone I meet wants to tell me what he was doing when I scored the winning goal in Moscow in that final game of the first big Canada–Russia hockey series. The more time passes, the more I appreciate the moment.

Just recently I went to meet a friend at the airport. In the short time I waited for him at the gate, five people came over to introduce themselves. As others passed by, I heard them whisper, "There's Paul Henderson."

My grandson Josh probably gets the greatest kick out of this recognition. He was born in 1983, but he knows all about the goal and has a picture of it in his room.

Josh stays with us for part of the summer holidays, and he loves it when people ask me for my autograph. If we're out and people approach us, he's quick to tell his grandmother, "They wanted Grampy's autograph and then wanted to talk about the goal."

The stories I've been told are happy, funny, often quite touching and say a great deal about the human spirit. Here are a few of the many I've collected.

One lady and her husband had just moved into a new

home. She was unpacking some dishes while the game was on television. At the moment I scored, she had a dish in each hand. Losing control for a second, she threw them into the air. The fine china went straight up, hit the ceiling and fell back, shattering into a thousand pieces. She said she didn't know whether to shout for joy or cry; the goal was one of the greatest thrills in her life.

A gentleman in Ontario wanted me to compensate him for his lost tackle box and fishing gear. He and two friends were out fishing in a small boat and had the game on the radio. When I scored he got so excited he jumped up and fell overboard, knocking his tackle box over the side. He was saved, but the box was lost. He felt I was responsible, so he thought it would be a good idea if I helped him replace his gear. Good luck!

Of all the letters I've received, one of the best was from a woman in Toronto. She and her husband had separated and were getting a divorce. On the day of the final game, he went over to the house to pick up a few items. He noticed she had the game on. The third period was about to start, and he asked if he could watch. So they sat before the TV without saying a word.

When I scored they jumped up, dancing and hugging. As they embraced, they looked into each other's eyes and realized they were still in love.

She wrote to me about three months later and said that I had given her the most wonderful Christmas gift ever. They had worked their differences out. If I hadn't scored, he might have left without looking at her again. A letter like that gives you a warm feeling inside.

At a convention in Kingston, Ontario, a guest speaker from the United States didn't know that a lot of people listening to him were also listening to the game on their transistor radios. When Yvan Cournoyer scored to tie the game at 5–5, there was a slight reaction in the audience.

The speaker was startled for a moment, but then continued his talk.

When I scored, the place went wild. The speaker must have thought his audience had gone temporarily insane. He was fairly certain it wasn't something he had said. Finally someone let him in on what had happened. I wonder if he saw the humor in it all.

Near Stratford, Ontario, a ploughing match was being held that day. The key to doing well in the contest was to maintain a straight line.

As one farmer set out, he placed a radio on top of his tractor. When he was about three-quarters of the way down the field, I scored the goal.

The farmer leaped onto the hood of the tractor and began dancing while the machine was still running. When he looked back, his rows swerved all over the place. He didn't win the match, but at least we made him happy by winning the game.

Patients got some of the quickest medical attention in history from a doctor in Mississauga. He was pushing them through so he could sneak out to the pharmacy next door where there was a small black-and-white TV. He would catch a glimpse of the game and then head back to his office for his next patient. With about five minutes to go, he told his receptionist: "I'm not seeing anybody else until the game's over. You'll have to tell them to wait."

Back at the pharmacy, a crowd had now gathered for the last moments of the series. They began to cheer: "We want Henderson! We want Henderson!"—probably because I had scored the winning goals in the sixth and seventh games. When I jumped into the play and scored the goal, they yelled, "We told you! We told you!"

A mother said that in the excitement of the afternoon her son and some other young boys had decided they wanted to play road hockey right after the game.

Problems began, however, when they all wanted to be Paul Henderson. The mother of this little guy had to settle the dispute.

Later he had his mother get a Paul Henderson helmet. No ordinary helmet would do. At that time not many NHL players wore helmets. This kid may have been one of the first to emulate a player who did.

The final game became an international event for one family. A young man found himself in England during the series. Before the last match he telephoned Canada and spoke to his father. "Now Dad," he said, "you be sure to phone me as soon as the game is over and let me know who won." The father agreed to do so.

As soon as I scored, the father called his son overseas. But he was yelling so loudly that the son couldn't understand a word.

"Dad, settle down. Who scored?"

Not until later could the son get a straight answer.

One woman told me the goal helped to mend a deep rift between her husband and son. The boy, fourteen, had not been talking to his father for several months.

Somehow the father and son watched the final game from Moscow together. After I put the puck past Vladislav Tretiak, they found themselves hugging each other. The strain in their relationship seemed to disappear instantly.

"You changed the whole atmosphere in my family," the mother told me. "I'll be eternally grateful."

My final story involves my own daughters, Heather and Jennifer, who watched the game at their Mississauga school. Heather was standing on a table when I scored. Her classmates charged, and she was knocked backward onto the floor. They mobbed her until a friend jumped in and offered her protection. The kids were so out of control that the principal had to dismiss the entire school.

Heather, nine, tried to find Jennifer, seven, so she could

take her home, where Wendy Sittler waited with our other girl, Jill. The Sittlers—Wendy and her husband, Darryl, my teammate on the Toronto Maple Leafs—had moved into our house to look after our daughters while we were away. With some difficulty Heather and Jennifer managed to get home, followed by a bunch of kids.

People began coming to the door looking for autographs and pictures. So many people came by that the girls put up a sign: "We have no autographs left." The phone rang so often that they had to take the receiver off the hook. Wendy didn't know what to do when people began nailing signs such as "Home of Paul Henderson" and "We love you" on the deck above our bedroom. Fortunately, Darryl, who had been out, got back in time to help her deal with the crowd.

Everywhere in Canada our victory in Moscow brought people together spontaneously. Many have told me they felt they had to go someplace where others were gathered; some headed to their local bar or to a mall where a television was set up.

People streamed out into the streets, stopping traffic and proudly waving the Canadian flag. After three tension-filled hours that ended with a sensational climax to a terrific hockey game and series, Canadians had a great need to demonstrate their love for their country.

I would have thought that by now the memories would have faded, but that hasn't been the case at all. The joy of that moment on Thursday, September 28, 1972, still burns bright in the minds of many Canadians.

Paul Henderson and Mike Leonetti

Nixon, Arizona

Christian was in his first year at Duke University, and we were attending a nationally televised game at the Meadowlands Number-nine Duke was playing number-two Arizona in a match-up of teams that had reached the Final Four the previous season.

The first half was encouraging for us when Arizona blew a nineteen-point lead. Once the Wildcats righted themselves, the teams stayed close, separated by more than two points only once during a twelve-minute stretch that ended when Sean Elliot hit a three-pointer with fifty-four seconds to play. This put Arizona ahead, 77–75.

Clutch play after clutch play followed. With six seconds to go, Danny Ferry grabbed a rebound, took a couple of dribbles and sent a long pass to my son, the freshman rookie. What had been an interesting game suddenly became my first moment of terror as a basketball mom.

With one second left, Christian was fouled by Ken Lofton. This meant that Christian would have to shoot a one-and-one and make both to tie the game. Arizona took a time-out to ice him. I put a jacket over my head. Christian missed, hitting the back of the rim. Elliott grabbed the long rebound. Arizona had the victory. Christian traveled back with the team. My husband and I took the long drive home, experiencing our first taste of what it felt like to swallow down a big loss. "George," I moaned, "Christian lost the game . . . on national TV! He must feel so bad."

"I'm sure Coach K won't let a missed foul shot ruin his outlook," he soothed. "Look at how Coach K ran out on the court and put an arm around him after the buzzer."

My brave husband later watched the game on tape. He called me into the living room. "Look," he said, pausing the tape on a pan of the crowd, "there's Richard Nixon."

A few days later I spoke with Christian on the phone and mentioned his dad's discovery. "I know, Mom," he replied. "He came into the locker room."

"You met Richard Nixon and *didn't tell me*," I exclaimed.

"Yeah. He hugged me."

I later read Wilt Browning's report in the *Greensboro News and Record* about the locker-room exchange:

> *Across the tomb of a dressing room, a door opened and a man wearing a gray pin-striped suit entered. [Coach] Mike Krzyzewski reached to greet former President Richard Nixon, who sought out Laettner in a far corner.*
>
> *"I know you feel badly, young man, but everything will be just fine. I know. I've won a few and lost a few myself. And I'll tell you this. This is the first basketball game I've attended in fifty-five years, and I will go away remembering the shots you made."*
>
> *Laettner, who hit all six of his field goal attempts, all in critical points in the game, smiled.*
>
> *"Thank you, sir," he said to the man who resigned the presidency after the Watergate revelations when Laettner was only a toddler.*

Bonita Laettner

Give the Kid the Ball!

Charity sees the need, not the cause.

German Proverb

It was a good evening to watch a ball game in the Bronx. The air was cool, and the Yanks' Ron Guidry was pitching. There were four of us, enjoying boys' night out.

In the second inning, a foul ball was hit in our direction. A boy of about nine was reaching for it when the ball was grabbed by a man of about thirty-five with horn-rimmed glasses. You could see that the kid was totally crushed. He had an oversized Yankees cap that came down over his eyes and a baseball glove that was too big for him. He seemed the kind of kid every other kid on the block beats up daily.

Suddenly someone shouted, "Give the kid the ball!" The chant was taken up by others around us: "Give the kid the ball! Give the kid the ball!"

Horn Rims shook his head and put the ball in his pocket. Yet inning after inning, the chant continued, until it spread throughout the lower left-field stands.

By the seventh inning, the kid must have had a stomach-ache. People around him were buying him peanuts, soda and ice cream. Then Sam, one of the fellows I was with, went over to talk to Horn Rims. I couldn't hear what Sam said, but I saw Horn Rims reach into his pocket, turn and give the kid the ball. The kid's eyes lit up.

Somebody yelled, "He gave the kid the ball!" The crowd was on its feet, clapping and yelling, "He gave the kid the ball! He gave the kid the ball!" The ballplayers were looking up in the stands. We were generating more excitement than the game.

Then a strange thing happened. A man in the front row who also caught a foul ball got up and gave it to the kid. Another thunderous ovation rocked the left-field stands.

In the bottom of the ninth, a young man with a Fu Manchu mustache was leaving. As he passed the kid, he took a ball from his pocket. "Here kid—here's another," he yelled, flipping the ball in the air. Surprisingly, the kid caught it. More cheers.

Hundreds of fans who had been halfheartedly watching a routine game were smiling and slapping strangers on the back. And the kid? He had three balls in his glove and a big grin on his face.

John J. Healey

Longest Line in the Universe Contest

Secretariat

It all began unfolding like some epochal scene of a drama turned suddenly surreal, with tricks being played by the lights and shadows of the late-afternoon sun, with the solitary silhouettes of the horse and rider floating out there, disembodied, toward the far turn. Through the rising, vaporous curtains of heat. Soundless, in the distance. All alone.

Secretariat had just rushed past the halfway mark of the one-and-a-half-mile Belmont Stakes in 1:09 4/5, the fastest six-furlong split in the history of the race, and now he was humming through the fourth quarter in :24 2/5, toward an opening mile in an unearthly 1:34 1/5. There, in that eerily dappled gloaming, Secretariat began turning the oldest of all the Triple Crown races into his own tour de force, drawing off to lead a beaten Sham by two lengths . . . four . . . six. Rarely in sport has a game's most brilliant competitor risen at precisely the right juncture in history—at the perfect coordinates of place, occasion and time—and seized the day by delivering a performance so original, so stunning in its clarity, that it raised to a new level the standard by which all who followed would be measured. And Secretariat, plunging toward the far turn, was raising it right then.

It was 5:40 P.M. on June 9, 1973, and what had begun thirty-eight months before had all quite suddenly come to this. On the night of March 29, 1970, the manager of The Meadow stud farm in Doswell, Virginia, Howard Gentry, hastily left a midnight game of pool in the basement of his home and headed in the darkness toward a solitary light that burned above the two-stall foaling barn in the corner of a field. Somethingroyal, one of the nation's preeminent brood mares, was about to give birth to her foal by Bold Ruler, America's prepotent sire. He was a good-sized foal, with hips so wide that Gentry feared he might have trouble clearing the breach. Nonetheless, at precisely ten minutes past midnight, with Gentry and a companion tugging on the forelegs, the whole roasted chestnut finally appeared. Gentry stood back and declared, "There is a whopper!"

It was a propitious declaration. In the course of his sixteen-month racing career, Secretariat rose higher and faster and larger than any U.S. horse of modern times. By the end of his 1972 season, he had so dominated the nation's juveniles, winning nearly every major stakes race on the East Coast, that he was unanimously voted Horse of the Year. It was the first time a two-year-old had ever been so honored. That winter, Secretariat became the most expensive animal in history when he was sold to a breeding syndicate for the then shocking sum of $6.08 million.

He had it all: impeccable bloodlines, a dazzling turn of foot and a physique so flawless that Charles Hatton, the aging dean of American turf writers, called him "the most perfect racehorse I have ever seen." Secretariat was the quintessential running machine, and he was never more keenly tuned than he was in 1973 for the greatest showcase of his sport, the Triple Crown. It had been twenty-five years since a horse had swept the three races—Citation, in 1948—and many had begun to wonder whether it would ever be done again.

So Secretariat's quest was all the more riveting. In the Kentucky Derby, after dropping back to last, he gradually picked up one horse after another, hooked Sham off the last turn and powered down the stretch to a still-record finish in 1:59 2/5. In a feat unprecedented for a ten-furlong race, Secretariat ran each successive quarter faster than the preceding one. Two weeks later in the Preakness, after again trailing early, he suddenly charged through a blazing second quarter of :21 and change, then sailed home to beat Sham by 2 1/2. The Pimlico teletimer had malfunctioned, obscuring the official final time, but two veteran Daily Racing Form clockers hand-timed Secretariat in 1:53 2/5, giving him his second track record in two weeks. (The official time was eventually recorded as 1:54 2/5, short of the record.)

It was as though, like a brilliant jazz musician, he was making the whole thing up as he went along, improvising something different for each race. All jockey Ron Turcotte had to do was hang on. He knew better than to interfere: Quiet, genius at work. With the country sunk in the Watergate abyss, Secretariat became the most diverting icon of the day, a $6 million equine Adonis with more presence than any horse in memory. And so it came about that the Belmont, on national TV, offered the ideal venue for the greatest performance in the history of the sport.

The colt came to it with more than the winds of history at his back. Secretariat was a prodigious eater—he was devouring fifteen quarts of oats a day during his Triple Crown season—and he needed extremely hard, fast workouts to burn this off and keep him fit. He was a morning whirlwind. Working out eight days before the Belmont, he bounded a mile in a sensational 1:34 4/5 and galloped out nine furlongs in 1:48 3/5, stakes-race time.

Clockers were checking their watches with each other.

What was going on here? The definitive answer would not come until sixteen years later, on the day Secretariat died, when Dr. Thomas Swerczek, a professor of veterinary science at the University of Kentucky, removed the animal's heart while performing the necropsy. Normal in all other ways, Secretariat's heart was about twice the size of the normal horse's pump and a third larger than any equine heart Swerczek had ever seen. "We were all shocked," he said.

No more so, though, than everyone who saw the Belmont. Sweeping into the far turn, leaving Sham behind, Secretariat widened his lead to seven lengths, then eight. Ten. Twelve. Fifteen. Twenty. He turned for home alone. In front by twenty-two. Turcotte did not move. Twenty-four. Twenty-six. The oldest horsemen on the grounds were struck dumb. Twenty-seven. Twenty-eight. Seventy yards from the wire, Turcotte glanced at the timer, saw 2:19 . . . 2:20. The record was 2:26 3/5. He looked away, then did a double take. He started scrubbing. Twenty-nine lengths. Thirty. The colt took a final leap. Thirty-one. The timer froze: 2:24. Twenty-one years later, it is frozen there still.

William Nack

Beyond Race

Let us not look back in anger or forward in fear, but around in awareness.

James Thurber

Autographs. Intrusive fans. A lot of stars grow to hate them. I never have. I've always loved being loved by fans. I admit that I have to wear a certain public face—a distant, sometimes vacant frown. It developed subconsciously over the years as I learned that the more open and approachable you appear, the more people will take advantage of you inappropriately.

One time I had a little stomach ailment on the road, which required frequent trips to the facilities. I was jogging toward the washroom in an airport when I heard a man calling me. I really couldn't stop. I hurried into a stall, but he had seen me. He thrust a piece of paper under the wall. "Mr. Lemon, I'm sorry to bother you, but I'm late for my plane and my son would never forgive me if I didn't get your autograph." I had to laugh. He got his autograph.

Then, blessedly, come the times when being accessible to people redeems all the occasional inconveniences. I remember the time when we played an all-black team before an all-white crowd, and when we went to the bus station afterward, we had to eat at a black-only diner in the back. A man came to me outside carrying his beautiful blonde daughter of about six. She wanted to meet me, to give me a hug and a kiss. She said, "I just love you, Meadowlark!" Her eyes shone, and her smile was radiant. She leaped from her father's arm into mine and squeezed me tight. I laughed. "Well, thank you, sweetheart. That's nice."

The man's eyes were moist. With her cheek at my ear, he leaned close to my other ear and said, "Thank you, Meadowlark. She's dying." It was all I could do to hang on to her. My strength seeped away. I held her close so she wouldn't see me crying.

"Thank you, thank you, Meadowlark," the little girl said. "You're so funny, and I love you and I wish I could take you home with me!" I choked, "I do, too, honey."

She was too young to see color.

And then there was the time I heard a little boy cackling at courtside. He just screamed and hollered and giggled as if he had never seen anything so funny in his life. And he kept calling, "Meadowlark Lemon! Meadowlark Lemon!" When the ball went out of bounds, the man next to him gathered it up and tossed it to me; I lobbed a pass toward the boy. It hit him in the chest and rolled back to me. When the ball came back, I tossed it to the boy again. Again, it hit him and rolled back. The crowd loved it, but I wondered what was going on. The man next to him told me by mouthing the words, "He's blind."

I took the ball to the boy and helped him hold it. He threw it back. I gave him a hug and heard him calling my name and cheering the rest of the game. He couldn't see color either.

Meadowlark Lemon
Submitted by Bill Bethel

Heart of a Champion

It had long since come to my attention that people of accomplishment rarely sat back and let things happen to them. They went out and happened to things.

Elinor Smith

In my third year as head coach of a small high school, I addressed a group of adults and students on the benefits of football. It was the traditional recruitment talk about teamwork and cooperation; I told the crowd that football was not just for star athletes.

Afterwards, a couple approached me. Their son, who had had a sickly childhood, really wanted to play football, even though they had tried to dissuade him. When they told me his name, my heart fell. Michael was five-feet-ten-inches and weighed about 108 pounds. He was a loner, the brunt of other kids' jokes and snide remarks, and as far as I knew he had never participated in sports.

I stammered through my clichés, trying to tell the parents it might not be a good idea. But so close on the heels of my "football is for everyone" speech, I said we could give it a try.

The opening day of practice Michael was the first player on the field. We went through thirty minutes of stretching and then a one-mile jog around the track.

Michael began near the back. At fifty yards he stumbled and fell. I helped him to his feet. "Michael," I said, "why don't you just walk the laps?" He began to get teary-eyed and stammered that he hadn't even tried yet. So I swallowed my heart and sent him on. Repeatedly he fell, each time picking himself up. After one lap I pulled him aside.

This occurred every day for weeks. During practice I assigned a coach to baby-sit Michael and keep him out of contact drills. It was tough to provide that kind of attention, but Michael's courage and tenacity made it impossible to do anything else.

As the season progressed Michael improved, physically and socially. He began to laugh and joke with team members, and I think most began to see him as some crazy kid brother. Instead of ridiculing him, they became touchingly protective.

By the last week of practice, Michael ran the mile without falling. We had won only one game that season, yet the team cheered louder for Michael's run than they had during our lone victory.

As I left my office for the last time that season, I was surprised to see Michael standing there; I told him how proud I was of him.

"Coach," he said, "I never played."

I started to say that I didn't want him injured.

Michael stopped me again. "I know why you couldn't play me, but I want you to next year. What can I do?" So I put together a schedule of weight training and exercises for him.

Michael wasn't in any of my classes, and I really didn't see much of him over the next couple of months, but I'd wave at him every night as I left school. He would be doing sit-ups or running, and it was obvious he was sticking to the program. Then one night I heard a knock at my door, and there was Michael. He had put on about ten pounds, and there seemed to be more color to his face. He wondered if I might beef up the program since it was becoming too easy. I laughed and added a few more exercises and doubled the running.

At the start of the next season, Michael ran the opening mile faster than anyone. Although he had a tough time in the drills, he did a pretty good job, so I made him a guard.

The following Monday after practice, I ran into one of the team captains. Steve was talented, but lazy and undisciplined. He was an honors student who rarely studied and was popular with his peers even though he could be heartless.

Steve pointed to the field where Michael was running and doing push-ups and asked me why he was still out there. I told Steve to ask him. The next night I was surprised to see Steve working alongside Michael.

Several weeks later we were preparing for one of our biggest games, and practice was grueling. I dismissed the team and started heading in. Only two kids left the field. The rest were huddled around Michael, who was giving them another workout. Steve had called on the players to join Michael and him in their post-practice workouts.

When the game began, we quickly fell behind by two touchdowns, and it was clear some kids had already given up. But not Michael, now an occasional starting guard. He was working so hard and imploring the team so much to keep trying that few had the courage not to. We won by one point with ten seconds remaining.

I picked Michael as player of the week, not so much for his play but because he was obviously the reason the others had kept fighting. We finished the season as one of the top teams in the state.

At the end-of-year banquet, the big award goes to the most productive player based on a strict point system. Although I would have liked to give it to Michael, I knew it belonged to Steve. I called him up to receive it.

"As much as I honor this award and what it stands for," Steve said, "there is someone who deserves it more than I do." The entire crowd went silent. "Everything I accomplished this season, and everything the team accomplished, is due to one person."

He turned towards Michael. It was hard for Steve to talk. "Michael, you used to say that I was your hero. If I were half the man you are, I would be proud, because there is no doubt you are my hero."

Michael ran up to the podium and hugged Steve so hard he almost fell down. The entire team cheered.

Michael is in the military today and I haven't heard from him in years. He and his parents always tried to tell me how much I had helped him. I don't think they realize that I was more of a bystander. I know I never found the words to tell Michael that he had done more for me than I had for him.

There are a lot more Michaels out there—kids who will never be "stars" but will probably give and get more from their association with sports than the athletically gifted. It's those kids that sports are for, and those who make me proud to be a coach.

Patrick L. Busteed

Knowing the Score

I stride briskly to the mound, reminiscent of Casey Stengel, to calm my pitcher. It is late in the game, and the ace of my staff has become unsettled. I tug at my manager's cap and summon up every bit of wit and savvy I command.

No, this is not Three Rivers Stadium with the bases loaded, bottom of the ninth. This is not even really baseball, nor is my pitcher precisely a pitcher. She is a little girl in tears, chased from the mound by a buzzing bumblebee. I take her by the hand.

I am a T-ball coach, a grizzled veteran who's just wrapped up his tenth surrealistic season attempting to bring some measure of order—and a smidgen of baseball skill—to six- and seven-year-old boys and girls.

Why do they call it T-ball? Think of baseball without any pitching, although a player fields the position. At home plate, the batter faces a rubber hitting tee (hence the name of the game) with a hard baseball sitting on top. The tee height can be raised or lowered; usually it's midway between the shoulders and waist. Other than the absence of pitching (which would be silly for children this age), the normal rules of baseball apply. Well, there's no scorekeeping either. It's game after game with no runs, no hits, no errors ever recorded.

I have coached T-ball in the rustic hills of Ohio and on the inner-city sandlots of Pittsburgh. I'm not sure what compels me to do this year after year. Rarely do sane adults coach the game for more than one year—and they're almost always parents of a kid on the team. I am a bachelor, and the world's most inept disciplinarian. First- and second-graders run roughshod over me. The meekest tyke turns brazen in my presence. So imagine the pandemonium when I try to reign over twenty kids equipped with wooden bats and hard balls with lots of open territory for them to roam. The bench-jockeys on my teams are always razzing *me*.

No T-baller has ever addressed me as "Coach"—much less as "Mr. Ehrbar." (One pun-loving ragamuffin did christen me "Mr. Error-bar" after I demonstrated the intricacies of fielding ground balls.) Instead, they all call me "Tommy," a kid's name. And the kids often go by adult-sounding handles like "Charles" and "Alexandra." No wonder there's confusion about who's in charge. The only time my players allow me grown-up, responsible status is at Dairy Queen, when someone has to spring for the ice cream.

But my role is the least of the reverses that T-ball is prone to. Topped balls that roll less than three feet frequently become home runs through a chain reaction of throwing mishaps. One time my catcher, Geoffrey, was having a rough day behind the plate, every single peg to first missing by a mile. On the next short grounder, rather than risk another errant toss, he gave chase after the batter. Weighed down by catcher's mask, chest protector and shin guards—and with baseball clenched in his raised right hand—he barreled after his quarry, around first base, second base, third and home. At which point the batter, realizing Geoffrey was still steaming after him, took off on yet another frantic lap around the diamond. So did Geoffrey. By the time the runner had reached home again he was exhausted and decided to stand his ground. What happened next was one of the great role reversals in sports history: guarding the plate was the *runner*, while the *catcher* came charging down the line, hell-bent for home. After the collision, Geoffrey staggered toward our bench. Out of breath, he gasped in my direction, totally pleased with himself: "I got 'im out, Tommy!"

Right field is another position that lends T-ball its piquant lunacy. Whenever T-ball players are assigned right field they immediately plunge into a daydream trance. Or worse, I remember a game when a ball was lofted into short right. As I followed the orbit of the sphere, I belatedly discovered that my fielder, Bartholomew, was peacefully asleep amid the dandelions. Defying odds greater than those against winning the Pennsylvania Lottery, the ball landed smack in Bartholomew's baseball mitt—the first catch of his T-ball career, about which we notified him after he woke up.

Because of the game's singular spirit, rain does not pose quite the same threat to T-ball as it does to big-league baseball. One time a furious thundershower swept across the field. The adult bystanders moved toward shelter en masse. Meanwhile the kids from both teams—and one conspicuous grown-up—took off their shoes, tossed their gloves aside and frolicked in center field beneath a spectacular rainbow.

And every year, always in surprising form, magic happens as the arc of summer moves from early June through late July. A kid just learning the game and understandably shy about fielding hard-hit balls will suddenly snag a line drive with unprecedented graceful dexterity, then await the next batter, his pose showing a tangible addition of assurance and pluck. Or a child embarrassed by frequently whiffing at a stationary ball will suddenly knock a fly way over everyone's heads. Rhonda, the little girl once scared by a bumblebee, turned into the finest athlete I ever coached. She's now a star sprinter and softball player in high school.

T-ball is that rare piece of life where there are no winners or losers, and the playing field is equal for all. Every kid gets the same number of at bats; each inning, fielders rotate to new positions.

All too soon, those who advance to Little League will face not only blazing fastballs, but the realities of competition: who will start and who will sit on the bench. Batting averages will be kept; so will scores. *I* prefer to remain at the level of T-ball.

For many years, I owned a massive and battered old Chevy convertible. Among my most joyous memories are a string of glistening Saturday mornings after T-ball: my Chevy jam-packed with rambunctious T-ballers, we're reliving the game, the wind in our faces, feeling as young and as wildly hopeful as a catcher named Geoffrey heading for home.

Tommy Ehrbar

In a play unprecedented in league history, Ned Felmley misreads the third-base coach's signals and steals the pitcher's mound.

A Cowboy's Last Chance

Courage is grace under pressure.

Ernest Hemingway

Joe Wimberly sat on a tree stump and stared at his house in Cool, Texas (population: 238).

"It ain't exactly the Ponderosa," Joe once told his wife, Paula, as he swept his arm toward their three acres of scrub grass. "But it's ours."

Earlier that day, the bank called Joe. The charge cards were full, the payments late and the checking account overdrawn. But being a cowboy was the only job Joe knew. He had been riding horses, herding cattle and climbing on the backs of steers since he was a kid. At eighteen, he set out for the last untamed range for the true American cowboy—the rodeo. There, he made a name for himself. Some days he walked around with $1,000 in his pocket. Other times he could not afford to eat. But there was never a day when he wanted to trade his chaps for a job with a boss looking over his shoulder.

It scared Paula to watch Joe on a bull. Still, she knew it put the sparkle in his eyes. So whenever he headed out the door, she would kiss him good-bye, cross her fingers and pray.

Joe was gone to the rodeo about two hundred days a year. He was a thousand miles away on the night that Paula gave birth to a daughter, Casey. They had no insurance.

"How we gonna pay for things, Joe?" Paula's voice cracked across the telephone wires.

"I'm gonna win," Joe told her. "And I'm gonna keep winning."

He was as good as his word. With the grace of a gymnast and the nerve of a bank robber, Joe dazzled crowds at little county fairs and big city stadiums throughout the West. In the 1980s he qualified five times to compete in the National Finals Rodeo. In his best year Joe won more than $80,000 in prize money.

However, with travel expenses and entry fees, times weren't easy, especially after the birth of another daughter, Sami. But bills got paid, and when Paula took a job in a pharmacy, they saved enough for a down payment on their house. Then Paula and Joe had a son, McKennon.

Joe had come back from hard times before, injuries, too. But by now weeks had passed since he'd put a paycheck on the kitchen table. *Maybe I'm just not trying hard enough,* Joe thought.

Mesquite, on the outskirts of Dallas, is the site of one of the best-known rodeos in America. One day a Dodge truck executive called rodeo owner Neal Gay with a promotional idea. If Gay would pick the meanest, wildest bull he could find, Dodge would put up a $5,000 prize for any cowboy who could ride it for eight seconds. The pot would grow by $500 every time the bull shucked a rider. The bull would be named after a new truck, Dodge Dakota.

Gay contacted Lester Meier, a rodeo producer who

owned a nightmarish black bull that weighed seventeen hundred pounds and had a single horn crawling ominously down the side of its white face. "You got your Dodge Dakota," Meier told Gay.

Of the thirty bull riders who competed at Mesquite every weekend, only one, assigned randomly by a computer, got a crack at Dodge Dakota. Week after week, the beast sent cowboys, even a former world champion, hurtling through the air. Joe was carrying a fifty-pound feed sack toward the horse pen at his ranch when he heard the screen door slam. Paula hurried over. "The rodeo called, Joe," she said. "You drew Dodge Dakota for Friday night."

Joe dropped the feed sack. The pot had grown to $9,500.

When it came time to face Dakota, Joe paced behind the chutes. He looked up in the stands and saw his family. When the spotlight found him, he pulled himself over the rails and settled on the bull's broad, humped back. He wrapped the rope around his right hand; the other end was twisted around the beast's belly.

The gate swung open. Dakota bolted and Joe's thighs squeezed tight. The beast bucked hard, lifting Joe into the air, then slammed down. The bull bellowed and twisted to its left. Foam spewed from its snout. The cowboy thumped back on his seat, the rope burning his hand. He shot in the air, his head snapping backward, hat flying off, but he hung on. The stands thundered—six thousand fans on their feet, screaming, shrieking, stomping. The clock flashed five seconds, six seconds. . . .

Dakota groaned in a voice from hell and bucked violently, four hoofs in the air. Suddenly the bull ran alone. When it was over, Joe brushed himself off, searched for Paula in the stands and slowly mouthed the words, "I'm sorry."

A second time that summer, Joe was paired with Dodge

Dakota. In an instant this time, the bull slammed his dreams into the dirt. Now Joe was scrambling for money. He shod horses. He entered jackpot bull-riding contests. He organized a rodeo school. But none of this put much of a dent in his debts. He was finally forced to place a newspaper ad to sell the house. "It's only boards and paint and siding," he told a tearful Paula. "If we stay together as a family, it doesn't matter where we are."

One Friday in September, Joe was riding at Mesquite. With all his troubles at home, Joe hadn't been thinking much about bulls. The purse for Dodge Dakota had grown to $17,000. Twenty-four times a cowboy had boarded the infamous bull, and twenty-four times the bull had won. The pot was big enough to save his house, to pay the bills, even to have a little extra.

At the arena they had stopped announcing ahead of time which cowboy would ride Dakota. Now they drew the name during intermission. Suddenly a rodeo official called out, "Hey, Joe Wimberly, you got Dakota."

Neal Gay came by. "Third time's the charm," the rodeo owner said with a wink. The cowboy pulled himself over the rails and straddled the bull that stomped inside its chute. The rope was wrapped around his hand as tight as a noose. One of his favorite phrases came to mind: "If you ain't got no choice, be brave."

The gate swung open, and the clock started to count the eight most important seconds of Joe Wimberly's life. The huge black beast bellowed. Nearly a ton of muscle and bone thundered by. Dakota's head snapped violently. Its eyes flashed fire. Dust rose from its kicking hoofs. And the clock ticked—two seconds . . . three . . . four. . . . Joe bounced on the bull's hard back, straining for balance. Then another punishing buck. He dangled at the edge, fighting gravity. Six seconds . . . seven seconds . . .

Joe crashed to the dirt as the horn sounded. A sudden

hush swept over the arena. An excited official raised his arms in the air, the sign of a touchdown. Joe had made it by two-hundredths of a second.

The cowboy dropped to his knees. "Thank you, Jesus!" Joe cried. Paula fell sobbing into the arms of a spectator. From his knees, Joe looked up and met Paula's eyes as she ran toward him with the kids. The roar of the crowd swept down on the arena floor, where the Wimberly family squeezed together in a ten-armed hug, their tears spilling on the dust.

It was past 2 A.M. when they got home. Joe went to the telephone and dialed the banker. "Who's this?" came a groggy mumble.

"Why, this here is Joe Wimberly," he said, "and I was just calling to say I got a check for you."

Dirk Johnson
Originally appeared in Chicken Soup
for the Country Soul

A Fragile Hero

Mickey Mantle was the classic baseball hero of the fifties and early sixties. At his peak, Mantle's dynamic combination of speed and power were breathtaking. There was something simultaneously charismatic and poignant about the Oklahoma lead-miner's son turned pin-striped hero. He reached people in ways his baseball feats alone could not fully explain. Part of it was Mantle himself. Part was what he represented—a time fondly remembered by baseball fans of the post-World War II generation. Whatever it was, Mantle's death in August 1995 touched a chord with millions of Americans. At Mantle's funeral in Dallas, Bob Costas spoke about those feelings, and about Mantle himself.

You know, it occurs to me as we're all sitting here thinking of Mickey, he's probably somewhere getting an earful of Casey Stengel, and no doubt quite confused by now.

One of Mickey's fondest wishes was that he be remembered as a great teammate, to know that the men he played with thought well of him.

But it was more than that. Moose (Skowron) and Whitey (Ford) and Tony (Kubek) and Yogi (Berra) and Bobby (Richardson) and Hank (Bauer), what a remarkable team you were. And the stories of the visits you guys made to Mickey's bedside the last few days were heart-breakingly tender. It meant everything to Mickey, as would the presence of so many baseball figures past and present here today.

I was honored to be asked to speak by the Mantle family today. I am not standing here as a broadcaster. Mel Allen is the eternal voice of the Yankees and that would be his place. And there are others here with a longer and deeper association with Mickey than mine.

But I guess I'm here, not so much to speak for myself as to simply represent the millions of baseball-loving kids who grew up in the '50s and '60s and for whom Mickey Mantle was baseball.

And more than that, he was a presence in our lives—a fragile hero to whom we had an emotional attachment so strong and lasting that it defied logic. Mickey often said he didn't understand it, this enduring connection and affection—the men now in their forties and fifties, otherwise perfectly sensible, who went dry in the mouth and stammered like schoolboys in the presence of Mickey Mantle.

Maybe Mick was uncomfortable with it, not just because of his basic shyness, but because he was always too honest to regard himself as some kind of deity.

But that was never really the point. In a very different time than today, the first baseball commissioner, Kennesaw Mountain Landis, said, "Every boy builds a shrine to some baseball hero, and before that shrine, a candle always burns."

For a huge portion of my generation, Mickey Mantle was that baseball hero. And for reasons that no statistics, no dry recitation of facts can possibly capture, he was the most compelling baseball hero of our lifetime. And he was our symbol of baseball at a time when the game meant something to us that perhaps it no longer does.

Mickey Mantle had those dual qualities so seldom seen—exuding dynamism and excitement, but at the same time touching your heart—flawed, wounded. We knew there was something poignant about Mickey Mantle before we knew what "poignant" was. We didn't just root for him, we felt for him.

Long before many of us ever cracked a serious book, we knew something about mythology as we watched Mickey Mantle run out a home run through the lengthening shadows of a late Sunday afternoon at Yankee Stadium.

There was greatness in him, but vulnerability, too.

He was our guy. When he was hot, we felt great. When he slumped or got hurt, we sagged a bit, too. We tried to crease our caps like him; kneel in an imaginary on-deck circle like him; run like him, heads down, elbows up.

Billy Crystal is here today. Billy says that at his bar mitzvah he spoke in an Oklahoma drawl. Billy's here today because he loved Mickey Mantle, and millions more who felt like him are here in spirit as well.

It's been said that the truth is never pure and rarely simple.

Mickey Mantle was too humble and honest to believe that the whole truth about him could be found on a Wheaties box or a baseball card. But the emotional truths of childhood have a power that transcends objective fact. They stay with us through all the years, withstanding the ambivalence that so often accompanies the experience of adults.

That's why we can still recall the immediate tingle in that instant of recognition when a Mickey Mantle popped up in a pack of Topps bubblegum cards—a treasure lodged between an Eli Grba and a Pumpsie Green.

That's why we smile today, recalling those October afternoons when we'd sneak a transistor radio into school to follow Mickey and the Yankees in the World Series.

Or when I think of Mr. Tomasi, a very wise sixth-grade teacher who understood that the World Series was more important, at least for one day, than any school lesson could be. So he brought his black-and-white TV from home, plugged it in and let us watch it right there in school through the flicker and the static. It was richer and more compelling than anything I've seen on a high-resolution, big-screen TV.

Of course, the bad part, Bobby, was that (Sandy) Koufax struck fifteen of you guys out that day.

My phone's been ringing the past few weeks as Mickey fought for his life. I've heard from people I hadn't seen or talked to in years—guys I played stickball with, even some guys who took Willie's side in those endless Mantle–Mays arguments. They're grown up now. They have their families. They're not even necessarily big baseball fans anymore. But they felt something hearing about Mickey, and they figured I did too.

In the last year, Mickey Mantle, always so hard on himself, finally came to accept and appreciate that distinction between a role model and a hero. The first he often was not, the second he always will be.

And, in the end, people got it. And Mickey Mantle got from America something other than misplaced and mindless celebrity worship. He got something far more meaningful. He got love—love for what he had been, love for what he made us feel, love for the humanity and sweetness that was always there mixed in with the flaws and all the pain that wracked his body and his soul.

We wanted to tell him it was okay, that what he had been was enough. We hoped he felt that Mutt Mantle would have understood and that Merlyn and the boys loved him.

And then in the end, something remarkable happened— the way it does for champions. Mickey Mantle rallied. His heart took over, and he had some innings as fine as any in 1956 or with his buddy, Roger (Maris), in 1961.

But this time, he did it in the harsh and trying summer of '95. And what he did was stunning. The sheer grace of that ninth inning—the humility, the sense of humor, the total absence of self-pity, the simple eloquence and honesty of his pleas to others to take heed of his mistakes.

All of America watched in admiration. His doctors said he was, in many ways, the most remarkable patient they'd ever seen. His bravery, so stark and real, that even those used to seeing people in dire circumstances were moved by his example. Because of that example, organ donations are up dramatically all across America. A cautionary tale has been honestly told and perhaps will affect some lives for the better.

And our last memories of Mickey Mantle are as heroic as the first.

None of us, Mickey included, would want to be held to account for every moment of our lives. But how many of us could say that our best moments were as magnificent as his?

This is the cartoon from this morning's *Dallas Morning News*. There's a figure here, St. Peter I take it to be, with his arm around Mickey, that broad back and the number 7. He's holding his book of admissions. He says, "Kid, that was the most courageous ninth inning I've ever seen."

It brings to mind a story Mickey liked to tell on himself. He pictured himself at the pearly gates, met by St. Peter who shook his head and said, "Mick, we checked the record. We know some of what went on. Sorry, we can't let you in, but before you go, God wants to know if you'd sign these six dozen baseballs."

Well, there were days when Mickey Mantle was so darn good that we kids would bet that even God wanted his autograph. But like the cartoon says, I don't think Mick needed to worry about the other part.

I just hope God has a place for him where he can run again. Where he can play practical jokes on his teammates and smile that boyish smile, 'cause God knows, no one's perfect. And God knows there's something special about heroes.

So long, Mick. Thanks.

Bob Costas

Funny You Should Ask

So we were lying on our backs on the grass in the park next to our hamburger wrappers, my fourteen-year-old son and I, watching the clouds loiter overhead, when he asked me, "Dad, why are we here?"

And this is what I said.

"I've thought a lot about it, son, and I don't think it's all that complicated. I think maybe we're here just to teach a kid how to bunt, turn two and eat sunflower seeds without using his hands.

"We're here to pound the steering wheel and scream as we listen to the game on the radio, twenty minutes after we pulled into the garage. We're here to look all over, give up and then find the ball in the hole.

"We're here to watch, at least once, as the pocket collapses around John Elway, and it's fourth-and-never. Or as the count goes to three-and-one on Mark McGwire with bases loaded, and the pitcher begins wishing he'd gone on to med school. Or as a little hole you couldn't get a skateboard through suddenly opens in front of Jeff Gordon with a lap to go.

"We're here to wear our favorite sweat-soaked Boston Red Sox cap, torn Slippery Rock sweatshirt and the

Converses we lettered in, on a Saturday morning with nowhere we have to go and no one special we have to be.

"We're here to rake in on a jack-high nothin' hand and have nobody know it but us. Or get in at least one really good brawl, get a nice shiner and end up throwing an arm around the guy who gave it to us.

"We're here to shoot a six-point elk and finally get the f-stop right, or to tie the perfect fly, make the perfect cast, catch absolutely nothing and still call it a perfect morning.

"We're here to nail a yield sign with an apple core from half a block away. We're here to make our dog bite on the same lame fake throw for the gazillionth time. We're here to win the stuffed bear or go broke trying.

"I don't think the meaning of life is gnashing our bicuspids over what comes after death, but tasting all the tiny moments that come before it. We're here to be the coach when Wendell, the one whose glasses always fog up, finally makes the only perfect backdoor pass all season. We're here to be there when our kid has three goals and an assist. And especially when he doesn't.

"We're here to see the Great One setting up behind the net, tying some poor goaltender's neck into a Windsor knot. We're here to watch the Rocket peer in for the sign, two out, bases loaded, bottom of the career. We're here to witness Tiger's lining up the twenty-foot double breaker to win and not need his autograph afterward to prove it.

"We're here to be able to do a one-and-a-half for our grandkids. Or to stand at the top of our favorite double-black on a double-blue morning and overhear those five wonderful words: 'Highway's closed. Too much snow.' We're here to get the Frisbee to do things that would have caused medieval clergymen to burn us at the stake.

"We're here to sprint the last 100 yards and soak our shirts and be so tired we have to sit down to pee.

"I don't think we're here to make *SportsCenter*. The really good stuff never does. Like leaving Wrigley at 4:15 on a perfect summer afternoon and walking straight into Murphy's with half of section 503. Or finding ourselves with a free afternoon, a little red 327 fuel-injected 1962 Corvette convertible and an unopened map of Vermont's backroads.

"We're here to get the triple-Dagwood sandwich made, the perfectly frosted malted-beverage mug filled and the football kicked off at the very second your sister begins tying up the phone until Tuesday.

"None of us are going to find ourselves on our deathbeds saying, 'Dang, I wish I'd spent more time on the Hibbings account.' We're going to say, 'That scar? I got that scar stealing a home run from Consolidated Plumbers!'

"See, grown-ups spend so much time doggedly slaving toward the better car, the perfect house, the big day that will finally make them happy when happy just walked by wearing a bicycle helmet two sizes too big for him. We're not here to find a way to heaven. The way is heaven. Does that answer your question, son?"

And he said, "Not really, Dad."

And I said, "No?"

And he said, "No, what I meant is, why are we here when Mom said to pick her up forty minutes ago?"

Rick Reilly

[EDITORS' NOTE: *John Elway retired in 1998.*]

More Chicken Soup?

Many of the stories and poems you have read in this book were submitted by readers like you who had read earlier *Chicken Soup for the Soul* books. We are planning to publish five or six *Chicken Soup for the Soul* books every year. We invite you to contribute a story to one of these future volumes.

Stories may be up to 1,200 words and must uplift or inspire. You may submit an original piece, something you have read or your favorite quotation on your refrigerator door.

To obtain a copy of our submission guidelines and a listing of upcoming *Chicken Soup* books, please write, fax or check one of our Web sites.

Please send your submissions to:

Chicken Soup for the (Specify Which Edition) Soul
P.O. Box 30880, Santa Barbara, CA 93130
Fax: 805-563-2945
Web site: *www.chickensoup.com*

You can also visit the *Chicken Soup for the Soul* Web site on America Online at keyword: chickensoup.

Just send a copy of your stories and other pieces to the above address.

We will be sure that both you and the author are credited for your submission.

For information about speaking engagements, other books, audiotapes, workshops and training programs, please contact any of our authors directly.

Supporting Sports Fans Everywhere

In the spirit of enjoying healthy, active lives, a portion of the proceeds from *Chicken Soup for the Sports Fan's Soul* will go to the following charities.

The **Children's Miracle Network** (CMN) is an international nonprofit organization dedicated to raising funds for children's hospitals. The hospitals associated with CMN care for all children with any affliction and ensure that care will be provided, regardless of the family's ability to pay.

Children's Miracle Network
4525 South 2300 East, Ste. 202
Salt Lake City, UT 84117
801-278-9800
Web site: *www.cmn.org*

After benefiting from a critically-needed cardiac procedure, Larry King knew more must be done to widen access to life-saving cardiac care. The mission of the **Larry King Cardiac Foundation** is to provide funding for life-saving cardiac procedures for children and adults who, due to limited means and inadequate insurance, would otherwise be unable to receive care.

Larry King Cardiac Foundation
575 Lynnhaven Parkway, Ste. 250
Virginia Beach, VA 23452
757-464-3831
e-mail: *lkcf@iaccess.net*
Web site: *www.ok.com/larryking*

Who Is Jack Canfield?

Jack Canfield is one of America's leading experts in the development of human potential and personal effectiveness. He is both a dynamic, entertaining speaker and a highly sought-after trainer. Jack has a wonderful ability to inform and inspire audiences toward increased levels of self-esteem and peak performance.

He is the author and narrator of several bestselling audio and videocassette programs, including *Self-Esteem and Peak Performance, How to Build High Self-Esteem, Self-Esteem in the Classroom* and *Chicken Soup for the Soul—Live.* He is regularly seen on television shows such as *Good Morning America, 20/20* and *NBC Nightly News.* Jack has co-authored numerous books, including the *Chicken Soup for the Soul* series, *Dare to Win* and *The Aladdin Factor* (all with Mark Victor Hansen), *100 Ways to Build Self-Concept in the Classroom* (with Harold C. Wells), and *Heart at Work* (with Jacqueline Miller).

Jack is a regularly featured speaker for professional associations, school districts, government agencies, churches, hospitals, sales organizations and corporations. His clients have included the American Dental Association, the American Management Association, AT&T, Campbell's Soup, Clairol, Domino's Pizza, GE, ITT, Hartford Insurance, Johnson & Johnson, the Million Dollar Roundtable, NCR, New England Telephone, Re/Max, Scott Paper, TRW and Virgin Records. Jack is also on the faculty of Income Builders International, a school for entrepreneurs.

Jack conducts an annual eight-day Training of Trainers program in the areas of self-esteem and peak performance. It attracts educators, counselors, parenting trainers, corporate trainers, professional speakers, ministers and others interested in developing their speaking and seminar-leading skills.

For further information about Jack's books, tapes and training programs, or to schedule him for a presentation, please contact:

Self-Esteem Seminars
P.O. Box 30880
Santa Barbara, CA 93130
Phone: 805-563-2935 • Fax: 805-563-2945
Web site: *www.chickensoup.com*

Who Is Mark Victor Hansen?

Mark Victor Hansen is a professional speaker who in the last twenty years has made over 4,000 presentations to more than 2 million people in thirty-two countries. His presentations cover sales excellence and strategies; personal empowerment and development; and how to triple your income and double your time off.

Mark has spent a lifetime dedicated to his mission of making a profound and positive difference in people's lives. Throughout his career, he has inspired hundreds of thousands of people to create a more powerful and purposeful future for themselves while stimulating the sale of billions of dollars worth of goods and services.

Mark is a prolific writer and has authored *Future Diary, How to Achieve Total Prosperity* and *The Miracle of Tithing.* He is coauthor of the *Chicken Soup for the Soul* series, *Dare to Win* and *The Aladdin Factor* (all with Jack Canfield), and *The Master Motivator* (with Joe Batten).

Mark has also produced a complete library of personal-empowerment audio and videocassette programs that have enabled his listeners to recognize and use their innate abilities in their business and personal lives. His message has made him a popular television and radio personality, with appearances on ABC, NBC, CBS, HBO, PBS and CNN. He has also appeared on the cover of numerous magazines, including *Success, Entrepreneur* and *Changes.*

Mark is a big man with a heart and spirit to match—an inspiration to all who seek to better themselves.

For further information about Mark, write:

MVH & Associates
P.O. Box 7665
Newport Beach, CA 92658
Phone: 714-759-9304 or 800-433-2314
Fax: 714-722-6912
Web site: *www.chickensoup.com*

Who Is Chrissy Donnelly?

Chrissy Donnelly is a bestselling author, speaker and entrepreneur. As coauthor of *Chicken Soup for the Sports Fan's Soul*, she helped capture the excitement, inspiration and true nature of our fascination with games and the lessons that we carry over to the game of life. Sports is second nature to Chrissy: She started gymnastics and dance lessons at age four and has accumulated more than twenty years of dance experience. A dozen years of gymnastics training included a stint on her high school varsity team. Chrissy performed with the Moving Force Dance Company for two years and competed in U.S. Gymnastics Federation competitions for six years. She has performed as a dancer and model for NIKE, Redken and Columbia Sportswear, and has appeared on television, both in commercials and on a weekly national aerobics program. She also ran track and is an avid golfer, hiker, skydiver and waterskiier.

Her enthusiasm, energy and skills have served her well in the business arena. After graduating from Portland State University with a bachelor's degree in business administration, Chrissy obtained her certified public accountant's license in 1991. She worked for Price Waterhouse from 1989 through 1995, acquiring Big Six international accounting experience.

She met her husband Mark in 1994 and together they cofounded Donnelly Marketing Group, developing and carrying out marketing, promotional and editorial activities that help spread the *Chicken Soup* message far and wide. The couple speaks in the national circuit about love and relationships, and the game of golf as a metaphor for life.

Chrissy is coauthor of the number-one *New York Times* bestseller., *Chicken Soup for the Couple's Soul* (January 1999) and *Chicken Soup for the Golfer's Soul* (June 1999). She and Mark are working on several other *Chicken Soup* titles.

Chrissy lives in Paradise Valley, Arizona, with her husband Mark. They can be reached at:

Donnelly Marketing Group, LLC
3104 E. Camelback, Suite 531
Phoenix, AZ 85016
Phone: 602-508-8956 • Fax: 602-508-8912
e-mail: *soup4soul@home.com*

Who Is Mark Donnelly?

Mark Donnelly is a bestselling author, entrepreneur, business owner and speaker. An all-around sports fan, he still recalls vivid memories of Little League days, especially the season that took his team all the way to the Babe Ruth State Championships. In high school he played varsity basketball and baseball, and ran track and field. Basketball was also his main sport in college. In addition to his on-field memories, Mark has also had some great times coaching youth soccer and basketball. He was introduced to golf at age three, and recalls one day following his dad to the golf course and finding a four-leaf clover. That day his dad won a prominent local amateur tournament.

Mark and his wife Chrissy Donnelly are the founders of two companies, Donnelly Marketing Group and Donnelly Productions Limited. Together they coauthored the #1 *New York Times* bestsellers, *Chicken Soup for the Couple's Soul* and *Chicken Soup for the Golfer's Soul*.

Mark built his success on foundations learned from his father and grandfather, who founded Contact Lumber in Portland, Oregon. Mark was Vice President of this family-owned company until 1996, when he resigned to pursue entrepreneurial interests with his wife. He currently serves as Vice Chairman of Contact Lumber.

A native of Portland, Oregon, Mark now lives in Paradise Valley, Arizona, with his wife Chrissy. He holds a Bachelor of Science degree in business administration from the University of Arizona, where he was in the Golden Key National Honor Society and president of his fraternity, Alpha Tau Omega. Awards received include his fraternity's Outstanding Senior Award in 1985 and all-region honors as a guard on the Mount Hood Community College basketball team.

Mark golfs, hikes, skydives and works out. He and Chrissy are working on several other *Chicken Soup* books. The couple also speaks nationally on the subjects of love and relationships, and golf as a metaphor for life.

Mark can be reached at:

Donnelly Marketing Group, LLC
3104 E. Camelback, Suite 531
Phoenix, AZ 85016
Phone: 602-508-8956 • Fax: 602-508-8912
e-mail: *soup4soul@home.com*

Who Is Jim Tunney?

As an educator, Jim has been a high-school teacher, coach, principal, district superintendent and headmaster. He serves on the boards of trustees for York School (Monterey, California) and Monterey Peninsula College.

His second career is in sports. During thirty-one years as an NFL official, Jim worked a record twenty-nine postseason games, including ten Championships, three Super Bowls and six Pro Bowls. Named *Sporting News* Best NFL Official and awarded The Gold Whistle by the National Association of Sports Officials, Jim was the first official named to the "All-Madden Team" and is in the Pro Football Hall of Fame (Canton, Ohio).

Recipient of All-Conference Honors in Basketball and Athlete of the Year at Occidental College, Jim started officiating out of college, first at the high-school level, then the PAC-10 and then for the NFL. He worked some of the most memorable games in NFL history, including the "Fog Bowl," "Final Fumble," "Snowball Game," "100th Game," "The Catch," "The Kick," "The Ice Bowl" and "The Field Goal." His book, *Impartial Judgment: The "Dean of NFL Referees" Calls Pro Football As He Sees It*, chronicles his career in the NFL.

Jim's third career is as a professional speaker. A past-president of the National Speakers Association, he is a charter member of its most prestigious group—the CPAE Speaker Hall of Fame—and holds every professional designation of the NSA, including the "Oscar of Professional Speaking"—The Cavett.

He established the Jim Tunney Youth Foundation in 1993 to support local community programs that develop leadership and work skills, wellness and self-esteem in youth. He and his wife, Linda, live in Pebble Beach, California. They have six children and nine grandchildren.

For further information, Jim can be reached at:

Jim Tunney Associates
P.O. Box 1500
Carmel-by-the-Sea, CA 93921
e-mail: *sportsfans@jimtunney.com*

Contributors

Some of the stories and poems in this book were taken from books we have read. These sources are acknowledged in the Permissions section.

Some of the stories and poems were contributed by everyday athletes and sports fans who are also professional speakers. If you would like to contact them for information on their books, tapes and seminars, you can reach them at the addresses and phone numbers provided below.

Many of the stories were contributed by professional athletes, coaches, owners, sports officials and others associated with professional sports in America. Others were contributed by readers like you who responded to our request for stories. We include information about each of these as well.

Scott Adamson, a native of Birmingham, has worked at *The Daily Home (Alabama) Newspaper* since 1987, and has served as sports editor there since 1988. A winner of numerous writing awards from the Associated Press and the Alabama Press Association, he is married to the former Pam Jones. The couple has a daughter, Cassady, and an obnoxious miniature dachshund, Otis.

Roger Angell is a baseball reporter and essayist for *The New Yorker* magazine. The publication of Roger Angell's *The Summer Game* (1972), a collection of twenty-one essays, set a new standard for baseball journalism, and was followed by such works as *Five Seasons: A Baseball Companion* (1977), *Late Innings* (1982) and *Season Ticket* (1988).

Larry Baltz believes that organizations achieve greatness only when the individuals in the organization achieve it personally. He is a professional speaker, trainer and consultant who helps individuals grow personally and professionally. Larry is committed to serving others by providing valuable content and stimulating messages. He is the owner of Dynamic Presentations, Nashville, Tennessee.

Dave Barry has been at the *Miami Herald* since 1983. He won the Pulitzer Prize for commentary in 1988. Barry writes about various major issues relating to the international economy, the future of democracy, the social infrastructure and exploding toilets.

Bill Bethel is a nationally recognized speaker (over 3,000 speeches and seminars). He has written three books, three television shows, plus dozens of magazine articles. As a marketing consultant, he has built a full resume of entrepreneurial experience. He can be reached at 800-548-8001.

Brian D. Biro is one of the nation's foremost speakers and teachers of leadership, possibility thinking and team-building. He is the author of the internationally acclaimed *Beyond Success! The Joyful Spirit!* and his brand-new *Through the Eyes of a Coach—The New Vision for Parenting, Leading, Loving and Living!* Brian has been featured on *Good Morning America*, CNN's *Business Unusual*, the Fox News Network and in the *New York Daily News*. You can reach Brian to book seminars and presentations for your organization by calling 828-654-8852, by fax at 828-654-8853, via e-mail at *bbiro@worldnet.att.net* or by calling Five Star Speakers and Trainers at 913-648-6480.

Thomas Boswell has been a *Washington Post* columnist since 1984. He is known for the many books he has written on baseball, including *How Life Imitates the World Series*.

Mark Bowden is the award-winning author of *Bringing the Heat* and *Doctor Dealer*. He has been a reporter at the *Philadelphia Inquirer* for nineteen years. He also writes for *Men's Journal, Sports Illustrated, Playboy, Rolling Stone, Parade* and other magazines.

Bill Bradley has been a leader for more than thirty years. From winning an Olympic gold medal in basketball in 1964, to representing New Jersey in the U.S. Senate from 1979–1996, to running for president, Bill Bradley exemplifies America's best qualities. A star professional basketball player for the New York Knicks from 1967–1977, he was inducted into the Basketball Hall of Fame in 1982. During his time with them, the Knicks won two NBA championships, in 1970 and 1973.

Patrick L. Busteed is a longtime teacher and coach in Colorado. He is presently teaching social studies and coaching football and track at Fort Collins High School. He has a wife, Robin, and two sons: Shawn, who is attending Vanderbilt University, and Chris, who attends Fort Collins High School.

Susan Butcher was raised in Cambridge, Massachusetts. She moved to the Wrangell Mountains of Alaska to pursue her first love—dog-sled racing and breeding huskies! A professional musher, dog breeder and veterinary technician, she is also the first person ever to win the Iditarod three consecutive times. Today, she is the foremost representative of dog-sled racing worldwide, appearing many times on national and global television. Her appearances include ABC's *20/20*, NBC's *The Late Night Show*, CBS's *CBS Sports Saturday*, The *Joan Rivers Show*, and PBS's documentary, *The Susan Butcher Story*.

Mike Celizic is an author, writer, commentator and Pulitzer nominee. He has spent his life traveling the world and writing about human triumph and tragedy with insight, compassion and humor, exploring not simply what is, but also what ought to be. He lives in upstate New York with his wife,

Margaret A. Sinnott; four children, Carl, James, Jane, and Zachary; and his little dog, Petey.

Dan Clark, C.S.P., is a primary contributing author to the *Chicken Soup for the Soul* series and author of ten of his own highly acclaimed books, including *Puppies for Sale and Other Inspirational Tales.* In 1982, Zig Ziglar sponsored Dan into the National Speakers Association. He has since spoken to more than 2 million people in all fifty states, Canada and fifteen foreign countries. An award-winning athlete, he fought his way back from a paralyzing injury that cut short his football career. He can be reached at P.O. Box 58689, Salt Lake City, UT 84108, 800-676-1121, or by e-mail at *SDANCLARKP@aol.com.*

Barney Cohen spent six years writing a magazine about raising kids through sports. His own kids, Ivan and Danica, are now raised and both are in show business. If they're applying *any* of the lessons they learned on the playing fields it will be a surprise to him. Mr. Cohen wrote and produced the movie, *Sabrina the Teenage Witch,* which became the hit television series. He wants everybody to know that the film/television rights to both of his stories in this book are available. Call his agent.

Bob Costas, with NBC Sports since 1979, is best known for his coverage of the Olympics and baseball, especially his play-by-play for the All-Star, play-off and World Series telecasts. His passionate commentary about the game's history and appeal has earned him the respect of millions. He has won twelve Emmy Awards and been named by his peers as National Sportscaster of the Year seven times. He lives with his wife and children in St. Louis, Missouri.

Joey Crawford is a twenty-four-year veteran official for the NBA, working in the finals the last thirteen years. He follows his father, Shag, who worked twenty years as a major-league baseball umpire, mostly as crew chief. Joey's brother, Jerry, is also a major-league baseball umpire, now in his twenty-first year. Married with three daughters and one grandson, Joey lives in Philadelphia, where he helps run the Comets, a women's AAU basketball team.

Gary D'Amato is an award-winning sportswriter/columnist for the *Milwaukee Journal Sentinel.* He has coauthored two books: *The Packer Tapes: My 32 Years with the Green Bay Packers* and *Mudbaths and Bloodbaths: The Inside Story of the Bears-Packers Rivalry.*

Gene Doherty was born into a family who loved and played golf from early ages—all nine brothers and one sister. Two brothers and one nephew are golf pros. As work, he started as a "grease monkey" and retired as general manager of the Chrysler–Plymouth dealership in Stoneham, Massachusetts. The Woburn CC is his home course.

Mack R. Douglas is the author of several bestselling titles about self-development that have been translated into multiple languages throughout the world. He is president of Discovery Seminars International.

Tommy Ehrbar is currently a freelance writer. He worked at the University of

Pittsburgh as director of feature services, writer and contributor to university publications. He previously held a similar position at Kenyon College. He is a graduate of Notre Dame University, a former congressional reporter for *The New Republic* and former TV weather forecaster.

Darlene Daniels Eisenhuth lives in rural South Newfane, Vermont, with her husband and their two teenage sons. She is a firm believer that the finer things in life are the simple ones. Most of her inspiration for her writing comes from her family and their experiences together.

Roy Firestone has won six Emmy awards, six ACE Awards for Cable Excellence, two Golden Mike Awards for sports reporting, and the Los Angeles Press Club Award for Best Sportscast. *Sports Illustrated* has called him "the best interviewer in sports." His book *Up Close and in Your Face with the Greats, Near-Greats and Ingrates of Sports* is available through Magic Turtle Productions, 818-789-0152. He lives in Los Angeles with his wife, Midori, and two children.

Tom Flores is one of only two people in NFL history to win the Super Bowl in all categories: player (Kansas City, 1969); coach (Oakland, 1976); and head coach (Oakland, 1980, and L.A. Raiders, 1983). The original quarterback for the Oakland Raiders (1960), he also played for Buffalo and Kansas City. He retired as the Raiders head coach in 1987, joined Seattle in 1989 as president/general manager, became head coach for three years and is currently a member of the Raiders Game Day Radio Team.

Dan Fouts was named Most Valuable Player twice and played on the All-Pro Team six times during his fifteen seasons as quarterback with the San Diego Chargers. He retired with forty-two team records and eight NFL records, including most three-hundred-yard passing games. Inducted into the Hall of Fame in his first year of eligibility, Dan transitioned into broadcasting, winning two Emmys as sports anchor for KPIX-TV in San Francisco. He is currently the game analyst for *Monday Night Football* on ABC.

Anita Gogno received Keystone Press Awards in 1998 and 1999 for her weekly "Faith Matters" column in *The Reporter*, Lansdale, Pennsylvania. Her work has been published in *Chicken Soup for the Couple's Soul*, magazines and newspapers. She also writes and edits for companies. Anita and husband Charlie live in Hatfield, Pennsylvania, with their three sons.

Bob Greene is a syndicated columnist with national bestsellers including *Hang Time: Be True to Your School*, and with his sister, D. G. Fulford, *To Our Children's Children: Preserving Family Histories for Generations to Come*. His new book is *The 50-Year Dash: The Feelings, Foibles and Fears of Being Half-a-Century Old*.

John Gross has reported more than three hundred network sporting events, including three Super Bowls, the Indy 500 and two Olympics. He covered the world champion Detroit Tigers in 1984 and the Detroit Pistons during their back-to-back world championships. Now a freelance ground cameraman for

NFL Films and working for KSTP-TV (ABC) in Minneapolis, he was named Indiana Division Two Photographer of the Year in 1996. He lives in Lakeville, Minnesota, with his wife and two children. His married daughter lives in Novi, Michigan.

Jack Hannah currently performs internationally with the Sons of the San Joaquin, a family trio that features songs of the cowboy and the American West. He is a poet, songwriter, avid roper and recreational cowboy. Recently inducted into the California State University at Fresno Baseball Hall of Fame and the Fresno Athletic Hall of Fame, he was a professional baseball player and thirty-year educator, national-award-winning coach and a counselor in the Fresno and Clovis public schools. He can be reached at the Sons of the San Joaquin by e-mail at *jhannah@gte.net*, or by fax at 559-222-3417.

Paul Henderson, a member of the Canadian Sports Hall of Fame, became a Canadian sports legend on September 28, 1972. His goal, with thirty-four seconds remaining in the final game, lifted Canada to victory in the "Series of the Century" against the Soviet Union. Incredibly, Paul scored the winning goal in each of the last three games of this historic first series between the two superpowers of hockey. That magical moment in Moscow is still considered the greatest in hockey history.

Brian Holloway is a Stanford All-American, five-time NFL All-Pro and now the most requested motivational futurist in the country. As chief executive officer of First Round Draft Picks.Com, he specializes in "Real" Team Building, the Art of Sales Mastery and Dynasty Crafting, and has worked with ninety-eight of the *Fortune* 500 companies. He lives with his wife, Tammy, and their seven children in Stephentown, New York. He can be reached through his Web site at *www.brianholloway.com*, or by fax at 518-773-6125.

Donald Honig is a former professional ballplayer and a novelist. *Baseball Between the Lines: Baseball in the Forties and Fifties, Man in the Dugout: Fifteen Big League Managers Speak Their Minds,* and *October Heroes: Great World Series Games Remembered by the Men Who Played Them* are all available in Bison Books editions.

Phillip M. Hoose's book *It's Our World, Too!* won the 1993 Christopher Award. *Hey, Little Ant,* written with daughter Hannah Hoose, was a Jane Addams Award finalist. He is a staff member of the Nature Conservancy, a director of the Children's Music Network and a performing musician. He lives in Portland, Maine.

Ricky C. Hunley is the motivational tool behind the Missouri Tigers as the associate head football coach in charge of the inside linebackers. A two-time consensus All-American linebacker at the University of Arizona, Ricky was the first Wildcat to earn those honors and the first UA player inducted into the College Hall of Fame (1997). He spent seven seasons starring in the NFL with the Denver Broncos, Phoenix Cardinals and Los Angeles Raiders. He resides in Columbia, Missouri, with his wife, Camille, and their two daughters, Alexis and Kenady. He can be reached at the University of Missouri, 100 Tom Taylor Bldg., Columbia, MO 65211, or by fax at 573-882-5588.

Ellen E. Hyatt, a fellow of the Western Pennsylvania Writing Project, teaches at Charleston Southern University in Charleston, South Carolina. Appearing in a variety of publications, her works have been honored by the Poetry Society of South Carolina and by the National League of American Pen Women.

Laura Ishler is an at-home mother and freelance writer. She has many wonderful years of experience coordinating programs for the poor and families in crisis. Her greatest joy is being Jerry's wife and Mark's mom. She can be reached at Rural Route #2, Curwensville, PA 16833.

Steve Jamison is a columnist, television host, acclaimed speaker, coauthor of *In the Zone,* and author of the successful book, *Winning Ugly and Mental Welfare in Tennis.*

Sharon Jaynes is the president of The Proverbs 31 Ministry, cohost for its international radio program, feature writer for its monthly newsletter and inspirational conference speaker. She is also the author of *Being a Great Mom—Raising Great Kids* and *At Home with God—Stories of Life, Love and Laughter* and can be reached at The Proverbs 31 Ministry, P.O. Box 17155, Charlotte, NC 28227 or 877-731-4663.

Barbara Johnson is the author of numerous bestselling books, including *Living Somewhere Between Estrogen and Death.* She lives in La Habra, California.

Rafer Johnson won the gold medal for the decathlon in the 1960 Olympic Games in Rome, posting a new Olympic record. After the Olympics, he devoted time to his family, his career and helping others. To this end, he became a sports commentator, worked with Robert F. Kennedy, is president of Rafer Johnson Enterprises and chairman of the board for the Southern California Special Olympics. His life story is told in *The Best That I Can Be.* He lives in Los Angeles with his wife and has two children.

Charlie Jones, a true pioneer of sports television, handled the *first* Super Bowl, AFL championship, NCAA Women's Final Four, World Cup Gymnastics, Senior Skins Game, World Cup Marathon and World Championships of Track and Field. He's covered twenty-eight different sports in forty-eight states and twenty-five countries, including three Olympics, fifty college football bowl games and thirty-eight years of NFL football. Winner of many awards and only the ninth broadcaster to be inducted into the Pro Football Hall of Fame, Charlie is the author of the *New York Times* bestseller, *What Makes Winners Win.* He lives in La Jolla, California.

Jack Kemp, the 1996 GOP nominee for vice president, is a codirector of Empower America. He served as secretary of HUD and represented Buffalo, New York, for eighteen years in the U.S. Congress. Mr. Kemp spent thirteen years as a professional quarterback. He was captain of the San Diego Chargers and later quarterbacked the Buffalo Bills, leading them to the American Football League championship in 1964 and 1965, when he was named the league's Most Valuable Player. He also cofounded the AFL Players Association and was five times elected president.

J. Michael Key is forty-four years old and has taught eighth grade for twenty-three years. He has coached basketball and softball during several of those years. He is also married with five children, ranging in ages from nine to nineteen, with whom he still enjoys playing basketball, softball and golf.

Jeff Kidd is the sports editor for the *Beaufort (South Carolina) Gazette*. He has written professionally for fourteen years, starting as a correspondent for South Carolina's largest daily newspaper, *The State*. Kidd's work has been recognized by the South Carolina Press Association eighteen times. He is also the author of a self-published baseball book, *The Total Hitter*.

Dave Kindred has eaten breakfast with Julie Krone, lunch with Muhammad Ali and dinner with Robert Redford. Between meals, he has written six thousand columns and six books. The 1997 National Sportswriter of the Year, he is a winner of sports journalism's highest prize, the Red Smith Award. He lives in Virginia with his wife, Cheryl.

Bernie Kish is the executive director of the College Football Hall of Fame in South Bend, Indiana. He served in the U.S. Army for more than twenty-nine years, retiring as a full colonel. He earned a Ph.D. in higher education from the University of Kansas, where he worked in the athletic department. He can be reached at 800-440-3263.

Zoe Koplowitz is the award-winning author of *The Winning Spirit—Life Lessons Learned in Last Place*. To date, she has completed fourteen marathons, all in last place, and in the process has set world records in New York, Boston and London. It is her personal mission, through her motivational speaking, to recreate the word "win" so that it takes on new meaning and context in the life of each individual. Speaking engagements can be arranged by e-mailing her at *TheWinningSpirit@aol.com*.

Tom Krause is a motivational speaker, teacher, coach and founder of Positive People Presentations. He speaks to teenagers, teaching staffs and any organizations dealing with teen issues, and to business organizations for motivation and stress reduction. His poem, "Just Me," appeared in *Chicken Soup for the Teenage Soul*. He can be reached at 4355 S. National Avenue, Suite 2206, Springfield, MO 65810, 417-883-6753, *justmetrk@aol.com*.

Bonita Laettner has been an elementary school teacher for twenty-seven years and has a master's degree in education. She has written two books about her family, which she hopes to have published, and is on the Newsletter Committee of the Mothers of Professional Basketball Players. She can be reached at 1225 Church Rd., Angola, NY 14006.

Sharon Landeen, a retired elementary-school teacher, is the author and illustrator of two bilingual picture books, *When You Get Really Mad* and *Really Riley.* She enjoys working with youth, was involved for twenty years with 4-H, and is back in the 4-H program again with her grandson. She's a volunteer teacher in reading and art, but still finds time to be "grandmother superior" as well as being an enthusiastic University of Arizona sports fan. She can be reached at 6990 E. Calle Arandas, Tucson, AZ 85750 or at *SLLandeen@aol.com.*

Walter W. Laos, D.D.S., grew up in Tucson and later served in the navy during the Korean conflict. After Korea he returned to Tucson to complete pre-dental-school training at the University of Arizona. From there he earned his Doctor of Dental Surgery degree at the Chicago College of Dental Surgery, Loyola. Upon graduation from dental school, Walter returned to Tucson to set up his dental practice, which has recently completed its thirty-seventh year. He wrote and self-published the novel, *Esparza,* about his father's mother's side of the family.

Clay Larson is vice chairman and a director of Pacific Capital Bancorp, a holding company for regional banks in central California. Voted Leader of the Decade by Leadership Monterey Peninsula (California) in 1992, he is a strong supporter of the community and an avid golfer. He and his wife, Sharon, have three children. He can be reached at P.O. Box 2178, Monterey, CA 93942.

Judge Keith J. Leenhouts is a pioneer of Volunteers in Courts, involving some 7 million citizens in reducing criminal convictions by eleven and one-half times (not percent) by federal government research of a court using volunteers (270/23 ratio). For information on the book, *Father, Son, 3 Mile Run,* the basis of *Race for Love,* and other information on court voluntarism, write Leenhouts at 830 Normandy, Royal Oak, MI 48073, or go to the Web site: *www.rj-systems.com.*

Meadowlark Lemon has been one of the creative forces behind the Harlem Globetrotters as well as the world's incomparable genius of comedic basketball. In 2001, he will celebrate his ten thousandth basketball game. This is the unmatchable equivalent of an NBA player playing a hundred games for a hundred years! An ordained minister since 1986, Meadowlark sponsors basketball camps all over the country called Camp Meadowlark. These camps emphasize the physical, psychological, social and spiritual aspects of basketball as a springboard for guiding kids to healthy techniques for dealing with the stresses they face in life. The Meadowlark Lemon Foundation raises money to ensure that no needy child is turned away for lack of camp fees. To learn more about Meadowlark Lemon or his foundation, please visit his Web site at *www.meadowlarklemon.com.*

Mike Leonetti is the author of *Shooting for Glory* (1992), the biography of hockey legend Paul Henderson. Since then he has completed *The Game We Knew* series of books for Raincoast Books of Vancouver, a three-volume set which covers hockey in a decade format as in the Fifties, Sixties and Seventies.

His most recent book was *Hockey Now!*, featuring biographies of current NHL stars. Leonetti is also the author of a children's book entitled *My Leafs Sweater*, which will be out in soft cover for the Fall of 2000.

Ed Marion, former president and executive director of the Professional Referees Association, was a head linesman in the National Football League for twenty-eight years. A graduate of the University of Pennsylvania, he is active in qualified retirement plans as a pension consultant. He can be reached at 1175 Hilltop Ln., Coatesville, PA 19320, 610-383-5542.

Mark H. McCormack is a pioneer and leader in sports marketing. Starting with a handshake with Arnold Palmer, McCormack revolutionized sports by establishing athlete representation as a distinct business discipline and by demonstrating the value of sports as an effective corporate tool, thus changing the definition of entrepreneurial leadership as well. His Cleveland-based company, IMG, is the world's largest sports and marketing conglomerate, representing top stars in all sports and areas of entertainment. He is also author of a string of bestselling books, including *What They Don't Teach You at Harvard Business School* and *Staying Street Smart in the Internet Age*.

Brian McFarlane is a member of the Hockey Hall of Fame and is one of Canada's best and most prolific hockey writers. He is the author of more than forty books, including *The Best of It Happened in Hockey* and *Proud Past, Bright Future*. As a broadcaster, he spent twenty-seven years with CBC's *Hockey Night in Canada* and has also been a commentator on NBC, CBS and ESPN.

Cary McMahon was raised in South Bend, Indiana. He played baseball and basketball through college and has coached both sports for seven years. He currently lives in Cincinnati, Ohio, with his thirteen-year-old son, Thomas.

David Meanor is a training consultant and founder of BUILD, a nonprofit training center that prepares people for construction projects. A former tennis and basketball coach, Dave assists his wife, Linda, with youth activities at their church. He enjoys writing poems on special occasions for family and friends. He and Linda live in York, Pennsylvania.

Nancy E. Myer is author of *Silent Witness: The True Story of a Psychic Detective, Angels and Pianos in Anthology* and *More Hot Chocolate for the Mystical Soul*. During her distinguished career as a psychic detective, she has appeared on *Unsolved Mysteries, Sightings, Paranormal Borderline, The Other Side* and many other shows. You can reach Nancy at P.O. Box 3015, Greensburg, PA 15601, phone: 724-832-3951, fax: 724-838-9837.

Chris Myers, an Emmy award-winning announcer, is currently an anchor on FOX Sports Net's *National Sports Report*. In addition to anchoring the nightly sports news show, he also hosts FSN's *Goin' Deep*, a weekly investigative sports magazine show, and *NFL This Morning*, a studio pregame show, during the football season. He previously worked at ESPN on *SportsCenter* and *Up*

Close. He can be reached at FOX Sports Net, FOX Network Center, 10201 W. Pico Blvd., Los Angeles, CA 90035.

William Nack, one of *Sports Illustrated's* most distinguished writers, joined the magazine in 1979. In addition to writing in-depth profiles, he has been a mainstay on the horseracing beat, winning six Eclipse Awards from the Thoroughbred Racing Association for excellence in magazine writing. He also authored *Secretariat: The Making of a Champion.* Nack's 1990 feature on Secretariat, entitled "Pure Heart," was selected for *The Best American Sports Writing of the Century* by editor David Halberstam.

Jim Nantz is the voice of CBS Sports. He anchors *The NFL Today,* CBS golf coverage and is the play-by-play voice of the Final Four. He anchored the 1992 and 1998 Winter Olympics. He lives with his wife, Lorrie, and their daughter in Connecticut.

Craig Neff has journeyed to thirty-one countries on assignment for *Sports Illustrated.* He added Panama to the list when he reported *Panama Canal: Bon Voyage* for *VIA.* Prone to seasickness, Craig had been on a ship only once before—when he boarded the *Saga Fjord,* docked in San Pedro, California, for dinner during the 1984 Olympics. Craig lives in New York City—not far from Canal Street—with his wife, Pamelia, and their cats, Hedda and Hopper.

Scott Nicholson is a fiction writer, journalist and Little League coach living in North Carolina. His story "The Vampire Shortstop" won the 1999 Hubbard Gold Award and appears in his collection *Thank You for the Flowers.*

Don "Ollie" Olivett presents motivational workshops and keynotes for businesses and professional organizations throughout the country, and serves as a motivational coach for professional, Olympic and college athletes and teams. He can be reached at Ultimate Performance, 305 Howard Circle, Emporium, PA 15834, or by e-mail at *dolivett@penn.com.*

Tim Palesky is a hairstylist, an aspiring motivational speaker and president of Skyway Productions. He designed the audiocassette program *You Were Born to Be a Winner,* establishing a program to help student-athletes achieve their goals. Tim is also editor-in-chief of *The Sports Page,* a publication dedicated to sports in New York and New Jersey. He can be reached at P.O. Box 513, Fairlawn, NJ 07410, or by fax at 201-796-6163.

Terry Paulson, Ph.D., C.S.P., C.P.A.E., of Agoura Hills, California, is the author of *They Shoot Managers, Don't They?* and *Paulson on Change.* As a speaker, he helps leaders and teams make effective change. He can be contacted through his Web site, *www.terrypaulson.com,* by phone at 818-991-5110, or by e-mail at *DrTerryP@aol.com.*

Tom Payne is an international speaker and author. He has spent more than sixty-five hundred hours delivering programs to organizations and people under pressure. He was a high school and college athlete who, until his junior year in high school, played without a facemask—which is why his picture does not accompany this story. Contact him via his Web site: *www.tompayne.com.*

Leonard Pitts Jr. writes a column for the *Miami Herald* on family and social issues that is syndicated in more than 150 papers nationwide. He is the author of *Becoming Dad: Black Men and the Journey to Fatherhood* and a forthcoming collection of his columns, *Living in America: Collected Reflections and Deadline Wisdom.*

Michael T. Powers is a freelance writer who resides in Wisconsin with his lovely bride, Kristi, and their two young boys. He is the founder of *Straight from the Heart,* a free daily e-zine that features inspirational stories, often by published writers. You can contact him via e-mail at *Thunder27@aol.com* or visit *www.StoriesFromMyHeart.com.*

Rick Reilly is a senior staff writer for *Sports Illustrated.* He has twice been named National Sportswriter of the Year and is coauthor with Marv Albert of *The Boz* and *I'd Love To but I Have a Game.*

Nancy Ann Richardson is the coauthor of *Riding for My Life,* celebrity jockey Julie Krone's autobiography, and *Feel No Fear,* the autobiography of legendary gymnastics coach Bela Karolyi.

Pat Riley is the Miami Heat head coach, and the former head coach of both the New York Knicks and the Los Angeles Lakers. He achieved his three-hundredth victory in fewer years than any other coach in history. Named one of the Top Ten NBC Coaches of All Time, he has taken his team to the playoffs in each of his sixteen seasons as a head coach. In the 1980s, he led the Lakers to four NBA championships, prompting the Associated Press to name him Coach of the Decade.

Grady Jim Robinson is a professional speaker and writer. His stories about growing up in Arkansas have appeared in *Sports Illustrated, Reader's Digest* and other magazines. He has earned a reputation as one of America's most entertaining speakers. His latest book, *Did I Ever Tell You About the Time . . . ,* shows how to develop and deliver personal stories. He can be reached through his Web site, *www.gradyjim.com.*

Harriet May Savitz is the author of twenty books and has taught creative writing courses. Her books include *The Lionhearted, On the Move* and *Run, Don't Walk,* which was an ABC afterschool special, as well as *Growing Up at 62,* an adult inspirational book. All books can be ordered through *www.amazon.com.* She lives in Bradley Beach, NJ, and can be reached by calling 732-775-5628.

Monica Seles was the top player in women's tennis in 1991 and 1992, having already won seven Grand Slam singles titles, including three consecutive French Open crowns. She returned to tennis in 1995, winning the Canadian Open, and won an eighth Grand Slam—the Australian Open—in January 1996.

Steve Smith is the publications director of Village Press in Traverse City,

Michigan, and editor-in-chief of *The Pointing Dog Journal* and *The Retriever Journal* magazines. A former schoolteacher and baseball coach, Steve is the author of more than a dozen books and a contributor to *Chicken Soup for the Pet Lover's Soul.*

Bart Starr, the winningest quarterback in NFL history, won five world championships in the 1960s; was NFL Most Valuable Player (MVP) in 1966 and Super Bowl MVP for Super Bowl I and Super Bowl II; has made six Pro Bowl appearances; was the first winner of the NFL's Byron White Award; and was NFL Man of the Year in 1969. He was inducted into the Hall of Fame in 1977. Today, chairman of Healthcare Realty Management, he can be reached at 2647 Rocky Ridge Ln., Birmingham, AL 35216.

Andy Strasberg is a native New Yorker, completed college and graduated cum laude from Long Island University. He realized a lifelong dream of working in major-league baseball when in 1975 he began a career with the San Diego Padres that lasted twenty-two years. Since 1997, Andy has opened ACME (All-Star Corporate Marketing Enterprises) and has, with his staff, provided valuable service to a diverse group of clients. Andy frequently is a guest lecturer at sports-marketing symposia and is a recognized innovator in creative marketing.

Ken Swarner writes the syndicated humor column *Family Man,* which appears weekly in dozens of newspapers in the United States and Canada. He lives in the Pacific Northwest with his wife and two children. He can be reached at 253-596-8553 or *swarnerkm@aol.com.*

Chris Tamborini is a former international freestyle skiing competitor, who took an interest in and documented the inspirational stories of several athletes while residing at the Olympic Training Center in Colorado Springs, CO. Both he and Chris Jerard are editors at *Freeskier* magazine, which showcases the lives of today's professional skiers.

William G. Tapply is the author of seventeen New England-based mystery novels, most recently *Scar Tissue.* Tapply has also published several books about hunting, fishing and the outdoors, including *Upland Days.* He's a contributing editor for *Field & Stream,* a columnist for *American Angler,* and editorial associate for the Writer's Digest School, and has written extensively on a variety of subjects for dozens of other publications. He teaches writing at Emerson College and Clark University, and lives in Pepperell, Massachusetts with Vicki Stiefel, his virtual spouse, and Burt, his Brittany spaniel.

Joe Theismann is a football analyst for ESPN and cohost of *NFL Countdown* and *Primetime.* He played twelve years with the Washington Redskins (1974–86), becoming the most productive quarterback in team history. He was the winning quarterback at Super Bowl XVII (1982) and was honored as NFL Man of the Year (1982) and MVP of the Pro Bowl (1983). He works with many charities concerned with the health and welfare of children and is a nationally known speaker on teamwork and stress management. He can be reached at JRT

Associates, 5661 Columbia Pike, Ste. 100-B, Falls Church, VA 22041.

Lee Trevino tops the Senior PGA Tour win list with more than two dozen victories and has been Senior Tour Player of the Year three times, including his rookie season (1990), in which he was also Rookie of the Year after capturing seven titles. He also won the PGA Tour's Rookie of the Year in 1967. He won six major titles—two U.S. Opens, two British Opens and two PGA Championships. His swing is entirely self-taught.

Lesley Visser, a pioneer among women journalists, has covered all major sports for print and electronic media. Voted Outstanding Women's Sportswriter in America in 1983, winner of the Women's Sports Foundation Award for Journalism in 1992 and the first woman assigned to *Monday Night Football,* she is a commentator for ABC and ESPN Sports. Married to sportscaster Dick Stockton, they reside in Boca Raton, Florida.

Dick Vitale is a former college and NBA coach, and a college broadcaster for ESPN and ABC.

David Wallechinsky is a renowned Olympics historian and NBC Radio's color commentator for the Olympics. He is the acclaimed author of a number of bestselling reference books, including *The People's Almanac Presents the Twentieth Century, The Complete Book of the Winter Olympics* and *The Book of Lists.* He has written pieces for *The New York Times Magazine* and *Parade,* and has appeared on television programs as diverse as *Late Night with David Letterman, Nightline, CBS Evening News* and PBS's *NewsHour with Jim Lehrer.* He divides his time between Santa Monica, California, and the south of France.

John A. Walsh is the executive editor of ESPN and oversees the editorial operation of all news and information on all ESPN networks and *ESPN The Magazine,* as well as *ESPN.com.* He was the founding editor of the original *Inside Sports* and held the title of managing editor at *Rolling Stone* and *U.S. News and World Report* magazines. He can be reached at ESPN, in Bristol, Connecticut.

William Wilczewski is a sergeant in the United States Army, serving at Fort Knox as sports editor for *Inside the Turret,* the post's newspaper. He and his wife, Bonnie Jean, have a four-year-old son, Daniel James Liam, a one-year-old daughter, Mary Ann Christine, and a one-year-old Black Lab named Fido.

Paul Winick, M.D., lives in Hollywood, Florida, with his wife, Dorothy. He practiced pediatrics there for twenty-eight years. He has two married children, Charles and Ruth, and two grandchildren. Dr. Winick graduated from Columbia College and S.U.N.Y. Downstate Medical School. He is a full professor of clinical pediatrics at the University of Miami Medical School.

Ernie Witham writes a humor column called "Ernie's World" for the *Monteceito Journal* in Montecito, California. His humor has also been published in the *Los Angeles Times,* the *Santa Barbara News-Press,* various magazines and several anthologies, including *Chicken Soup for the Golfer's Soul.*

Steve Young was the starting quarterback for the San Francisco 49ers from 1991 until he retired in June 2000. He holds many career honors, including Most Valuable Player (MVP) of Super Bowl XXIX, National Football League MVP and the highest quarterback rating in NFL history. He is active in many charities, including the Forever Young Foundation; the Sport, Education and Values Foundation; and the Children's Miracle Network.